This book of daily
devotions belongs to:

_____

From:

_____

Date:

_____

Walk With Jesus

366 DAILY DEVOTIONS WITH THE WAY AND THE TRUTH AND THE LIFE

Jan de Wet

CHRISTIAN ART
PUBLISHERS

Originally published by Christian Publishing
Company under the title *Wandel met Jesus*

Copyright © 2000

English edition published by CHRISTIAN ART PUBLISHERS,
PO Box 1599, Vereeniging, 1930.
Christian Art Publishers, Lombard, IL.

Copyright © 2001
First edition 2001
Second edition 2003

Translated by Haidee Kotze

Edited by The Livingstone Corporation.
Project staff: Joan Guest, Mark Childers, Mary Horner Collins.

Cover designed by Christian Art Publishers

Scripture taken from the *Holy Bible*, New International Version®.
NIV®. Copyright © 1973, 1978, 1984 by International Bible Society.
Used by permission of Zondervan Publishing House. All rights reserved.

Set in 12 on 14 pt Weidemann Book by Christian Art Publishers

Printed in China

ISBN 1-86920-277-5

03 04 05 06 07 08 10 11 12 13 – 10 09 08 07 06 05 04 03 02 01

PREFACE

Walking with Jesus is a wonderful adventure. He is, after all, Immanuel – God with us. When the disciples of Emmaus had the opportunity of walking with him, their hearts were filled with joy and warmth (see Luke 24:13-35).

This collection of daily devotions takes you on a journey through the books of the Bible, from Genesis to Revelation. The men and women walking alongside us are ordinary folk, people just like you and me. They are people with dreams, people who have tasted success as well as failure.

We learn lessons from their experiences. We sometimes feel very sorry for them. We often rejoice with them.

But each of these people also points to Jesus, who is the only One who can tell us how we ought to approach our walk through life. After all, he is the way, the truth, and the life. He remains the very best example that we could possibly have.

Come, let us walk alongside Jesus Christ every day of this year.

– Jan de Wet –

God

THEY CALL HIM ELOHIM

In the beginning God created the heavens and the earth. (Genesis 1:1)

The very first name used to refer to God in the Bible is Elohim. This name refers to a God who is three, but also one. This is something that is difficult for us to grasp. Actually, the word just wants to tell us that God is the only true God.

Elohim also tells us that God is in control, that he is powerful, that he is mighty. Yes, as a matter of fact, God is almighty. He is the only true God among all the gods. He is the greatest of them all. There is none like him.

How wonderful it is that you and I can have a personal relationship with this great God. After all, Jesus helped us to make peace with this God. That is why we needn't be afraid of his all-powerfulness. We are not afraid that he might destroy us. We are not afraid that he might kill us. We are not afraid that he will be angry with us, because Jesus brought us back to him. Now he is not only Elohim, the great and powerful God, but also our Father. We call him Abba, Daddy, and he calls us his children. What a privilege!

Kneel before this great God. Thank him for becoming your Father through Jesus Christ. This God is with you today.

W.W.J.

Jesus came to show us what Elohim is like.

January 1

Adam

HE WAS PART OF GOD'S PLAN

The LORD God formed the man ... and the man became a living being. (Genesis 2:7)

When the Lord created the heavens and the earth, at first there were no trees or greenery because the Lord had not yet sent rain to fall on the earth and there were no human beings to cultivate the soil. Then the Lord caused the first rains to fall, and he also created the first person. The whole earth was like a big, wonderful garden, and the man that the Lord had created lived in this garden. Adam, the first human being, lived in the garden to cultivate it and to take care of it. Adam also gave all the animals their names. God's plan for the man was that he would be very happy and would always remain close to him.

The Lord also created you, just as he created me. Even though much sin has come into the world since the creation, you and I can be assured that God has a very specific plan for our lives and that he wants to achieve his goals by working through us. He knows each one of us by name. He knows where we live, what we look like, and what he wants to accomplish through us. He also very much wants us to be close to him. That is why he gave us Jesus to be our Savior on the cross.

Take some time right now to thank the Lord for making you, just as he made Adam.

W.W.J.

The Lord loves me, he knows me, and he is with me every moment of every day.

Adam

WORK IS A GOOD THING

The LORD God took the man and put him in the Garden of Eden to work it and take care of it. (Genesis 2:15)

After the Lord created Adam, he put him in the Garden of Eden and told him to cultivate it. This was probably the most beautiful garden that has ever existed on earth. There were a variety of trees that were pleasing to the eye and good for food. In the middle of the garden stood the tree of life and the tree of the knowledge of good and evil. Adam probably spent all his days nurturing the fruit of the garden and naming the multitude of animals. A river flowed from Eden, and from it the garden was to be watered.

Some people think that work only came into existence after humans fell into sin. Many people think that work is a punishment and that it would be much better if every single day could be a holiday. However, this is not how the Lord created us. People are created to work. And when we do work that means something to someone else, we immediately experience a good feeling in our hearts. That is why we should thank God for the work that we can do.

It makes no difference whether you are going to school, helping out at home, or washing the car – these are all good things with which to keep yourself busy. The Lord wants us to be hardworking and energetic in all our work.

It is a pleasure to see people enjoying their work. Watch how ants work. They are always busy and industrious, and the Bible tells us that we should learn from them. If there is something that you have to do today, do it enthusiastically and without complaining. God wants us to be busy and to enjoy our work.

W.W.J.

Jesus was a carpenter and later he became a teacher and healer of people. If we walk with him, we will also be good workers.

Satan

He Wears a Mask

Now the serpent was more crafty than any of the wild animals the LORD God had made. (Genesis 3:1)

If the devil approached Eve openly and frankly, she would probably have realized that his words were a lie. However, he did not approach her openly. He is much too sly and clever to have chosen the straight-forward way. That is why he devised a different plan and instead went to Eve in the form of a serpent, or snake.

You might have seen someone wearing a mask before. When you put on a mask, no one can see your real face. When you wear a mask you are hiding, and you don't look at all like the person you really are.

The devil always comes to us wearing a mask. He approaches us with all kinds of lovely words and beautiful ideas. Sometimes he comes to us in the form of an irresistible offer that someone makes us. Sometimes he comes bearing money in his hands. He usually whispers sweet little words in our ears and promises us all that is beautiful and wonderful. But he is the biggest liar and deceiver that has ever existed, and he never means what he says. We should always be sure that what we are doing, or what we want to do, is in line with God's will. Fortunately, we have the Bible and the Holy Spirit in our hearts, both of which help us to know whether something is right or wrong.

W.W.J.

When we are with Jesus, we can be just who we are. In his company all our masks are removed.

Eve

DISSATISFIED ABOUT NOTHING

When the woman saw that the fruit of the tree was good for food and pleasing to the eye ... she took some and ate it. (Genesis 3:6)

There were many things to enjoy in the garden that God created for the first people. Adam and Eve could eat as much as they wanted of the fruit that God created, every day of their lives. When they were thirsty they could drink some of the cool water from any one of a number of streams, because all the water was completely clean and pure. They could go wherever they wanted and could enjoy laughing and playing and sleeping whenever they wanted.

Unfortunately, a very sad thing happened. We read in the Bible that the devil, who is also called Satan, disguised himself and went to Eve in the form of a serpent, or snake. He told Eve that she really shouldn't be so contented; after all, there was one tree in the garden from which they were not allowed to eat. Satan lied to Eve, making her question God's prohibition. Perhaps God didn't really love them if there was something he held back from them. Satan told Eve that God did not want them to eat the fruit of this tree because God knew that they would become like him if they did. And this is how the devil persuaded Eve to go against the will of the Lord.

Eve started feeling dissatisfied that she couldn't have fruit from that one tree (even though she had everything else). She started believing that the devil may have been right – that she and Adam could be just like God – so she ate the fruit of the tree. Suddenly sin came into her life and changed everything. From that day on sin has been the cause of death and suffering, pain, accidents, and sorrow. If only Eve had been content with the Lord's instructions, you and I and the whole world would never know pain. Let's learn from Eve to be content with what the Lord gives us and to trust that what he wants us to do is for our good.

W.W.J.

When we walk with Jesus, we should always be contented. He is the source of living water and the true bread of life.

January 5

Adam and Eve

THEY HID FROM THE LORD

Then the man and his wife ... hid from the Lord God among the trees of the garden. (Genesis 3:8)

As we have been reading, Adam and Eve were the very first people the Lord created. They lived happily in a wonderful garden. They could play with all the animals that God created. They could eat the fruit of all the trees in the garden, but God told them that there was one tree from which they were not allowed to eat the fruit. This was the tree of the knowledge of good and evil. He gave them a choice – they could choose to obey God, or choose to disobey. If they did not eat of the fruit of the tree, he would know that they really loved him.

Unfortunately, Adam and Eve disobeyed God. They ate the fruit of the tree of the knowledge of good and evil. The moment they did this, sin came into this world. The very first thing that Adam and Eve saw was that they were naked. They felt so ashamed that they went and hid themselves among the trees in the garden.

Adam and Eve hid from God because they were scared of what God would say about their disobedience. It is exactly the same with us. When we commit a sin or when we rebel against God, we feel ashamed before the Lord. We want to hide, and we are afraid. Fortunately, Jesus died for our sins so that we can say that we are sorry. This is the only way for us once again to stand before God, clothed in the garments of forgiveness.

W.W.J.

When we walk with Jesus, we never have to feel ashamed or afraid. With him at our side, we will always be walking in the light.

January 6

Adam

HE ALLOWED HIMSELF TO BE PERSUADED

The man said: "The woman you put here with me – she gave me some fruit from the tree, and I ate it." (Genesis 3:12)

The Lord created all things to be beautiful. The sea, the animals of the field, the clouds, the mountains – actually, all of creation was beautiful. On the last day of creation, God also created man. The first man's name was Adam. Adam was very happy, but God saw that he needed a helper, a mate. That is why he created Eve. She was the first woman and was Adam's mate. The two of them were very happy together.

But unfortunately, Eve listened to what the snake – no, actually the devil – told her. She ate the fruit of the tree of the knowledge of good and evil. She thought that it was a truly delicious fruit. She found it incredibly beautiful and alluring because she believed it would give her and Adam unlimited knowledge. Then she went to Adam and persuaded him to eat of the fruit also.

Adam knew what the Lord had told them about this tree's fruit. Adam should have corrected Eve right then and there by telling her that the fruit of that tree was off-limits to them. But when Eve spoke such tempting words, when she showed him the fruit and he smelled its delicious fragrance, when she told him that they would surely prosper if they ate the fruit, he believed her. As a result, he joined Eve in sinning against God.

Sometimes our friends, or other people, try to convince us to do things that we know are wrong. Let's learn a lesson from Adam. Afterward he was very sad because he had listened to Eve, and they both had to face severe consequences for their disobedience. We should listen to God first, and then to the opinions of other people. God's words are always the most important.

W.W.J.

Walking with Jesus means that we always listen to what he tells us to do.

Cain

The First Murderer

Now Cain said to his brother Abel, "Let's go out to the field." And while they were in the field, Cain attacked his brother Abel and killed him. (Genesis 4:8)

Cain and Abel were brothers. They were the children of Adam and Eve. Cain worked the land and produced fruit, vegetables, and grain. Abel kept flocks of sheep, cattle, and other animals.

One day Cain was feeling very discontented with the Lord. He was also very angry with his brother Abel because the Lord had accepted Abel's offering and rejected Cain's. So Cain decided to do a terrible thing. He killed his younger brother. Afterward, he just continued with his work and pretended that nothing had happened. But God had seen everything Cain did.

The Lord then spoke to Cain and asked him where his brother was. Cain gave the Lord a very rude and grumpy answer. But then the Lord said that he knew that Cain had killed his brother. As punishment, Cain would become a restless wanderer on the earth. Cain was cursed and driven from the land where he had killed his brother. The soil would also no longer yield its crops for Cain. He would be forced to wander aimlessly from place to place.

It was because Cain fostered bad feelings in his heart that he murdered his brother. You and I should always work to be at peace with our family, and we should always talk problems through in the calmest way. We should never hurt one another. We should also never attack our family or friends with a sharp tongue. When we say cruel things to each other, it is almost as bad as committing murder. Let us love one another instead.

W.W.J.

Jesus taught us to love one another sincerely and to never hurt one another.

Noah

COULD IT BE TRUE?

And Noah did all that the LORD commanded him. (Genesis 7:5)

Noah lived in a time when people were becoming more and more wicked and corrupt each day. People did just as they pleased and no longer paid any attention to the Lord's words. The earth was full of sin, and people did many evil things. The Lord was sorry that he had created these people, because they did not do what he wanted them to do. He then decided to wipe humanity off the face of the earth, together with all the sins that they had committed.

God saw that Noah loved him. Noah always tried to do what the Lord asked. So God went to Noah and gave him an assignment. He asked Noah to build a big ark. This ark was a huge ship, and a male and female of each kind of animal on earth had to be brought in pairs onto the ship so that they could survive. Noah and his family also had to go into the ark.

Then old Noah started building. He spent years and years building, and I think everyone must have had a good laugh at his expense. They probably thought that old Noah had gone completely off his rocker. Why would he want to build a big ship when there wasn't even any water around? Perhaps Noah himself wondered whether God's instructions to him were right. Did God perhaps make a mistake?

After many years had passed, God sent heavy rains on the earth. It rained for forty days and forty nights, and the floodwaters rose so high that all the people on earth drowned. Noah, his family, and all the animals that had been taken into the ark were the only ones who survived.

Sometimes the Lord gives us instructions, too. When this happens we should do what the Lord asks of us, even when people laugh at us and even when we wonder if we heard the Lord right. God never makes a mistake. Let's do everything that he tells us to do in his Word.

W.W.J.

We walk with Jesus when we do as he commands us.

January 9

The Babylonians

THEY WERE ARROGANT

Then they said: "Come, let us build ourselves a city, with a tower that reaches to the heavens, so that we may make a name for ourselves." (Genesis 11:4)

After the flood, the people on earth started increasing again. All the people all over the world spoke the same language. The people settled in a plain in Shinar. This is where they learned to use bricks instead of stone to construct buildings. They were so proud of their bricks that they decided to build themselves a really big building.

The people made bricks and baked them thoroughly in a furnace. Then they started building. They built and built and built, until they eventually built a very high tower. Every day they continued to build it higher and higher because they wanted it to reach to the heavens. They imagined that if they could build a tower that high, they would be almost like God. They were nothing but stuck-up braggarts.

The Lord saw the tower, but he also looked deep into their hearts. He saw that they thought themselves more important than God. He knew that if he left them to continue this way, they would simply do something even more arrogant the next time. God decided that he would come down from heaven and confuse their language so that the people would be unable to understand one another. While the Babylonians were still happily chatting along, they discovered that they could no longer understand each other at all. They scratched their heads and struggled for a long time, but try as they might they could not communicate with one another. They decided to stop building the city, and each of them went in his or her own direction. They called the place of the tower "Babel," which means "to confuse," because there the Lord confused the language of the whole world.

The Lord dislikes people who think too highly of themselves. Today, let us be humble before the Lord and before all people in everything we do.

W.W.J.

Jesus said that those who are meek in spirit are blessed.

January 10

Abram

Yes, Lord

The LORD had said to Abram, "Leave your country ... and go to the land I will show you." (Genesis 12:1)

Abram was the son of Terah. Terah decided to go to Canaan. But when he and his family reached a place called Haran, they settled there instead. Terah eventually died in Haran.

Because he had a very specific plan in mind for Abram, the Lord told Abram that he had to leave his country and go to the land that the Lord would show him. The Lord also promised Abram that he would bless him and make him a very important man. Abram left his country in obedience to the word of the Lord. The Lord led Abram to the country of Canaan. There he appeared to Abram and said to him: "To your offspring I will give this land." Then Abram built an altar and worshiped God.

It could not have been easy for Abram to leave his familiar environment just like that in order to follow the Lord. But he was obedient to the Lord's word, and therefore the Lord blessed him. When the Lord asks us to do something for him, we would be very foolish to say no to him. Every boy or girl or man or woman who acts according to his or her own will and opposes the will of the Lord is looking for trouble and will never really be happy. Let us follow Abram's example and simply say: "Yes, Lord."

W.W.J.

When the Lord leads us in a particular direction, we follow him step-by-step.

Abram

HE WAS AFRAID

"Say you are my sister, so that I will be treated well for your sake and my life will be spared because of you." (Genesis 12:13)

When Abram arrived in Canaan, there was a terrible famine in the land. Abram and his family went to live in Egypt so that they could survive. Just as they were about to enter Egypt, Abram said to his wife Sarai, *"I know what a beautiful woman you are. When the Egyptians see you, they will say, 'This is his wife.' Then they will kill me but will let you live"* (Genesis 12:11-12). Abram told her to lie. He told her to say that she was his sister, so that his life would be spared. Abram was very scared. He didn't believe that the Lord would be able to save and protect him. That is why he made this silly little plan.

Matters turned out just as Abram had predicted. The Egyptians saw that Sarai was very beautiful. They praised her to Pharaoh, who took her into his palace as his wife. Everyone thought that she was Abram's sister. Because of Abram and Sarai's lie, terrible trouble nearly befell them all. The Lord had to intervene, and he inflicted serious diseases on Pharaoh and his household. Pharaoh then sent Abram and Sarai away from Egypt.

Even when we are very afraid, we should trust in the Lord rather than trying to take things into our own hands to "fix" them.

W.W.J.

When we are walking with Jesus, we need not be afraid and tell lies. He will help us.

January 12

Abram

A Very Wrong Plan

So after Abram had been living in Canaan ten years, Sarai his wife took her Egyptian maidservant Hagar and gave her to her husband to be his wife. (Genesis 16:3)

Sarai really wanted to have a child, but she had not been able to have a baby. The Lord did promise Abram that he and Sarai would have children, but Sarai was becoming discouraged with waiting. So she made a plan. Unfortunately, it was a very wrong plan.

She decided to give one of her maidservants, named Hagar, to her husband. She knew that Hagar could bear children, and she believed that this could be a solution to their problems, because then she and Abram could have a child. But things went terribly wrong. After Hagar had given birth to Abram's child, Sarai and Hagar got into a big argument, and Hagar ran away. The child Hagar had with Abram was called Ishmael. The Lord knew that Isaac would be born, and that is why he was not pleased with Sarai and Abram's little plan. To this day there is still war between the descendants of Isaac and those of Ishmael.

From this we learn that we should wait patiently. We should not become impatient and make our own decisions when God has already revealed his plan to us. If we do this, we invariably make a mess of everything.

W.W.J.

Jesus is the One who will teach us what to do.

Sarah

She Laughed

Then the Lord said to Abraham, "Why did Sarah laugh?" (Genesis 18:13)

The Lord promised that Abram and Sarai would have children, and he also changed their names to Abraham and Sarah. But after many years had passed, there was still no sign of a child. They probably thought that the Lord had forgotten his promise. But the Lord never forgets a promise.

One day three visitors arrived at Abraham's tent. It was a very hot day and Abraham offered them some water to wash their feet and invited them to rest awhile in the shade of a tree. He offered them food as well.

The men told Abraham that he and Sarah would have a son within the next year. Sarah was listening at the entrance to the tent, and when she heard the news about a son, she laughed to herself. She could not believe what the man was saying. She thought that she was much too old. Surely no one who was ninety years old could have a baby!

As it turned out, it was the Lord's messengers who had brought the good news. Even though it was the Lord speaking, Sarah still laughed in disbelief at his words.

There are many people who laugh at the things that the Lord has promised us. Some of them even laugh at and mock the Lord. But he laughs best who laughs last. Later, Sarah was probably very ashamed that she had laughed at God.

W.W.J.

Let us walk with Jesus, even when our friends ridicule and laugh at us because of what we believe.

January 14

Lot's Wife

SHE TURNED INTO A PILLAR OF SALT

One of them said, "Flee for your lives! Don't look back!" (Genesis 19:17)

Lot and his family lived in Sodom. Sodom was a very wicked place. People did just as they pleased and did not listen to God. God decided to put an end to Sodom and all its sin. Abraham pleaded with God to spare the people of Sodom. The Lord told Abraham that he would spare the city if he could find merely ten people in the city who loved him and wanted to follow his ways. But there were not even ten righteous people in all of Sodom.

The Lord, however, did decide to spare Lot and his family. He sent angels to them, and the angels told them that they all had to flee from Sodom. One of the angels also told them that they should not look back, otherwise they would surely die. At the coming of dawn, the angel told Lot that he should take his wife and two daughters and get out of the city. Just as the sun rose over the land, the Lord rained down burning sulfur on Sodom and Gomorrah. Lot's wife made the mistake of looking back at the scene, and something terrible happened to her. She turned into a pillar of salt.

Sometimes the Lord gives us specific commands in his Word. For example, he says that we must not commit murder and that we must not steal. It is a really foolish person who would then go and do precisely what the Lord has commanded us not to do. Let's learn a lesson from Lot's wife. We should do as the Lord tells us.

W.W.J.

If we walk with Jesus, we have to live according to his commands.

Abraham

At Last He Became a Daddy

Abraham was a hundred years old when his son Isaac was born to him. (Genesis 21:5)

One night, the Lord appeared to Abraham and told him to look up at the stars and to try to count them all. But you and I know that Abraham would never have been able to count the number of stars in the heavens! The Lord then told Abraham that he would have as many children as there are stars in the heavens. It was very difficult for Abraham to believe these words.

At that time Abraham and his wife Sarah were still childless, yet they knew that God had promised them offspring. Even though Abraham and Sarah were doubtful, God kept his word. When Abraham was a hundred years old, Isaac was born. Isaac fathered children, and his children had children, and they all had children, and now, after many, many years, the descendants of Abraham are too many to count – just like the stars in the heavens. God kept his word.

There are many promises in the Bible. God gives all of these promises to us. When God makes a promise, we should hold on to it, because he will always keep his word.

W.W.J.

To walk with Jesus means to hold on to his promises from day to day.

January 16

God

There he called upon the name of the Lord, the Eternal God. (Genesis 21: 33)

There is an unusual name for God that we find in the Bible. This is the name El Olam, and it means "the Eternal God." This is the name that Abraham gave to the Lord when he planted a tamarisk tree in Beersheba and worshiped the Lord there. (A tamarisk is a very beautiful tree.)

Abraham declared that God is an eternal God. All the other gods worshiped by the pagan nations were just manmade objects, and they would all pass away and eventually disappear. But not the God of Abraham. He is a God who has existed from eternity, and who will continue to exist for all eternity. He is the One who lives forever. Time begins in him and runs its course in him, but it has no effect on him. Long after people and time have passed away, God will still be there. All earthly things pass. Holidays pass. School passes. The fun of parties passes. But the Eternal God will always be there.

It is nice to know that there is someone who is always the same and who will live forever. This is God. If we give our lives to the Lord and have the right kind of relationship with him, God gives us a wonderful gift. He gives us a little piece of his eternity. He gives us eternal life. Even though our lives here on earth will pass and our bodies will eventually die, our hearts and spirits will live with God forever. Thank the Lord that you can have eternal life with him. Worship him as the Eternal God.

W.W.J.

Jesus said that he gives us eternal life, and that no one will be able to tear us from his hand.

Abraham

That's Terrible!

Then God said, "Take your son, your only son, Isaac, whom you love, and go to the region of Moriah. Sacrifice him there as a burnt offering." (Genesis 22:2)

The Lord wanted to accomplish great things through Abraham. Abraham would be the father of many nations. When the Lord wants to use someone, he expects that person to be faithful to him. The Lord wishes us to love him wholeheartedly and to show our love for him by our lives. Perhaps that is why he decided to test Abraham.

God told Abraham to sacrifice his only son, whom Abraham loved very much. To us, this sounds outrageous. We are almost tempted to say that this is just too much to ask of someone. How could God do something like that? It almost seems as if the Lord is heartless, as if he does not care. But the Lord only wanted to test Abraham.

Abraham's heart was very heavy while he was walking toward Moriah where he had to sacrifice his son. Initially, Abraham couldn't find it in his heart to tell Isaac about everything that God had said. He simply said that he believed that the Lord himself would provide a lamb for the burnt offering. Just as Abraham picked up the knife to slay his son, the Lord intervened and stopped him. Then God said to Abraham, *"Now I know that you fear God, because you have not withheld from me your son, your only son"* (Genesis 22:12). Suddenly Abraham saw a ram caught by its horns in a thicket nearby, which he took and sacrificed as a burnt offering. Abraham then called that place "The Lord Will Provide."

Sometimes the Lord tests us to see whether we truly love him. May we pass the test, just as did Abraham.

W.W.J.

When we walk with Jesus, our faith will be tested many times. However, he will always provide for all our needs.

January 18

God

ENOUGH FOR YOU, TOO

So Abraham called that place The Lord Will Provide. (Genesis 22:14)

You will remember that the Lord asked Abraham to sacrifice his only son as a burnt offering to him. God made this demand because he wanted to test Abraham, to see whether Abraham truly trusted him. Abraham was faithful to the Lord, so he took his son Isaac and went to the region of Moriah. In his heart, he prayed and believed that the Lord would provide.

Just as Abraham was about to sacrifice his son, God called out to him from heaven and told him to stop. When Abraham looked up he saw a ram caught by the horns in a nearby bush. He then took the ram and sacrificed it – instead of Isaac – as a burnt offering to the Lord. Then Abraham called that place "The Lord Will Provide."

This name of God tells us that the Lord wants to provide for all our needs. When the Lord sees that we need him and that we serve him, he likes to provide for us. To provide for someone means to give him or her something because you know that person needs it. All the treasures of the Lord are available to us. God gladly provides for us, as long as it is within his will and in our best interests. His provision in our lives should also serve to glorify him.

What do you lack? What do you need urgently? God can provide all these things. He is also called the Provider. Ask him to help you and to provide for you. Trust him with your life. Praise and worship him. Serve him with all your heart. Then God will gladly provide for you.

W. W. J.

Jesus said that we should first seek his kingdom and righteousness, and then he will provide us with everything else (Matthew 6:33).

Ephron

A Kind Man

Abraham went to mourn for Sarah and to weep over her. (Genesis 23:2)

While Abraham and his family were living near Hebron, his wife Sarah died. Abraham was very sad and mourned for her and wept over her. It is always a very sad thing when someone you love dies. Abraham then had to bury Sarah. But Abraham did not own his own land, and he was a stranger in a foreign country. He therefore had to ask permission to buy some property for a burial site where he could bury his wife.

Abraham went to the Hittites and asked them if they would sell him some property. One of the Hittites was named Ephron, and he told Abraham that he had some land. Abraham wanted to pay for the land, but Ephron told him to take the land as a gift. At first Abraham did not want to, but then Ephron said to him, *"Listen to me, my lord; the land is worth four hundred shekels of silver, but what is that between me and you? Bury your dead"* (Genesis 23:15). Ephron was kind to Abraham. He knew that Abraham's heart was filled with grief, and he wanted to do something to help him feel a little bit better.

We read about people dying every day, and we also see it on the news. Sometimes people close to us die. Sometimes a family member of one of our friends dies. When this happens we should go out of our way to be kind to those who have lost their loved ones. Is there someone you can console today? Write a note or a card, or phone someone and tell him or her that you care.

W.W.J.

Jesus was sad along with Martha and Mary when their brother, Lazarus, died. He taught us to care for those who are mourning and grieving (John 11:35-36).

Eliezer

LORD, SHOW ME ...

Then he prayed ... (Genesis 24:12)

Eliezer was the chief servant of Abraham's household (Genesis 15: 2-3). Abraham sent him to a distant country to find a wife for Isaac. Eliezer very much wanted to please his master and probably wondered if he would be able to make the right choice. Because he was a child of God, he decided to trust the Lord to show him which woman to choose. In those days, a family usually chose the children's future husbands or wives.

Eliezer had a serious conversation with the Lord and prayed that the Lord would show him the right girl. He asked God to give him a sign. The Bible says that even before he had finished praying, Rebekah came out with her water jar on her shoulder. Eliezer quickly realized that this was the woman the Lord had sent.

You and I should always talk to the Lord about everything – no matter how important or unimportant it may seem. We need to learn God's will in order to be able to follow it. He wants to lead us, and he will always help us. Ask him for wisdom and clarity.

W.W.J.

Walking with Jesus also means talking to him regularly.

January 21

Rebekah

A Good and Hardworking Young Woman

"Drink, my lord," she said. (Genesis 24:18)

Abraham was very old, and he had a son named Isaac. He knew that Isaac needed a wife, but he was very worried that Isaac would marry the wrong woman. It is, after all, very important for us to marry the right person. That is why Abraham decided to send his servant to his native land. There the servant was to find a good woman for Isaac to marry.

After the servant had traveled a very long distance, he was thirsty and tired. He arrived at a well. While the servant sat beside the well, a very beautiful young woman arrived and filled her jar with water. The servant then asked, "Please give me a little water from your jar." She answered, "Drink, my lord." And then she offered to draw water for his camels, so that they could also drink their fill. Camels drink a lot of water, and it probably took her a very long time to draw enough water for all of them. The servant saw that she was a good, hardworking young woman. In his heart, he knew that the Lord wanted to give this woman to Isaac to be his wife.

Let us learn from Rebekah not to think of ourselves only. We should share whatever we have with others. As a matter of fact, we should go beyond just sharing and give more than what is expected of us.

W.W.J.

A person who walks with Jesus quickly learns that other people's needs are very important.

Jacob

He Hatched His Own Little Plans

Jacob replied, "First sell me your birthright." (Genesis 25:31)

Jacob and Esau were twins. They were the sons of Isaac and Rebekah. Esau had red hair and became a skillful hunter who liked walking around in the open countryside. Jacob was a quiet boy who preferred to stay at home. Isaac favored Esau because he really liked wild game. Rebekah favored Jacob.

One day, when Esau came home from hunting, he was very tired and absolutely famished. Jacob was cooking a delicious stew and Esau wanted some of it. Then Jacob devised a clever little plan. He wanted to have the birthright that belonged to Esau, the firstborn. In those days, the firstborn son was the most important, and he inherited all the most valuable things. So Jacob told Esau that he could have some stew if Esau would sell his birthright to him.

Esau thought that his birthright probably wasn't that important anyway, and he made a deal with Jacob. If Jacob would give him some stew, he would give his birthright to Jacob. This was not a very nice thing for Jacob to do. This is perhaps why Jacob's name means "trickster." He deceived Esau just so that he could have his own way and improve his own position. Christians should always be honest and open. They should never devise double-dealing plots to get their own way. Let's learn from Jacob and decide to never take someone else's possessions just so that we can be wealthier and better off.

W.W.J.

A person who walks with Jesus puts an end to all underhanded dealings.

Jacob

FOURTEEN YEARS OF HARD WORK

Jacob was in love with Rachel and said, "I'll work for you seven years in return for your younger daughter Rachel." (Genesis 29:18)

Because Jacob had deceived Esau (which made Esau very angry), Jacob had to flee his home. He went to live in a distant country with his Uncle Laban's family. When he arrived there, he saw a beautiful girl. Her name was Rachel. He found her so beautiful that he immediately wanted to marry her. Jacob told Laban that he would work for him for seven years if he could marry Rachel in return.

It seems as if Laban had just as many tricks up his sleeve as Jacob did. After Jacob had worked hard for seven years, Laban gave Leah instead of Rachel to Jacob. Because his bride was veiled during their marriage, Jacob did not realize that the woman he was marrying was not his beloved Rachel. He was very angry when he realized that Laban had deceived him. But there wasn't much he could do about the situation, even though he did not really love Leah. Then Laban told him that he could have Rachel too, but he would have to work for Laban another seven years! Perhaps the Lord felt sorry for Jacob, because during these seven years Jacob was very blessed and became a wealthy man.

You and I are also occasionally deceived by dishonest people. Perhaps someone has stolen something that belonged to you. Or perhaps a friend did not keep a promise to you. It is not a nice feeling when something like this happens. Fortunately, the Lord sees all these things, and he will always take care of us. So why not forgive the people who have treated you badly?

W.W.J.

Walking with Jesus does not mean that we will never be disappointed. Fortunately, Jesus will never deceive us.

Leah

Is There Anybody There?

"It is because the LORD has seen my misery. Surely my husband will love me now." (Genesis 29:32)

Leah's story is a very sad tale. It is the story of a woman whose father used her to make a profit. Jacob was in love with Leah's sister, Rachel, and wanted to marry her. Her father, Laban, told Jacob that after seven years of work he could have Rachel as his wife. After the seven years, Laban did a very deceitful thing and gave Leah, instead of Rachel, to Jacob. Only after Jacob had married Leah did he find out that she was not Rachel. He didn't like this one bit. He also didn't really love Leah. Nevertheless, he had no choice but to live with her.

For the rest of her life, Leah tried to win Jacob's love. However, she never quite managed to do so. Even the fact that she eventually bore Jacob nine sons never really made him love her. Leah was trapped in a loveless marriage. At night, she may have cried into her pillow because her husband did not really care about her. Sure, he looked after her, but he never truly loved her.

Leah probably often asked herself whether there was anyone who really loved her for who she was. Later in Genesis 29, she answers her own question when she says that she started to praise the Lord for all the children that he had given her. Leah eventually learned to find her joy in the Lord.

There are many women and men who are unhappy in their relationships. The most important lesson to be learned is that happiness does not come from your friends or your companion in life, but from the Lord. Only the Lord can make a person truly happy. This is something that Leah had to learn with time. Pray that the Lord will give you the right marriage partner when you grow up, someone who will love you just as you are. But find your joy in the Lord. He will always love you for who you are.

W.W.J.

Jesus does not have favorites – he treats all people as equals and loves everyone the same.

January 25

Rachel

She Sat on Top of the Household Gods

Now Rachel had taken the household gods and put them inside her camel's saddle and was sitting on them. (Genesis 31:34)

Rachel was Jacob's wife. She was also the daughter of Laban. Laban knew of the Lord, but unfortunately, was not very faithful to him. In those days, many people kept statues of idols in their homes. They did not trust in the Lord, but preferred to put their trust in these household gods. Laban should have known better. He served the Lord, but he also wanted to cling to his idols.

His daughter grew up with these little statues of the gods in the house, and therefore she wanted to have them around her. She thought that the statues would help and protect her. When she and Jacob moved out of her father's house, she stole the household gods. She hid them inside her camel's saddle and sat on them.

When her father realized that the household gods were gone, he went after Jacob and Rachel. He was furious. He searched everything and made them unpack all the luggage. Rachel pretended to be ill and did not get off her camel. In this way, she made sure that her father would not find the statues.

It is a pity that Rachel was just as faithless as her father. She too clung to those useless little idols. Very often we are exactly the same way. We tell the Lord that we love him and trust in him, but then we hold onto all kinds of other things. Some people hold onto predictions made by astrologers. Others put their trust in money or popularity. Let us learn that we should serve the Lord wholeheartedly. We should not take idols along on our journey.

W.W.J.

When we follow Jesus, we leave our idols behind.

Jacob

HE STRUGGLED WITH GOD

So Jacob was left alone, and a man wrestled with him till daybreak. (Genesis 32:24)

Jacob went away from Laban's household with his family and all his flocks. One night, they camped next to a river. Even though Jacob was known for his underhanded trickery and even though he was called a trickster, the Lord still had a plan for his life. God never gives up on anyone. He always wants the best for us.

Because Jacob was afraid of what his brother, Esau, would do to him when he arrived home, he prayed to God. A long time before, the Lord had promised Jacob that he would be with him and bless him. Now Jacob reminded the Lord of his promise and asked the Lord to help him. While he was sitting all by himself next to the river, a man suddenly appeared and started wrestling with Jacob. They wrestled the entire night. Jacob became very tired. Then the man hit Jacob on the hip so hard that his hip was wrenched from its socket. It turned out that it was the Lord who was wrestling with Jacob. The Lord wanted to teach Jacob to be more dependent on him. The Lord also gave Jacob a different name. He would no longer be called Jacob, the "trickster," but Israel, "one who struggles with God and wins." In this way, the Lord blessed Jacob.

W. W. J.

When we walk with Jesus, we must always ask him, as Jacob did, to bless us.

January 27

Joseph

JEALOUSY IS AN UGLY THING

When his brothers saw that their father loved him more than any of them, they hated him and could not speak a kind word to him. (Genesis 37:4)

Jacob had twelve sons, but only two of them were children of his wife Rachel. He loved Rachel very much, but Rachel just could not have very many children. She had prayed and pleaded for the Lord to give her a child. The Lord had heard her prayer, and she brought Joseph into the world. After that, she also gave birth to Benjamin. These two children were very special to Jacob. Of course he loved all his children, but he had a special place in his heart for Joseph. He even gave Joseph a beautiful, bright, colorful coat with long sleeves. When Joseph's brothers saw that their father gave him preferential treatment, they did not like it at all. They became very jealous of him. They were so jealous that they decided to kill him.

Jealousy often causes us to do horrible things to other people. It is never nice to see other people being treated better than you. Sometimes it seems as if your mom or dad has a soft spot for your brother or sister, and then you feel a little bit neglected. When you feel this way, you should talk to your mom or dad about it. It is important that we don't start thinking mean thoughts about other people because we are jealous of them. Remember that the Lord has a plan and a place for every one of us. You should also remember that the Lord never has any favorites. He doesn't give preferential treatment. We are all equally important to him. The Bible says that the Lord is no respecter of persons. This means that no one is more important than anyone else.

W.W.J.

It seems as if Jesus had a special place in his heart for his disciple John but he loved all his disciples just the same (John 13:23). He also loves us very much.

January 28

Joseph

THE DREAMER

"Here comes that dreamer!" they said to each other. (Genesis 37:19)

The Lord loved Joseph very much and had a special plan for his life. That is why the Lord spoke to Joseph in a special way, even when Joseph was still young. He gave Joseph dreams, which all had a particular meaning. Joseph told his brothers and his father all about his dreams, but they did not understand what he was trying to say to them. They thought Joseph was just conceited.

One day, Joseph's father sent him to his brothers, who were tending the flocks in a distant region. Joseph's brothers saw him from a distance, and then and there they decided to kill him. They simply could not understand his relationship with the Lord and all the strange dreams that he had. Fortunately, the Lord made sure that Joseph was not killed by his brothers.

If you walk with the Lord and accept that he has a very specific plan for your life, there will always be people who won't be able to understand you. It may be that the Lord speaks to you in a special way. You may know deep in your heart that he has certain things in mind for your life. If you share these things with other people, they may doubt what you are saying. Perhaps it would be a good idea to talk to the Lord about these things in your quiet time. And if you have a special friend, you can share your thoughts with him or her. But you should be willing to accept that people will fail to understand what you are saying. You must also be willing to accept that people may even reject you while the Lord is busy fulfilling his plan for your life.

W. W. J.

When we walk with Jesus, we will not always be popular.

January 29

Reuben

HE STOPPED THEM

Reuben said this to rescue him from them ... (Genesis 37:22)

Joseph had eleven brothers. The name of his oldest brother was Reuben. Reuben did not agree with his brothers' plan to kill Joseph. He said that they should not kill Joseph, but should instead throw him in a dry well in the desert. He said this so that he could later rescue Joseph and send him back to their father. So the brothers grabbed Joseph, stripped off his clothes, and threw him down the well.

After this, the brothers sat down to eat their meal. When they looked up from their food, they saw a caravan of Ishmaelite traders coming their way. The Ishmaelites were on their way to Egypt, and their camels were loaded with merchandise. Reuben was not there at that time, and one of the other brothers suggested that they sell Joseph, because then they could get some money for sparing his life. So the brothers sold Joseph to the Ishmaelite traders who were on their way to Egypt. When Reuben returned, he was very upset that Joseph had been sold by his brothers. Fortunately, the Lord made sure that Joseph arrived safely in Egypt.

Sometimes we are around people who are plotting cruel plans against others. Perhaps they gossip or say mean things about other people. Perhaps they are planning on stealing something from someone. Perhaps they are being bullies. In situations like these, you can do something good by making a suggestion that will show people a better way to behave. If your friends are planning on doing bad things, I hope that you will be like Reuben and persuade them not to go through with their wickedness.

W.W.J.

Jesus said that we should be like the salt of the earth and like a light that shines in the darkness (Matthew 5:13-14).

January 30

Joseph

HE RAN AWAY

But he ... ran out of the house. (Genesis 39:12)

When Joseph arrived in Egypt, he was sold as a servant (or slave) and went to work in the household of Potiphar, a very important official in Egypt. The Lord was with Joseph and blessed him. Because Joseph was a good, hardworking, and virtuous young man, he also did his work well. He was quickly noticed by others, and everything that he did turned out to be successful. Joseph found favor in Potiphar's eyes, and he was eventually put in charge of Potiphar's entire household and everything he owned.

Potiphar's wife started keeping an eye on Joseph. Joseph was handsome and well-built. Potiphar's wife started having wicked thoughts about Joseph and wanted to tempt him to sin with her. Joseph knew that if he did this, he would be acting contrary to the will of God. He didn't want to disappoint God and so he said "no" to Potiphar's wife. She kept nagging him, but Joseph knew that he would never be able to do something like that because he would be sinning against God. One day, Potiphar's wife grabbed him by the cloak, but Joseph ran away and left his cloak in her hand.

When you and I feel that people want to force us to commit a sin, we should simply run away. It is better to run away than to do wrong things.

W.W.J.

Jesus always loved sinners but fled from sin.

Joseph

GOD CONSOLES

The LORD was with him; he showed him kindness. (Genesis 39:21)

After Joseph ran away from Potiphar's wife, he was in deep trouble. She called the other household slaves and told them that Joseph had tried to hurt her, and that is why he ran away. She claimed that when she screamed, Joseph became frightened and fled, leaving his cloak beside her. When Potiphar heard this story, he was very angry. He had Joseph arrested and thrown in prison.

It must have been very hard for Joseph to endure suffering in prison, all the while knowing that he was innocent. Prison life is not nice at all. In addition, everybody now thought that Joseph was a bad person. But the Bible says that while Joseph was in prison the Lord was with him there as well, and he showed Joseph kindness.

In the same way, the Lord wants to console us when we are hurting, especially when we have to suffer for something we did not do. God consoled Joseph, and what is more, God made sure that Joseph found favor in the eyes of the prison warden. Later he put Joseph in charge of all the prisoners held captive in that prison. The Bible says, *"The LORD was with Joseph and gave him success in whatever he did"* (Genesis 39:23), even in prison.

W.W.J.

The fact that the Lord is always near us should be our consolation. He knows everything, even when we are suffering for something we did not do.

Joseph

FROM PRISON TO PALACE

Thus he put him in charge of the whole land of Egypt. (Genesis 41:43)

The Bible tells us that God was with Joseph while he was in prison. He consoled Joseph, looked after him, and gave him success. The cupbearer and the baker of Egypt's king were also in prison with Joseph. These two each had a dream the same night. When Joseph came to them the next morning, he saw that they were dejected. They told him about their dreams. The Lord then gave Joseph the wisdom to interpret their dreams. Unfortunately, the news he had for the baker was very sad: he would be killed in three days. The cupbearer would be set free in three days. Everything happened just as Joseph predicted.

Two full years later, while Joseph was still in the same prison, the king also had a dream that disturbed him greatly (Genesis 41:1). No one could explain his dream to him. Then the cupbearer remembered about Joseph. He told the king all about Joseph, and the king sent for Joseph in prison. Joseph then interpreted the king's dream for him. The dream had to do with the future of Egypt – and Joseph even had a plan for how the king could handle it. The king was so happy that he put Joseph in charge of all Egypt; only Pharaoh himself held a more important position. God performed a miracle by helping Joseph – rescuing him from prison and taking him right into a palace.

Perhaps you are in trouble today, but remember that God can help you.

W.W.J.

We experience wonderful things when we walk with Jesus.

February 2

Joseph

HE FORGAVE

And he kissed all his brothers and wept over them. (Genesis 45:15)

While Joseph was in charge of Egypt, the country experienced seven years of great abundance. The harvests were plentiful, and Joseph stored huge amounts of grain to prepare them for a coming famine, which God had predicted through Joseph. When the famine struck, it devastated nearby lands. When Jacob, Joseph's father, heard that there was grain in Egypt, he sent his sons there to buy some. And this is how it came about that Joseph's brothers traveled to Egypt.

Joseph was the governor of Egypt, and he himself sold the grain to people. His brothers went to him and bowed down before him with their faces to the ground. When Joseph saw his brothers, he immediately recognized them. They, however, did not recognize him. Joseph questioned them about their homeland and pretended not to know them. The youngest brother, Benjamin, was not there with the rest of the brothers, and Joseph very much wanted to see him. So he commanded that one of the brothers stay behind while the other brothers returned home with the grain. They then had to come back and bring Benjamin to him. Joseph's brothers were very afraid, but they did as he told them.

When Joseph saw Benjamin, he started crying. He told his brothers everything. They were afraid that Joseph would do something to punish them, but Joseph assured them that he had forgiven them completely. Joseph knew that God had used all the horrible things that had happened to bring about something wonderful.

Sometimes we see only the cruel things that people do to us, and we do not understand that something good can come from these bad things. When God is in control of our lives, he can use the horrible things to make good things happen. Let's forgive those who do bad things to us.

W.W.J.

Just think of how people abused Jesus on the cross, and yet this is how he became our Savior.

February 3

Joseph

He Saved His Country

"You have saved our lives," they said. (Genesis 47:25)

After seven years of abundance, a famine came to Egypt. The famine lasted seven years. The Lord had warned Pharaoh beforehand in a dream that there would be seven years of abundance followed by seven years of famine. This was the dream that Joseph had interpreted for Pharaoh. The Lord then gave Joseph wisdom, and for seven years Joseph stored up all the grain that he could so that there would be enough grain for the seven years of famine.

When the famine had spread over the whole country and there was no food left, the people came to Joseph for grain. Joseph took their livestock in exchange for grain. When they no longer had any livestock, they gave him their land in exchange for grain. In this way Joseph bought all the land in Egypt for Pharaoh. Then Joseph told the people, *"Now that I have bought you and your land today for Pharaoh, here is seed for you so you can plant the ground. But when the crop comes in, give a fifth of it to Pharaoh. The other four-fifths you may keep as seed for the fields and as food for yourselves and your households and your children"* (Genesis 47:23-24). The people were very glad and saw that Joseph was very clever. They told him that he had saved their lives and that they would serve him and Pharaoh.

Joseph was the leader of Egypt, and the Lord gave him wisdom. He was a good ruler, and therefore the Egyptians prospered, despite the famine in the land. We too require good leaders like Joseph. Every country needs good rulers. That is why we should pray for our leaders and ask the Lord to give them wisdom, as he gave Joseph wisdom. If our leaders follow the Lord and love him, our country will also prosper, and we will be able to praise and worship the Lord for helping us. Take some time to pray for our political leaders today.

W. W. J.

When we walk with Jesus we honor our leaders and do good to others.

February 4

Moses

THE BABY IN THE BASKET

But when she could hide him no longer, she got a papyrus basket for him and ... placed the child in it. (Exodus 2:3)

Moses was born in Egypt. In Egypt, many years after Joseph died, all the Israelites had become the slaves of the Egyptians. The Bible tells us that Moses was a very beautiful baby. His mother hid him for three months, because Pharaoh had ordered all the newborn boys of the Israelites to be thrown into the Nile. He did this because he was afraid that the Israelites would continue to multiply and become too numerous to control. But after three months, Moses' mother could no longer hide him. So his mother made a different plan.

She got a papyrus basket and coated it with tar and pitch to make it waterproof. She placed Moses in the basket and put it among the reeds along the bank of the Nile. Moses' sister stood at a distance to see what would happen to him. Pharaoh's daughter came to the Nile to bathe in the water, and there she saw the basket. When she saw the beautiful baby boy, she felt sorry for him and decided to raise him as her own. This is how it came about that Moses was raised in Pharaoh's palace. Everything happened this way because the Lord had a special plan for Moses' life. Moses was rescued from the hands of Pharaoh's soldiers – and by none other than Pharaoh's own daughter. Only the Lord could have devised a plan like that!

The Lord had been working on a plan to rescue the Israelites from the hands of the Egyptians for a very long time. God saw that the Israelites had to work very hard, and he saw how badly they suffered in Egypt. The Lord's plan was to train Moses to be a leader so that he could set the Israelites free. The Lord has a plan for your life, too. He knows where you have been raised and what kind of personality you have. You too can be an instrument in his service.

W.W.J.

When we walk with Jesus, we find out all about God's big plan for our lives.

February 5

God

They Call Him Yahweh

God said to Moses, "I am who I am." (Exodus 3:14)

If we know the names of the Lord, we may be able to understand him a little bit better. We may also appreciate him more. God's names tell us something about who he is. These names are not nicknames, but proper, true names. They tell us about his personality and his characteristics.

The name most often used for the Lord is Yahweh. This is the name that God told to Moses. When the people asked Moses who sent him to Egypt, Moses would say that Yahweh, had sent him – the One who is who he is.

It is rather a strange name, isn't it? Actually the Lord simply wants to tell us that we cannot fully describe him. We cannot really say who he is. Our intellects, our minds, are simply too small. He is too big and too wonderful and too different from us. He is who he is. We cannot prove his existence. We cannot define him. We cannot give an accurate description of him. He is simply what he is. Because he is so great, we can do nothing but bow before him.

God is still this big and wonderful God in your life today. Kneel before him. Accept that he is completely different from you. Know that he is much bigger and much more powerful than any human being. He will reveal himself to you in each and every circumstance of your life.

W.W.J.

Jesus tried to teach his disciples who the Father is. They didn't quite understand what he was telling them. But the day came when they finally understood.

February 6

Moses

A MAN OF MANY EXCUSES

But Moses said, "O LORD, please send someone else to do it." (Exodus 4:13)

The Lord wanted to use Moses to lead his people out of Egypt. Perhaps Moses almost wrecked God's plan, because we read in the Bible that at one time Moses became so angry about his people's suffering in Egypt that he killed an Egyptian. As a result, Moses had to flee to a faraway country, or else he would have been in deep trouble. In this distant country, Moses tended flocks in the desert to make a living. One day the angel of the Lord appeared to him in flames of fire from within a bush. The Lord then spoke to Moses and told him to return to Egypt and liberate the people of Israel from Pharaoh's oppression.

Even though the Lord was speaking to him, Moses did not want to go. He asked, "Who am I, that I should dare go to Pharaoh and bring the Israelites out of Egypt?" The Lord assured Moses that he would be with him and help him. But Moses had another excuse: "Suppose the Israelites do not believe what I tell them and refuse to listen to me? What if they say that the Lord did not really appear to me?" The Lord assured Moses that his strength would help Moses and would convince the Israelites that he was telling the truth. Again Moses had an excuse: "O Lord, I am slow of speech and tongue and can't really speak all that well in front of crowds." But the Lord assured him that it would not be a problem. Still Moses was not done with his excuses: "Please Lord, send someone else to do it." Then the Lord became angry at Moses, and Moses realized that he really had no choice but to go.

When God is on your side, you will always be successful. I hope you will not have as many excuses as Moses did when the Lord wants to use you. Sometimes we think that we are not good enough for the Lord to use us. But this is not true at all. It is not because we are good that the Lord wants to use us, but because we are willing.

W.W.J.

Jesus shows us that we can be instruments in his hands.

February 7

Moses

GOD IS THE MOST POWERFUL

"Then I will lay my hand on Egypt and with mighty acts of judgment I will bring out ... my people the Israelites." (Exodus 7:4)

Moses and Aaron went to Pharaoh, who was not at all willing to listen to a bunch of his slaves. So, Aaron threw his staff on the floor before Pharaoh and his officials, and the staff turned into a big snake. The Egyptian magicians then did the same thing with their staffs. But Aaron's staff swallowed up all their staffs. Despite this, Pharaoh remained stubborn and refused to let the people go.

After this, God brought ten plagues upon Egypt. All the water turned into blood. Millions of frogs crawled all over everything: in the houses, in the ovens, and even in the kneading troughs. Trillions of gnats came upon men and animals – every little particle of dust turned into a gnat. A plague of flies ruined the land throughout Egypt. A plague broke out among the livestock and killed thousands of horses, donkeys, camels, cattle, sheep, and goats. Boils broke out on the bodies of all the Egyptians and they were in terrible pain. Devastating hailstorms wreaked havoc upon the land. Then the Lord sent locusts that devoured what little was left after the destruction of the hail. After this, there were three whole days of complete darkness and the people were very afraid. The last plague was the most terrible. All the firstborn sons of the Egyptians died in one single night. The magicians of Egypt could imitate many plagues, but the last one was just too terrible. Then Pharaoh realized that God was more powerful than all his magicians, and he decided to let the Israelites go.

The Lord is more powerful than anyone else, be it a human being or any other god or idol. He proved his might against Pharaoh. Ask that the Lord will make his strength and power visible to others through your life.

W.W.J.

When we walk with Jesus, we have the God of the universe on our side.

February 8

Moses

An Entire Army Drowns

The LORD swept them into the sea. (Exodus 14:27)

After the tenth plague, Pharaoh gave his permission for the Israelites to leave Egypt. They were overjoyed to be free and started traveling toward the Red Sea. During the day, the Lord went ahead of his people in a pillar of cloud to guide them on their way, and by night, a pillar of fire gave them light. Thus, the Israelites could travel by day or by night.

When Pharaoh realized that the Israelites were gone for good, he regretted his decision and decided to pursue them. He realized that he would no longer have enough slaves to work for him. He had his chariot made ready and took his entire army with him. They pursued the Israelites and eventually overtook them as they camped by the Red Sea, near Pi Hahiroth, opposite Baal Zephon. When the Israelites saw Pharaoh's army approaching, they were terrified. But Moses told them not to be afraid, because he believed that the Lord would save them. The Lord then commanded Moses to raise his staff and stretch his hand over the sea to divide the water. Then an amazing miracle happened: the waters divided and the Israelites walked all the way through the sea on dry ground.

As the Israelites passed over the dry sea bed, Pharaoh's army tried to follow them. When the entire army was in the middle of the sea and the Israelites safely on the other side, the Lord sent the water of the sea back to its place, and all the Egyptians drowned.

Sometimes there are things in our lives that scare us, and then it always seems as if there is no way out of our problems. It is in times like these that we should trust in the Lord, as the Israelites and Moses did. The Lord often helps us to overcome our most difficult troubles. Nothing is too difficult for him to do.

W.W.J.

Jesus himself said that we should not be afraid because he will be with us for all eternity.

February 9

Miriam

SHE SANG AND DANCED

Then Miriam ... took a tambourine in her hand, and all the women followed her, with tambourines and dancing. (Exodus 15:20)

One of the most beautiful songs recorded in the Bible is the song that Miriam sang after the Lord had saved the Israelites from the Egyptian army. Miriam was Aaron's sister. Remember, the Israelites were terrified when they saw Pharaoh's army storming toward them. But when they saw how the Lord had helped them and how all the Egyptians had drowned, they were so happy that they simply had to rejoice and sing.

Miriam was overjoyed and so she grabbed a tambourine and started dancing. She sang a song praising the Lord for his greatness. All the Israelites probably joined in the singing and started rejoicing and clapping their hands with gladness.

Christians are people who like praising and worshiping the Lord. They always sing about the wonderful things that the Lord has done to save them from all their difficulties. The most important of all these wonderful things is the fact that Jesus Christ died for us on the cross, thereby saving us from the devil and an eternity without God. The God who saved the Israelites when Pharaoh tried to take them back to Egypt is the same God who is our Father and Savior in Jesus Christ. He redeems us from sin. That is why we too sing and dance with joy, as Miriam did. Today, why not take some time to praise the Lord for being so good and wonderful? Perhaps you would like to sing a song to him right now.

W.W.J.

Our Savior, Jesus Christ, fills our hearts and mouths with songs of praise.

February 10

Moses

Food from the Heavens

"At twilight you will eat meat, and in the morning you will be filled with bread. Then you will know that I am the LORD your God." (Exodus 16:12)

Despite the fact that the Lord liberated the Israelites from the bondage of Egypt, they soon started grumbling. You and I are much the same. All too often we are just so dissatisfied about what we don't have that we can't be happy about what we do have. The Bible says that we should be grateful for everything and thankful at all times. The Israelites were not. They longed for the abundance of food they had in Egypt and did not like the uncertainty and difficulty of life in the desert. They were also afraid that they would starve to death in the desert, even though the Lord promised them that he would take care of them.

The Lord then told Moses that he would rain down bread from heaven for them every day. Each day, the people were to go out and collect enough provisions for the day. This would keep them from starving. In the evening the Lord sent quail (small birds) into the camp, and the Israelites could then catch, cook, and eat the birds. In this way they had meat to eat together with the bread that the Lord rained down for them from heaven. This bread was called manna.

The Lord provided the Israelites with food every single day. When the Israelites tried to store some of the food, it spoiled and became filled with maggots. They had to trust the Lord to provide for them every day, and he never failed them.

In the Lord's Prayer, Jesus taught us to pray to our heavenly Father to give us our daily bread (Matthew 6:11). The Lord always looks after his children, and he will look after you today. All you need to do is trust in him. The Bible tells us that the children of the righteous will never go hungry.

W.W.J.

Jesus taught us that we should seek his kingdom first, and then he will give us everything we need.

February 11

Aaron and Hur

THEY HELD HIS HANDS UP

... so that his hands remained steady till sunset. (Exodus 17:12)

The Israelites had to go to battle against the Amalekites. Moses knew that they would need the strength of the Lord to help them overcome the Amalekites. Moses trusted that the Lord would help them as long as he kept the staff of God up, holding it over his head with his two hands. Moses, Aaron, and Hur went to the top of a hill. From there they could look down on the battle between the Israelites and the Amalekites.

As long as Moses held up his hands, the Israelites were winning. When he lowered his hands, the Amalekites were winning.

After a while Moses' arms started growing tired. This posed a big problem, because as soon as Moses lowered his hands, the Amalekites started winning. Then Aaron and Hur took a stone and put it under Moses so that he could sit down on it. Aaron and Hur then stood on either side of Moses, and each of them held up one of his arms. In this way, Moses' hands remained steady until sunset, even though by this time his arms were very numb. That day Israel won a very important victory over the Amalekites.

It was not really Moses' hands that brought them this victory. It was his faith. Moses built an altar on that place and said that the Lord had given them the victory.

There are many men and women who work for the Lord. They are like Moses: they are holding up their hands in the battle against the devil. But they also grow tired. That is why we should support them just as Aaron and Hur supported Moses. Pray for your spiritual leaders. Support them and encourage them. Keep their hands up.

W.W.J.

Jesus very much wanted his disciples to keep watch with him in the garden of Gethsemane. He needed them to hold up his hands as well.

February 12

Jethro

Too Much for One Guy

"You and these people who come to you will only wear yourselves out."
(Exodus 18:18)

Jethro was Moses' father-in-law. He had heard of everything that the Lord had done for Israel and for Moses by leading them out of Egypt. One day, Jethro left his home and went to where Moses and the Israelites were living in the desert.

Jethro was very surprised and very glad to see how the Lord had used Moses in his plan. Jethro was also delighted to hear how the Lord had rescued the Israelites from the hands of the Egyptians. One day, after Moses had spent the entire day hearing people's court cases against one another, Jethro gave him some good advice. Jethro saw that the task of leading the people and making decisions on their behalf was too heavy for Moses to bear. He saw that Moses would soon become completely worn out because of all the work. He then told Moses to appoint leaders over a thousand people, over one hundred people, over fifty, and over ten. They had to serve as judges for the people at all times. Only the most important or difficult cases were to be brought before Moses. In this way, Moses' workload would be much lighter, while the people would still receive fair and just treatment from the judges. This was very sound advice indeed. When Moses followed Jethro's advice, the situation immediately improved.

Some people think that they are very important and want to do all the work there is to do by themselves. They trust no one else to accept responsibility for a job. Eventually, such people simply have too much work to do, and then they become tense and worried and have sleepless nights because their workload is too heavy. Teamwork is much better than individual work. When everyone contributes his or her share, the work gets done very quickly. I hope you enjoy working together with others in a team.

W.W.J.

Jesus often gave his disciples small tasks to complete. They worked together well as a team.

February 13

Moses

Ten Good Rules

And God spoke all these words. (Exodus 20:1)

The Lord knew that the people of Israel would need some guidelines by which to live. A guideline is really a rule. It is almost like fencing in a camp with barbed wire so that the sheep or cattle can safely graze inside the fenced area. The barbed wire ensures that no predators can get in to get them and that they won't stray away and get lost.

The Ten Commandments that the Lord gave to Israel were intended to keep them safe and well. If they followed the commandments, no difficulties or problems would be able to overwhelm them. They would be safe as well as happy. The Bible tells us that later, when Jesus came, God wrote his laws and rules in our hearts through the working of his Holy Spirit.

Let us follow the will of the Lord and do as he commanded us in his Word. His words are guidelines or rules intended to help us to live better and happier lives. If we break his rules, we are only hurting ourselves. It will cause us endless pain and our lives will become uncertain and dangerous.

W.W.J.

Jesus is the way and the truth and the life (John 14:6). If we walk with him, he will keep us safe.

February 14

Moses

His face was radiant

The Israelites could not look steadily at the face of Moses because of its glory. (2 Corinthians 3:7).

When the Lord gave the Ten Commandments to Moses while he was on Mount Sinai, Moses was in the presence of the Lord for a long time. While Moses was with God and listening to the words of the Lord, something wonderful happened: God's glory started to radiate from Moses' face. This means that Moses' face started shining. When someone comes close to God, God's light shines upon that person, and then it is as if his or her face changes completely.

Jesus too was filled with glory, and he wanted to share his glory with all of his followers. We read in John 17 how Jesus prayed to the Father to give to us the same glory that the Father gave to him. However, it is only when we spend time with the Lord, hear his words, and do as he tells us that the glory of the Lord can shine in our lives. Jesus said that we should be light for a dark world and that people should see our light wherever we go. This light is simply his presence living inside us. It is his glory that changes our lives.

The farther we stray from the Lord, or the more sin there is in our lives, the darker our lives become. When this happens, the glory of the Lord disappears from our lives.

When Moses came down from Mount Sinai, the people could see the glory of the Lord upon his face. You and I can have the glory of God in us every day of our lives. Let us try to live as close as possible to the Lord.

W.W.J.

The Bible says that Jesus had exactly the same glory as the Father. He was filled with grace and truth. We share in his glory if we walk with him.

Moses

He Pleaded with God

The LORD would speak to Moses face to face, as a man speaks with his friend. (Exodus 33:11)

Moses was an ordinary person, much like you and me. Do you remember how Moses objected when the Lord called him to lead the Israelites from Egypt? The Bible says that the Lord even became angry at Moses for objecting. Nevertheless, Moses decided to do the will of the Lord, and he returned to Egypt. From that time on, his walk with the Lord was truly remarkable. He continually sought the Lord's advice, constantly prayed, and learned many lessons from the Lord. Moses had a very special relationship with the Lord – the Bible says it was like they were best friends.

Even though the Lord is so great and so different from us, he wants us to get to know him as a Person. He is not a powerful force that exists somewhere beyond the clouds; he is a person and he wants us to get to know him as he is. He is, after all, a God of love who cares for us deeply. He proved his love by sending Jesus to earth for us. The Bible says that the Lord was like a friend to Moses, and that they talked with each other as friends do. The Lord wants us to know him personally as our most wonderful Friend. We get to know him as a Friend when we love him and do as he tells us. If his Word lives in our hearts, we cannot help getting to know him better and appreciating him more. When we know him, we share everything in our lives with him: our schoolwork, our dreams, our hurts, our questions, our doubts, and also our joy. Today, talk to the Lord like you would talk to a friend. Share everything in your heart with him.

W. W. J.

Jesus said that when we walk with him, we are not his servants, but his friends.

February 16

Bezalel

WHAT A CRAFTSMAN!

"Bezalel ... to whom the LORD has given skill and ability ..." (Exodus 36:1).

The Lord set aside a place where the people could come to worship and serve him. This place was called the Tent of Meeting. The Lord commanded Moses and the Israelites to make this tent, also called the tabernacle. This tent was to be set up quite a distance from the Israelites' camp. Everyone who wanted to know the will of the Lord could go to the Tent of Meeting. When Moses entered the tent on behalf of the people, a pillar of cloud came down from heaven and hovered over the entrance of the tent, and then the Lord spoke to Moses.

There were many different pieces of furniture in the tabernacle. The Lord gave strict instructions as to how these pieces of furniture were to be made. The people willingly brought many offerings to the Lord to be used in the construction of the tabernacle and its contents. Some brought pins and rings, while others brought earrings and necklaces and all kinds of other objects made of gold. Then the Lord chose Bazalel to do the work of constructing the tabernacle. The Bible says that the Lord equipped him with the Holy Spirit so that he could do any kind of work with skill, ability and knowledge. He could make anything from gold, silver, and bronze; he could cut, polish, and set precious stones; and could also do woodwork. The Lord gave all these talents to him, and the Holy Spirit taught him how to use these talents well.

Today, the Lord still gives certain talents to every person. You also have certain talents. When the Lord gives his Holy Spirit to you, you can use your talents to glorify him. Take some time to think about the things that you can do or would like to do. Ask the Lord to teach you through his Holy Spirit how to use these abilities to glorify him.

W. W. J.

When we walk with Jesus, we realize that every person is special and that each and every one of us has received unique talents.

February 17

Miriam

"Has the LORD spoken only through Moses?" they asked. "Hasn't he also spoken through us?" (Numbers 12:2)

Moses had brought the people of Israel out of Egypt. Because he thought that he was no good at talking, the Lord used Aaron to help him with this problem. Aaron's sister, Miriam, also helped Moses. One could say that these three were the leaders of the Israelites. However, it is very clear that Moses was the most important leader of the three.

While he had lived in Midian many years earlier, Moses had married a woman who was not an Israelite. Miriam and Aaron began to criticize Moses about this. We don't know what caused the problem, but we do know that when they came to Moses about it, they weren't at all kind. In fact, they placed themselves at Moses' level of leadership, basically saying that the Lord had spoken to them too, and that they knew better than Moses did what was right. The Lord heard this and was not at all pleased. The Lord told Aaron and Miriam that he spoke to Moses personally and that he thought Moses was the most reliable man in his service. In a nutshell, the Lord told them to back off and leave Moses alone.

We might imagine that before Aaron and Miriam complained to Moses himself, they must have been talking behind his back. Saying bad things about other people behind their backs is always vicious and mean. God also doesn't like it when we think we know better than anyone else does. Gossip and pride are very dangerous. We should always be careful of our attitudes toward and our words about others.

W.W.J.

When we walk with Jesus, there is no place in our lives for gossip. Instead, we ought to support and inspire one another.

February 18

Joshua and Caleb

ONLY TWO BELIEVED

"The LORD is with us. Do not be afraid of them." (Numbers 14:9)

The Lord told Moses to send men to explore the land of Canaan. Twelve men were sent out to see what the land was like, what the people living there were like, and how the Israelites should go about conquering the land. Twelve men went to Canaan as Moses told them and saw many exciting things. They learned that the land was fertile – so fertile, in fact, that a cluster of grapes was so massive that two of the men had to carry it on a pole between them! The men spent forty days exploring Canaan and then they returned to Moses and the Israelites.

When the spies arrived back in the camp, they spoke to Moses, Aaron, and the other Israelites. They told the Israelites that it was a truly wonderful land, but they also pointed out that the people living there were very tall and powerful. These people were called the descendants of Anak, or children of the giants. Ten of the spies said that the Israelites had absolutely no chance of conquering these huge, strong people. Joshua and Caleb, however, said that the Lord would help them to overcome the sons of Anak. They encouraged Moses to lead the Israelite army into Canaan so that they could take the land in possession. However, the ten frightened spies had caused the Israelites to become afraid. They wept and once again started grumbling against Moses and Aaron.

There are always people who prefer only to focus on the dark side of a situation. Their attitude is always negative. They always see only the difficulties in life and how impossible every task seems. They never see their way clear to do anything. They are easily frightened and choose to withdraw from the situation. However, with God on our side, we need never be afraid, for he can help us conquer even the "giant" problems. What are you afraid of today? Believe in God, as Joshua and Caleb did.

W.W.J.

With Jesus on our side we are always part of the winning team.

February 19

Moses

LORD, FORGIVE!

"I have forgiven them, as you asked." (Numbers 14:20)

When Joshua and Caleb returned from Canaan with the rest of the spies, they said that the Lord had blessed his people with a land that was flowing with milk and honey – a picture of its lush abundance. All the other spies, however, did nothing but complain and grumble. They also incited the crowd to become negative. Moses quickly had to intervene, because the people wanted to stone Joshua and Caleb right there and then. Then the Lord became very angry. He asked, *"How long will these people treat me with contempt? How long will they refuse to believe in me, in spite of all the miraculous signs I have performed among them?"* (Numbers 14:11). Then the Lord decided that he wanted to destroy the Israelites.

Moses was a good man, and he had a gentle spirit. He pleaded with God not to hold the Israelites accountable for their rebellion, but to forgive them. Moses intervened and God listened. The Lord told him that he would forgive the Israelites.

We see people who rebel against God around us just about every day. They don't really believe in him. They don't really want to walk in his footsteps. Some people even slander the Lord. They also slander Christians. We should ask the Lord to forgive such people, just as Moses pleaded with the Lord to forgive the Israelites. Perhaps the Lord will have pity on them and they will eventually find the Lord and serve him. It is better to forgive others than to judge them.

W.W.J.

Even on the cross we heard Jesus saying, "Father, forgive them, for they do not know what they are doing" (Luke 23:34).

February 20

Korah, Dathan, and Abiram

CONSEQUENCES OF REBELLION

The earth opened its mouth and swallowed them with their households ... and all their possessions. (Numbers 16:32)

While the Israelites were on their way to Canaan, Korah, Dathan, and Abiram – together with 250 other leaders rebelled against Moses. They asked Moses and Aaron, *"Why then do you set yourselves above the LORD's assembly?"* (Numbers 16:3). They forgot that God himself had appointed Moses and Aaron to lead the people, so they had become jealous and wanted to have more leadership power themselves.

When someone is called to be a leader, it does not mean that person is receiving preferential treatment. Jesus taught us that the best leader is someone who serves others. Life is often very difficult for someone in a position of leadership, because a leader sometimes has to make unpopular decisions. The men who rebelled against Moses and Aaron thought that Moses and Aaron were trying to pretend that they were more important than anyone else.

Moses pleaded with them not to do anything against the will of the Lord. But they did not want to listen to Moses. The Lord became very angry. Moses pleaded with God on their behalf and prayed to the Lord to have mercy on them. However, the Lord knew that he could not allow this kind of rebellion among his people, and that is why he caused the ground to split open beneath all the rebels. The earth swallowed Korah, Dathan, and Abiram and everyone who was with them.

We should examine our hearts carefully to make sure that we are not rebelling against those people whom God has placed in positions of authority. Even when we don't really like our leaders, we should always pray for them.

W.W.J.

Jesus taught us to respect our leaders.

Moses

THE BRONZE SNAKE

"Make a snake and put it up on a pole; anyone who is bitten can look at it and live." (Numbers 21:8)

The Israelites were a real bunch of grouches. They always found something to complain about. They were never satisfied with what they had. The Lord brought them out of Egypt and looked after them every day while they were in the desert. The Lord also had taken them to a beautiful land, but they had been too afraid to go in. So here they were, wandering around in the desert, never content, always finding something to complain about. One day, they asked the Lord why he had brought them out of Egypt only to let them die in the desert. There was no bread and no water, and they complained that they detested the "miserable food," the manna that the Lord had graciously been providing for them to eat.

The Lord does not like people who constantly complain. He wanted to teach them a lesson, and so he sent poisonous snakes among the people. The snakes bit the people, and many Israelites died. Then the people felt sorry for what they had said and confessed that they had sinned against the Lord. They asked Moses to help them and to pray to the Lord to take the snakes away from them.

The Lord then told Moses to make a bronze snake and put it up on a pole. Those who were bitten by one of the snakes only had to look up at the bronze snake and they would survive the poisonous bite.

Do you remember that Jesus was also put up on a wooden pole when he was crucified? In doing so, Jesus saved us so that we do not have to die in sin but can have eternal life. Just think of Jesus hanging on the cross. When you look up at him, you can choose eternal life by believing in him as your Savior.

W. W. J.

Jesus gave his life for us so that we would not have to suffer eternal death, but could have eternal life.

February 22

Balaam

Just Listen to What He is Saying!

"I summoned you to curse my enemies, but you have blessed them these three times." (Numbers 24:10)

Balak was the king of the Moabites. The Moabites were terrified of the Israelites and tried to make all kinds of plans to keep the Israelites from attacking them. One of their plans was to find a sorcerer, fortune-teller, or magician to put a curse upon God's people.

Balak then summoned the sorcerer Balaam and asked him to speak evil words and put a curse upon the Israelites. Perhaps Balaam knew about the existence of the God of Israel, but he was not really a prophet of God. He was, after all, a fortune-teller and sorcerer. When Balaam was on his way to go put a curse on the Israelites, God spoke to him and told him not to curse the Israelites, because they were his special people. Nevertheless, Balaam continued his journey, because he knew that he would be handsomely rewarded for doing his evil work against the Israelites. He was traveling along when suddenly his donkey refused to take another step. Balaam couldn't see it, but the donkey saw an angel of the Lord standing in the middle of the road. Balaam beat the donkey, and then the donkey suddenly spoke to Balaam. Then Balaam knew that the Lord meant serious business. Instead of cursing the Israelites, he blessed them. God was using Balaam to do his will.

God can even use people who are not yet his children as instruments to do his will. He does this because he is a great God and because he wants to fulfill the purpose and plan that he has for our lives. Just think of how the Lord worked in Balaam's life. Our God is all-powerful. He can do anything.

W.W.J.

Even though evil people wanted to harm Jesus, God used them to achieve his goal.

February 23

Joshua

A New Leader

"Take Joshua ... a man in whom is the spirit, and lay your hand on him." (Numbers 27:18)

The time came for a new leader to be appointed over the Israelites. By this time Moses was very old and God had said that he could not enter Canaan. That is why God decided to appoint a new leader.

The Lord always keeps in mind the people whom he wants to use as leaders. Leaders are important because they have to guide people in the right direction. God knew this very well, and that is why he decided to appoint Joshua as the new leader of Israel. Joshua had been watching Moses lead the Israelites for many years. He probably learned a lot about leadership from Moses. And yet Joshua was very different from Moses. He had his own distinct personality and did things in his own way. The Lord trusted Joshua, and that is why he made him leader of the Israelites. Do you remember that Joshua was only one of two spies who believed that the Lord could help Israel conquer the land, while the other ten spies were frightening the Israelites?

Take some time to pray for the leaders around you today. Pray for the government leaders, the leaders in your church congregation, in your class, and in your school. Support them and help them. Perhaps you too occupy a position of leadership. If so, you should have faith in God and walk according to the guidelines of his Word, just as Joshua did.

W.W.J.

Jesus was the best leader who ever lived on earth.

Rahab

THE SCARLET CORD

But Joshua spared Rahab the prostitute, with her family (Joshua 6:25)

Rahab lived in the city of Jericho. She worked as a prostitute, which means that she sold her body in exchange for money. Earlier, when the spies had gone into Jericho to see whether they could conquer the city, they stayed in Rahab's house. Her house was close to the wall and the spies should not have aroused much suspicion. However, someone apparently got suspicious.

When the king of Jericho heard that some Israelites staying in Rahab's house had come to spy out the land, he sent a messenger to Rahab, telling her that she had to send the men out so that he could kill them. But Rahab chose not to obey the king. She hid the men and sent a message to the king that they had already left. When night fell, she would help them get away safely. She told them that she knew that the Lord wanted to give the land of Canaan to his people. She had heard how the Lord had brought the Israelites out of Egypt. Then she spoke in faith: she said that the Lord is God in heaven above and on the earth below. She asked the two spies to promise to spare her life and the lives of her family members when they came to conquer the city. The spies promised, and then Rahab let them down by a rope through the window. They agreed that Rahab would tie a scarlet cord or rope in that same window so that the Israelites would know which of the houses belonged to her when they came to take Jericho.

Perhaps it was because Rahab started to believe in God that the Lord spared her life. From that time on she served the Lord with the Israelites. She married, had children, and her descendants included King David and Jesus. No one is ever too wicked or sinful to change and live according to the will of God. We should never look down on other people who we think are sinners. We should rather pray for them and help them to believe in God.

W.W.J.

Jesus spoke to sinners about his kingdom. He came so that sinners could be shown the right way.

February 25

Achan

THE FLY IN THE OINTMENT

Achan ... took some of them [the devoted things]. So the LORD's anger burned against Israel. (Joshua 7:1)

The Israelites were ready to take possession of all of Canaan. To do so, they would have to go into battle against the other nations living in Canaan. The first city they wanted to take was Jericho. The Israelites were not afraid, because they believed that the Lord was with them in their conquest. The Lord gave them very clear instructions that they had to follow, and Joshua had to make sure that they did everything exactly as the Lord had told them. The Lord had said that the people were not allowed to take any of the articles of silver, gold, bronze, and iron for themselves. These things were sacred to the Lord. They had to be taken to the treasury and used in the house of the Lord.

The Lord delivered Jericho into the hands of the Israelites. Unfortunately, there was a man named Achan who disobeyed God and took some of the things for himself. He thought that no one would ever know what he had done. And then a terrible thing happened.

After the fall of Jericho, the Israelites thought that they would be able to conquer the small town of Ai very easily. They sent only a small part of their army to Ai. However, the Israelites suffered a terrible defeat there. The Israelites could not believe that such a small town could defeat them after such a big victory at Jericho. What could the reason be? The Lord gave Joshua the answer to this question: someone had taken some of the devoted things from Jericho. It quickly became known that Achan had committed this wrong.

We often do things and think that no one will know what we have done. But God always knows. Let's do what is right – even when we think no one will know.

W.W.J.

Judas walked with Jesus and yet he turned against him. Judas thought Jesus didn't know about his underhanded plot, but he was mistaken.

February 26

Acsah

SHE ASKED NICELY

Caleb asked her, "What can I do for you?" She replied ... (Joshua 15:18-19)

Caleb was one of the spies who encouraged the Israelites to go into Canaan with faith in their hearts. Because of this, God was pleased with him. That is why he allowed Caleb to remain alive and enter the promised land.

Caleb had a daughter named Acsah. From what the Bible tells us, Caleb seems to have been very proud of her. He loved her very much and did not want to give her in marriage to just any man. That is why he said that he would give Acsah to any man who could conquer a certain group of very hostile people. They were the people of Debir. Only a man of great courage would be able to do this. Othniel was such a man.

After Othniel had conquered the enemy, Caleb gave his daughter Acsah to him to be his wife. Acsah was a very clever woman. She immediately realized that they did not have a good piece of land upon which to live, so she went with her husband to her father and asked him very nicely if he would also give them some fertile soil with permanent water. Caleb gave her a piece of land with beautiful springs of water.

Perhaps there is something that you would really like to have. Perhaps your parents would like to give it to you if you would only ask very nicely – as Acsah did. Don't be afraid to ask your parents. Always make sure that you have a good relationship with your parents. Honor them and show them that you love them. Parents enjoy giving things to their children when their children do nice things for them too. And don't be afraid to ask God for good things as well.

W.W.J.

Our heavenly Father likes giving us things, simply because Jesus made it possible for us to receive his gifts.

February 27

Joshua

CHOOSE TODAY

"Choose for yourselves this day whom you will serve." (Joshua 24:15)

Joshua was a very good leader. At the end of his life, he summoned all the tribes of Israel to assemble at Shechem, and there he spoke to them. He reminded them of how the Lord had freed them from slavery in Egypt and how he had been faithful to them through the years. He also reminded them of how the Lord had given them the victory over all their enemies in Canaan. Then Joshua asked the Israelites to serve the Lord with sincerity and faithfulness. He asked them to throw away all their idols and to love only the Lord.

Because Joshua knew that many of the Israelites served the Lord half-heartedly while simultaneously worshiping foreign gods, he told them to choose once and for all whom they would serve. He said that they had to serve either the Lord or the gods of the foreigners. They had to make a choice. They could not serve both at the same time. And then Joshua said a very beautiful thing: *"But as for me and my household, we will serve the LORD"* (Joshua 24:15). Joshua was single-minded. He decided that he wanted to serve only the one true God, and that was the God of Israel. The Israelites then told Joshua that they too wanted to choose God, as Joshua had done. Then Joshua told them that they first had to destroy all the foreign idols that were among them and then yield their hearts to God completely. To yield your heart to God means to be completely devoted to the Lord and to follow and serve him with all your heart.

I sincerely hope that you are not serving the Lord half-heartedly. Decide today to serve the Lord wholeheartedly, just as Joshua did.

W.W.J.

Jesus also gave his disciples the choice of following him.

February 28

Gideon

AN ORDINARY GUY

"I am the least in my family." (Judges 6:15)

It is a good thing not to have too high an opinion of yourself. However, it is also a good thing not to belittle yourself. When you know that you are a child of the Lord and that he has a plan for your life and loves you just as you are, you will also know that you are very valuable. You are important because you are important to God.

Gideon was very important to the Lord. Gideon lived in the time before Israel had a king. Other nations were constantly attacking the Israelites and making life very difficult for them. The Midianites, for example, regularly invaded the Israelites' land and destroyed their crops and killed all their livestock. When the Israelites asked the Lord to help them overcome the Midianites, the angel of the Lord visited Gideon. Gideon was an ordinary farming boy. While he was busy going about his daily work in the fields the angel greeted him, *"The LORD is with you, mighty warrior"* (Judges 6:12). Gideon didn't think that he was all that mighty a warrior, and he was very surprised at the angel's words. Then he told the angel all about the Midianites who were giving them so much trouble. The angel said to Gideon, *"Go in the strength you have and save Israel out of Midian's hand. Am I not sending you?"* (Judges 6:14). But Gideon did not have a very high opinion of himself and did not think that the Lord would be able to use him. He came up with all kinds of excuses: he said that he was a very ordinary guy and the least important man in his family. But God wanted to use him, and he did.

Today, the Lord wants to use you, too.

W.W.J.
Jesus sends ordinary people like us to be his disciples all over the world.

February 29

God

The Lord is Peace

So Gideon built an altar to the Lord there and called it The Lord is Peace. (Judges 6:24)

When the angel of the Lord appeared to Gideon, telling him to go to battle against the Midianites, Gideon was very afraid. But the angel told Gideon not to be afraid. Gideon then built an altar to the Lord and proclaimed that God's name is "The Lord is Peace." In Hebrew it is Yahweh-shalom.

Oh, how the Israelites yearned for peace and tranquillity in their country. They were living in perpetual fear. The Midianites were constantly harassing them. Things were not going well for the Israelites, and they decided to ask the Lord please to give them peace and quiet. Then the Lord appeared to Gideon and promised Gideon that he would bring peace to the Israelites. God is always eager to bring peace to troubled people.

All the earth yearns for the peace and calm of the Lord. Every country desires to have peace. Our country is no exception. There are so many people in pain, so many who suffer, so many who are murdered, so many who are raped. Only God can give us peace and calm. That is why we call him the God of peace, Yahweh-shalom.

Let us pray that the Lord will bless our country with his peace. But before we can have his peace, we must first decide to do the Lord's will. In doing his will, we find peace and tranquillity. You and I first have to make our peace with God, with the help of Jesus, our Peacemaker.

W . W . J .

Jesus said that he would give us peace – not the kind of peace that the world gives, but the kind of peace that he alone can give (John 14:27).

Gideon

WHO DID THIS?

"Gideon son of Joash did it." (Judges 6:29)

When Gideon realized that the Lord wanted to use him, he listened to everything the Lord told him to do. God instructed him to tear down his father's altar to Baal and to build a proper altar to the Lord in its place. Then he had to sacrifice a bull in honor of the Lord. This was quite a difficult task that God gave Gideon, don't you think? Gideon probably wondered what would happen to him when people found out what he had done. He also probably worried that his father would be very angry at him.

Because Gideon was afraid of his father's family and all the men of the town, he decided to tear down the altar during the night. He worked through the night to destroy the altar, and when the people got up the next morning they saw that Baal's altar had been demolished. In its place stood an altar to the Lord. Then the men of the town asked one another, "Who did this?" They inquired everywhere, and finally someone said that Gideon was the culprit. Then the men became very angry, and told Joash, Gideon's father, "Bring your son out of the house. He has to die!" But Joash protected Gideon and convinced the people that they first had to prove that Baal was actually greater and stronger than God.

When God calls us to do something for him that is bound to make us unpopular, we are sometimes afraid, like Gideon. Fortunately, the Lord always sends us help, and sometimes our help comes from a completely unexpected place. Gideon was afraid of what his father would say, but in the end it was his father who protected him.

W.W.J.

The road that we walk with Jesus is often called the narrow road. This is often a very unpopular road to walk.

March 2

Gideon

"There are still too many men." (Judges 7:4)

We often think that the Lord can only work through us if we are very good or very strong or very clever. We also often think that the Lord can only use us if there are many of us together in a group. But this is not the case at all. The Lord wants us to know that we need to rely on nothing but his strength, his presence, and his assistance.

This is the lesson that the Lord wanted to teach Gideon. Initially, Gideon was very unwilling to be used by the Lord because he did not have a very high opinion of himself. But God is always the most powerful, and if he is on your side, you will always be victorious. Gideon blew on a trumpet and went around summoning men from everywhere to join him in fighting the Midianites. In the end, Gideon had a very large army.

However, the Lord told Gideon that there were too many men in the army. God wanted the victory to depend on him alone – and not on a powerful army. All the men who were afraid were allowed to return home. Twenty-two thousand men left for home, and only ten thousand remained. But the Lord told Gideon that there were *still* too many men. While the men were drinking water, Gideon chose three hundred men. Imagine – only three hundred men in an army! And this while the Midianites were so numerous that they couldn't be counted. How could the Israelites possibly win?

But God gave Gideon a plan. One night the Israelite army made lots of noise just outside the Midianite camp. The Midianites thought they were surrounded by a huge army, so they ran away in fear. In this way, Gideon and his men conquered the army of the Midianites.

We do not win because we are clever or rich or strong or fast, but because the Lord wins through us. That is why we should never boast about our own accomplishments.

W.W.J.

Jesus entrusted the spread of his gospel message to a small group of disciples, who then turned the world upside-down.

March 3

Gideon

THE GOLDEN GARMENT

Gideon made the gold into an ephod, which he placed in Ophrah, his town. (Judges 8:27)

After Gideon and his three hundred men conquered their enemies, the Israelites were overjoyed. They held Gideon in very high esteem. They even wanted Gideon to be their king. But Gideon knew that God was their King, and therefore he said that he could not be the Israelites' king.

However, Gideon did ask one thing from the Israelites. He asked each one of them to give him a small golden earring from their share of the plunder they had taken from the Midianites. They then spread open a garment and each man threw an earring onto it. The weight of all the golden earrings combined came to about forty-three pounds. Gideon took this gold and made a golden ephod from it.

An ephod is a garment. The Israelites wore it over their other clothes. It is almost like a waistcoat that is worn over a shirt. We don't really know why Gideon decided to make a golden ephod. Perhaps he just wanted to remember how the Lord had used him to conquer Midian. Unfortunately, this golden image, which Gideon placed in his hometown of Ophrah, became more important to the Israelites than the Lord himself. All of Israel streamed to the town to look at the golden ephod, and this caused them to wander from the Lord's path. In their hearts, they thought that Gideon and the ephod were more important than the Lord, who was actually the One who had given them the victory.

We should be very careful not to think that our achievements or trophies or awards are more important than the Lord. Always remember that it is he who gives us the victory. Glorify and honor him for all his great deeds.

W.W.J.

Jesus said that where our hearts are, there our treasure will also be. (Matthew 6:20-21)

March 4

Jephthah

A Rash Promise

"Whatever comes out of the door of my house to meet me ... will be the Lord's." (Judges 11:31)

Jephthah lived in the time of the judges. This was the time when Israel did not have kings. However, God sent specific men and women to lead the Israelites. In Jephthah's time, the Ammonites were a great threat to Israel. Jephthah gathered some men together, and they set out to do battle against the Ammonites. He also made a vow to the Lord. A vow is when you promise the Lord something. When you make such a solemn promise, you have to keep it. Jephthah promised that if the Lord gave them victory over the Ammonites, he would give to the Lord the first thing that came out of his house to meet him when he returned from the war. This was a very strange promise, and also, as it turned out, a very impetuous and unfortunate one.

Jephthah and his men fought the Ammonites, and God made sure that they were victorious. When Jephthah returned from the war, he probably thought about the promise that he had made to the Lord. Who would come out of the door of his house first to greet him? As it turned out, it was his only daughter, whom he loved very much. When he saw that it was his daughter, Jephthah tore his clothes, because now his daughter would have to be offered to the Lord. This meant that she would never be allowed to marry or have children. It is really a pity that Jephthah made such an impetuous vow to the Lord.

We must be careful not to make rash promises to the Lord. You might think that you can persuade the Lord to do something for you by making promises. Sometimes you need his help so badly that you make all kinds of thoughtless promises. Trust in the Lord and believe in him, but be careful not to make just any promise to him. Once you have made a promise, you have to keep it.

W.W.J.

Jesus taught us that our yes should be yes, that our no should be no, and that we should never have to back up our words with promises. (Matthew 5:37)

March 5

Delilah

Why Did She Do It?

"Each one of us will give you eleven hundred shekels of silver." (Judges 16:5)

Delilah definitely does not have a good name. Even today, when someone talks about a wicked woman, they use the name "Delilah." Why? Because she so cunningly deceived Samson.

Samson fell in love with a young Philistine woman named Delilah. She must have been a very beautiful woman, and Samson wanted her all to himself. She knew this all too well, and so did the Philistines. Now the Philistines were Israel's enemies and they kept fighting with Israel. Samson, however, was an extremely strong man who was often foiling their plans. So some leaders of the Philistines went to Delilah and asked her to lure Samson into telling her the secret of his great strength. In return, they offered her a large amount of money. This sounded like a very appealing plan to Delilah. She did not really care for Samson, but she did care a whole lot about the money. So she made a plan to trick him into telling her his secret.

She flirted with Samson, and it wasn't long before the two of them were involved in a relationship. Delilah was a very wily woman. She seduced and tricked Samson for the sake of money. She pretended to care for him, but she didn't really.

There are many people who do not have honest intentions. They might try to get into our good favor, but not because they really love us or care for us, but because they want something from us. You should watch out for such people. Ask the Lord for wisdom. Ask him to show you who your true friends are: people who don't just use you, people who really care for you and who really love you.

W.W.J.

Jesus knew people's hearts. He knew when they came to him with devious plans in their hearts.

March 6

Ruth

She Chose the Best

"Your people will be my people and your God my God." (Ruth 1:16)

Naomi and her husband and two sons had gone to a country called Moab when a famine came over the land of Judah. Naomi's sons had married while there. Eventually, Naomi's husband died, and then her two sons also died. Naomi decided to return to Judah, her homeland, and she told her two daughters-in-law that they could remain in Moab.

Ruth was Naomi's daughter-in-law. Ruth loved her mother-in-law dearly. She was very sad when she heard that Naomi wanted to return to Judah. She decided that she wanted to accompany Naomi. Naomi tried to convince her that it would be best for her to stay in her own country, where she would have her own religion and her own home. Naomi's other daughter-in-law, Orpah, decided to remain behind in Moab. But Ruth said to Naomi, *"Don't urge me to leave you or to turn back from you. Where you go I will go, and where you stay I will stay. Your people will be my people and your God my God"* (Ruth 1:16). Ruth made a choice. Not only did she want to remain with her mother-in-law, she also wanted to become one of God's people. Moreover, she wanted to accept the Lord God of Israel as her God. What a marvelous choice! She forsook her own gods and chose to accept the one true God.

In the Bible we read that the Lord blessed Ruth, probably because of the choice she made. She met a good man by the name of Boaz. He was wealthy and successful. He also believed in God. He decided to marry Ruth, and they were very happy together. Ruth was the great-grandmother of King David.

When we choose the Lord and follow him wholeheartedly, we can expect him to shower his blessings upon us.

W.W.J.

When you walk with Jesus, life is always worthwhile.

Hannah

Pray and You Will Receive

"I prayed for this child, and the Lord has granted me what I asked of him."
(1 Samuel 1:27)

There once was a woman by the name of Hannah. She could not have children. This troubled her very much because she really longed to have a baby. Her husband was also married to another woman besides Hannah, and this woman ridiculed and humiliated Hannah for being childless.

One day Hannah was in the tabernacle at Shiloh. She was very unhappy and pleaded with the Lord to give her a baby. While she was busy praying to the Lord, the priest was watching her. He thought that she was drunk because she cried so much and pleaded so earnestly with the Lord. "No, sir," she said, "I have not been drinking. I was pouring out my soul to the Lord" (1 Samuel 1:15). The priest then understood what was going on and assured her that the Lord had heard her prayer and granted her request. When she heard this, Hannah was no longer so sad.

The Lord is pleased when we ask him to help us and show him that we need him. He heard Hannah's earnest prayer and decided to grant her request. Hannah became pregnant and gave birth to a beautiful baby boy. She called him Samuel, which means that the Lord heard her prayer. In her prayer, she had promised to give her little boy to the Lord, to be in the Lord's service all the days of his life. So Samuel grew up in the temple of the Lord from a very young age. He later became one of the greatest figures in the history of Israel.

You and I should also rest assured that the Lord always listens to our prayers. When there is something we really want, we should not be shy to pray and plead with the Lord to help us. He will give us what we ask if it is in our best interests. We should simply trust in him and believe that he knows best. Take some time right now to tell the Lord all about your heart's desires.

W.W.J.

Jesus said that we have to pray in order to receive.

March 8

Eli

A Careless Dad

"His sons made themselves contemptible, and he failed to restrain them."
(1 Samuel 3:13)

Eli was a priest who worked in the temple of the Lord. He had two sons, Hophni and Phinehas. They were wicked boys and did not live according to the will of the Lord. Like Eli, they worked in the house of the Lord. However, they did not want to obey the Lord regarding their service in the tabernacle. Instead, they ignored God's commands and did some pretty horrible things.

People told Eli about his sons' corrupt behavior, but he did not punish them. He just chatted with them about their behavior. So the Lord decided to do something about the situation. Through Samuel, God sent Eli a message that he was going to punish Eli's sons.

When the Israelites went to battle against the Philistines, Hophni and Phinehas carried the ark of the Lord to the battlefield, without the Lord's permission. The Philistines defeated the Israelites in the battle, and they took the ark of the Lord with them to their country. This was truly terrible. The ark was, after all, the place where the Lord spoke to his people. And now it was in a foreign country, surrounded by idols! All of this happened because Hophni and Phinehas were disobedient and did wicked things. On the same day that the ark was captured by the Philistines, Hophni and Phinehas were killed. When Eli heard the news of his sons' deaths and the capture of the ark, he fell backwards off his chair and broke his neck (1 Samuel 4:18). This is how Eli died.

It is very dangerous to live in a way that opposes the will of the Lord. God loves us and wants to draw us ever closer to him, but if we continue doing wrong things, we will quickly find ourselves in deep trouble. If your mom or dad reprimands you or punishes you for doing wrong, don't complain about it. Rather be happy that they are trying to help you.

W.W.J.

When Peter acted improperly toward Jesus, Jesus gave him a serious reprimand.

March 9

Dagon

A False God Bows Down

There was Dagon, fallen on his face on the ground before the ark of the LORD! (1 Samuel 5:3)

Do you remember that the Philistines captured the ark of the Lord and took it to their own country? This happened because Hophni and Phinehas disobeyed the Lord. The Lord then allowed the Philistines to defeat the Israelites in battle. When the Philistines arrived in their country with the ark of God, they decided to put it in the temple of their own gods, next to a statue of their god, Dagon.

Imagine that! The ark of God (which embodied God's presence in the tabernacle in Israel) was standing next to an idol! The next morning, after the Philistines had placed the ark next to Dagon, they saw that the idol was lying on its face on the ground before the ark of the Lord. They picked Dagon up and put him back in his place. But the following morning when they rose, there was Dagon, again fallen on his face on the ground before the ark of the Lord! His head and his two hands had been broken off and only his body remained. Furthermore, the Lord brought devastation over the Philistines, and all the people started getting tumors all over their bodies. The Philistines realized that all this was happening because they had the ark of God with them.

God is greater than any idol. All the gods of the world have to bow down before the great God of Israel and the Father of Jesus Christ. The Bible also tells us that every knee will bend before him and every person will acknowledge that he is the King and the Lord and the only true God. Let us bow down before the Lord, today.

W.W.J.

When Peter walked with Jesus, he realized that Jesus was the only true Lord. He said to Jesus: "You are the Christ, the Son of the living God". (Mark 8:29)

Saul

He Followed His Own Mind

"To obey is better than sacrifice." (1 Samuel 15:22)

Saul was the first king of Israel. He was a tall, strong young man who clearly surpassed all the other men, and the Lord chose him as king so that he might lead God's people. You will remember that the people were not content with having only the Lord as their King. They wanted an earthly king, just as all the other nations had. God hoped that Saul would be a good king and lead the Israelites well.

Initially things went very well. However, it wasn't long before Saul started following his own mind instead of listening to what the Lord asked him to do. After he had been king for about two years, he one day brought an offering or sacrifice to the Lord by himself, something that he was not allowed to do. The Lord was very angry with Saul and sent the prophet Samuel to rebuke him. Another time, after the Israelites had defeated the Philistines in battle, Saul did something else that was very wrong. The Lord instructed the Israelites to destroy all the cattle, sheep, camels, and donkeys belonging to their enemies. Saul did not obey the Lord's command and kept some of the best livestock. Saul's excuse was that he wanted to use the animals as offerings to the Lord, but Samuel knew that this was probably not completely true. In any case, Saul had disobeyed God, and he would have to pay the consequences. Samuel told Saul, *"You have rejected the word of the Lord, and the Lord has rejected you as king over Israel"* (1 Samuel 15:26).

The Lord wants to use each and every one of us, but we have to ask him what he wants us to do and not follow our own thoughts.

W.W.J.

When we love the Lord, we gladly obey his commands and instructions.

David

God Sees Inside

"The LORD does not look at the things man looks at. Man looks at the outward appearance, but the LORD looks at the heart." (1 Samuel 16:7)

Saul's rule as king eventually came to an end. Because Saul was disobedient, the Lord no longer wanted to use him. A king who does not do God's will is, after all, a dangerous king. The Lord then decided to choose a new king. He instructed Samuel to go to Bethlehem, to the house of a man named Jesse. The Lord told Samuel that he would show him the man who would be the new king of Israel. *"You are to anoint for me the one I indicate,"* God said (1 Samuel 16:2).

When Samuel arrived at Jesse's house, he invited all seven of Jesse's sons who were at home to come to him. He thought that he was to appoint a king from among them. Samuel scrutinized the boys and wondered which one God had chosen. God then quietly told Samuel that he should not consider their outward appearance, but should rather trust the Lord to point out the right one, because God looks at people's hearts. He sees what is going on inside a person. It is not necessarily the tallest, the prettiest, or the strongest person who will be chosen, but the one whose heart is true to the Lord.

After Samuel had seen all seven of Jesse's sons, God still had not shown him who was to be king. Then Samuel asked Jesse whether he perhaps had another son, and Jesse answered, *"Yes, there is still the youngest one, but he is in the fields tending the sheep."* When Samuel saw the boy, the LORD said, *"Rise and anoint him; he is the one"* (1 Samuel 16:12). That boy's name was David.

Our outward appearance does not matter to the Lord, but our hearts are very important to him.

W.W.J.

Jesus said that some people are like whitewashed graves: clean and neat from the outside, but filled with bones on the inside. (Matthew 23:27)

David

Music Has Power

Then relief would come to Saul; he would feel better, and the evil spirit would leave him. (1 Samuel 16:23)

After God had rejected Saul as king, Saul's life started deteriorating really fast. Saul's heart grew more and more evil by the day. The devil started to work in Saul's heart, and an evil spirit began tormenting him. This evil spirit made Saul very agitated, and he was always in a bad mood.

One of Saul's servants suggested that they should get David to play the harp for Saul and make him feel better. David was very good at playing the harp. He wrote many songs and was continually singing to the Lord. David then came to Saul and played the harp for him. Whenever David played the harp for Saul, Saul calmed down and the evil spirit left him.

Music is a wonderful gift from the hand of God. Music can make you peaceful or it can make you restless. Music can upset you or it can make you feel happy. Music that is intended to honor the Lord is almost like medicine that the Lord can use to heal someone's spirit. We can almost say that music has power. When a singer sings to glorify God or a musician plays his instrument to honor the Lord, God's strength and power work through that music. What kind of music do you listen to? Does your music glorify God?

W.W.J.

Jesus and his disciples often sang songs to praise God. (Mark 14:26)

March 13

David

NOW THAT'S WHAT YOU CALL FAITH!

"Let no one lose heart on account of this Philistine." (1 Samuel 17:32)

When David arrived on the battlefield of the war between the Israelites and the Philistines, he immediately saw that all the Israelite men were afraid of Goliath and the Philistines. No one wanted to go out and fight Goliath: he was a giant, much too big and strong for any normal solider to be able to defeat in hand-to-hand combat. Whenever Goliath stood in the middle of the battlefield and, with a mighty roar, challenged the Israelites to come out and fight him, the Israelites trembled with fear.

Then David asked, "Who does this Philistine think he is to mock and belittle the armies of the living God?" David went to King Saul and told Saul that he would fight Goliath. At first, Saul did not want to allow it, because he thought that David was way too young and too small. But David told Saul that the Lord had saved him from the claws of lions and bears that had tried to attack his sheep, and so the Lord would also save him from the hand of the Philistine. Now that's what you call faith! David saw this huge guy standing in front of him, but in his mind's eye he also saw a God who was even bigger and who could do anything.

If only you and I had as much faith as David did! Tell the Lord that you trust him and him alone – even in the face of "giant" problems.

W.W.J.

Follow David's example and trust only in God.

Goliath

What a Big Bully

And the Philistine cursed David by his gods. (1 Samuel 17:43)

One day, David's father told him to take some food and provisions to his brothers who were in the Israelite army. The army was at war with the Philistines. When David arrived at the battlefield, he was astonished. His brothers weren't in a good mood at all, and the Israelite army was faring very badly against the Philistines. As a matter of fact, the Israelites were all hiding in fear. Every day, a Philistine giant by the name of Goliath came out onto the battlefield. In a loud voice, he insulted the Israelites, he humiliated them, and then he challenged one soldier to come out and fight him. But no one was willing to fight Goliath.

Despite the fact that David was very young and rather small, he was not afraid of Goliath. He was indignant because this Philistine giant dared to defy the army of the Lord. David decided that he would go out and fight Goliath. When David approached Goliath, the giant started cursing him in the names of the Philistine gods. Goliath was really a big bully. But David was not afraid of him, because he knew that the Lord was on his side.

There are always people who try to intimidate us because they think that they are better than we are. They are almost like Goliath: big bullies. They belittle us, and even ridicule our God. However, you should always remain faithful to God, just as David did. With God on your side, you have nothing to fear.

W.W.J.

In Jesus' time there were many bullies who tried to hurt him, but he continued to believe that what he was doing was right. He always did his Father's will.

March 15

God

Millions on His Side

"... but I come against you in the name of the Lord Almighty, the God of the armies of Israel." (1 Samuel 17:45)

In the Bible the Lord is often called Yahweh-sabaoth. This actually means "Lord of hosts." Or "God of the multitudes." Or "God of the regiments." What does this mean?

This name tells us that God is never in the minority. He never has too few hands to help him. He is never embarrassed because there are not enough people to do his work. No, God is always in the majority. Millions upon millions of angels serve him and are always ready to obey his instructions. He also has millions of Christians, all of whom he has saved, at his call. All of them belong to him. Furthermore, God can even use unbelievers to accomplish his goals here on earth. God is in control. He is always in the majority.

You and I need never be afraid that God will not be able to fulfill his promises. All by himself, he is already a majority, for he is all-powerful. Even more so, he has millions ready to serve him at a moment's notice.

W . W . J .

God's angels were ready to save Jesus after he was arrested, but God did not allow it, because he wanted us to be saved by Jesus' death on the cross. (Matthew 26:53)

David

THE BEST WEAPON

"This day the LORD will hand you over to me." (1 Samuel 17:46)

When David was standing before the giant Goliath, he probably knew that he would never be able to defeat this enormous man – at least not in his own strength. The giant was simply too big. Even the tallest, strongest men in Israel were afraid of the giant Goliath. They all ran away as fast as they could whenever Goliath merely glanced in their direction.

It wasn't because David was foolish that he decided to fight Goliath. It was also not because he was arrogant. Neither was it because he had a really good weapon to use on Goliath. After all, the only weapon in his hand was a sling. So why did David decide to stand up to Goliath?

Whenever David had been in trouble before, he had called upon the name of the Lord God. Yes, the name of the Lord is like a strong fortress. If we call upon his name, God hears us in heaven and he can send millions of angels to help us. The name of our Savior God is like a wonderful key that can unlock the gates of heaven to us. That is why David said to Goliath, *"You come against me with sword and spear and javelin, but I come against you in the name of the LORD Almighty, the God of the armies of Israel, whom you have defied"* (1 Samuel 17:45). You see, David's weapon was not what he was holding in his hand, but rather who was in his heart. David fought in the name of the Lord. His weapon was the best weapon anyone could possibly have – the name of God.

The only weapon that will ensure you of victory is to take the name of the Lord on your lips and to trust in God. Having God at your side and the Holy Spirit in your heart is better than all the weapons in the world combined. Make the Lord your strongest weapon today.

W.W.J.

Jesus invited us to ask in his name so that our joy could be complete. (John 15:11)

Saul

SUDDENLY JEALOUS AND AFRAID

Saul was afraid of David, because the LORD was with David. (1 Samuel 18:12)

Because Saul did some wrong things, the Lord decided that he would no longer be king over Israel. The Lord had David anointed as king. From the moment David was chosen, the Spirit of the Lord started to lead and guide David. God's Spirit was with David in a very special way.

After David had defeated Goliath, the women came out from all the towns of Israel singing and dancing, *"Saul has slain his thousands, and David his tens of thousands"* (1 Samuel 18:7). Saul was very angry about this and he grew increasingly jealous of David. He was afraid that David would take his place as king. The Bible says that Saul started to become very distrustful of David. An evil spirit took possession of Saul, and while David was playing the harp for Saul, Saul tried to kill David by throwing a spear at him. Fortunately, David managed to duck in time, and the spear missed its target. Saul realized that the Lord was with David, and he became very afraid of David. Saul put David in command of a thousand men in his army. He hoped that the enemy would kill David during a battle. However, David was successful in everything he did because the Lord was with him. All Israel and Judah loved David, and he led them in all their war campaigns.

It is very easy to become jealous of someone who has the hand of the Lord upon him. Seeing God bestowing his favor on someone else and giving that person success in everything he or she does isn't always a pleasant experience for us. However, we should not make the mistake that Saul made. If the Lord has given someone else talents, we should be glad for that person and give him or her the praise that he or she deserves. After all, the Lord has also given us many talents. We should all simply do the will of the Lord. Don't be jealous of someone else's success.

W.W.J.

Jesus taught his disciples to love one another and not to be jealous of one another. (Mark 10:43)

March 18

David

Be Humble

"Who am I ... that I should become the king's son-in-law?" (1 Samuel 18:18)

Because the Philistines and Goliath caused the Israelites so much trouble, King Saul promised his daughter in marriage to the man who could defeat Goliath. After David defeated Goliath, Saul said that he would give his oldest daughter, Merab, to David as his wife. But because Saul's heart had already turned against David, he changed his mind and decided to give his other daughter, Michal, to David instead. Despite Saul's bad temper and the fact that he was constantly changing his mind, David did not hold these things against him. Even though Saul had tried to kill David by throwing a spear at him, David still said in humility, *"Do you think it is a small matter to become the king's son-in-law? I'm only a poor man and little known"* (1 Samuel 18:23). David felt as if he were not worthy to be the king's son-in-law. He knew that Saul had been anointed by the Lord, and therefore he had to be respected, even though he was not a good man.

What a wonderful attitude. It shows us that David was a humble man who did not have too high an opinion of himself. Perhaps David eventually became such a great and important man precisely because he was so humble. He always respected other people and never thought that he was more important than they were.

David married Michal and the Lord blessed them. Saul became even more fearful of David and grew increasingly hostile toward him. The Philistines attacked Israel a number of times, but every time David was more successful in his battles against them than all of Saul's other officers. As a result, David was held in high esteem by just about everybody. Don't think better of yourself than you should. Be humble and trust the Lord.

W.W.J.

Jesus was very humble. He who was the Son of God even respected mere earthly leaders.

March 19

David and Jonathan

BEST FRIENDS

And Jonathan had David reaffirm his oath out of love for him, because he loved him as he loved himself. (1 Samuel 20:17)

Saul had a son named Jonathan, who was a good man. Despite his father's jealousy of David, Jonathan got to know David and the two of them became good friends. They often visited each other and did all kinds of things together. They shared the deepest secrets of their hearts with each other. When Saul started to hate David and wanted to kill him, Jonathan pleaded with his father to spare David's life. Jonathan also gave David some advice about how he should act in Saul's presence. What is more, Jonathan made sure that David could flee from Saul when Saul wanted to kill David. Jonathan and David prayed together and even wept together because of all the appalling things that Saul kept trying to do to David.

Friends are a gift from the Lord. We all need friends to support us, understand us, and listen to us when we really need to talk to someone. I hope that you have a good friend: someone you can open your heart to, someone you can pray with, someone who understands you, and someone that you can support and help in turn. Pray for your friends and help them as much as you can. Be faithful to your friends and don't say mean things about them behind their backs. Thank God for your friends. Pray with your friends, and above all, be someone else's best friend.

W.W.J.

Jesus did not call his disciples his servants; he called them his friends (John 15:15). He lived with them, and they all loved one another.

David

Repay Evil with Good

"You have treated me well, but I have treated you badly." (1 Samuel 24:17)

King Saul wanted to kill David. Once when David found out about one of Saul's plans, he talked to Jonathan about it, and they decided that it would be best if David fled for his life. Saul pursued David and ordered all his men to find David and kill him. David had to hide from Saul and his army all the time. He even hid among the people of foreign nations, and many of these people told Saul that David was hiding among them.

One day, while David was hiding from Saul in the Desert of En Gedi, Saul chose three thousand men from his army and set out to track down David and the few men who were with him. At one point in the pursuit, Saul went into a cave, unaware that David and his men were in the back of the cave. David's men told him that he should kill Saul right then and there, because Saul would be taken completely by surprise. While Saul was in the cave, David sneaked up behind him and cut off a corner of his robe. Saul did not even notice what had happened. David did not want to kill Saul. After Saul had left the cave, David called after him and then bowed down before the king. David showed the corner of the robe to Saul and told him that this was proof that he did not intend to harm Saul. David then asked Saul not to kill him. Saul started weeping and said that David was a much more righteous man than he could ever be. After this incident, Saul stopped persecuting David for a while.

Even though Saul wanted to kill David, David's attitude always remained honorable. He did not want to commit murder. He gave Saul another chance to have a change of heart. Let's learn from David not to repay evil with evil. Let's be as forgiving as David was and give other people, even those who wrong us, a second and a third chance.

W.W.J.

Jesus taught us to love even our enemies. (Luke 6:27)

March 21

Abigail

A Clever Woman

She was an intelligent and beautiful woman. (1 Samuel 25:3)

While David was in the Desert of Maon, he heard about a very wealthy man named Nabal. His wife's name was Abigail. She was an intelligent and beautiful woman, but Nabal was a really mean and rude man.

David sent a few of his men to Nabal to give him a message of goodwill. David very much wanted to live in peace with Nabal and his family. However, Nabal insulted David and treated his men rudely. When David's men told him what had happened, David decided to teach Nabal a lesson. By this time, David had about six hundred men with him. He wanted to teach Nabal not to be so rude and impolite to people.

Nabal's clever wife heard that David and his men were on their way to teach Nabal a lesson. Abigail knew that there would be big trouble if she did not do something, so she devised a very clever plan. She quickly took two hundred loaves of bread, two jars of wine, five roasted sheep, five buckets of roasted grain, a hundred cakes of raisins, and two hundred cakes of dried figs. All this she loaded on donkeys. Then she rode out to meet David and greeted him very respectfully. She politely apologized for her husband's rude behavior. Her kind and courteous disposition caused David to change his mind. He praised her for her good judgment, which had prevented him from unnecessarily shedding blood by taking the law into his own hands.

Abigail saw that trouble was on the way and made a plan to keep the peace. Blessed are the peacemakers, for they will be called children of God. I hope you are a peacemaker: someone who tries to avoid fights by acting in a kind and courteous manner.

W. W. J.

Jesus taught us to be peacemakers. (Matthew 5:9)

March 22

Saul

He Went to a Witch

"Consult a spirit for me," he said, "and bring up for me the one I name."
(1 Samuel 28:8)

Because Saul was disobedient to the Lord, the Lord no longer spoke to Saul or answered his requests. Saul's heart was filled with evil and he was no longer led by the Holy Spirit. When the Philistine army was preparing to attack the Israelites, Saul was afraid and wondered whether the Lord would help him. He inquired of the Lord whether he would help the Israelites, but the Lord did not answer Saul. Then Saul devised a different plan.

Saul decided to go to a witch, or a spirit medium. Witches' power does not come from the Lord, but from evil sources. They conjure up the spirits of the dead, and then evil spirits speak through these people. Saul went to a witch in Endor. Because he did not want people to recognize him, he disguised himself and went to see the witch at night. He then asked her to bring up Samuel from the dead. God worked through this witch – in fact, she was terrified – and Saul was told that the Lord had turned against him and that he and his entire army would be defeated by the Philistines.

In his Word, the Lord forbids us to have anything whatsoever to do with witches or spirit mediums. The Lord does not want us to make use of strange powers. Consulting the dead is not right. The Lord wants to lead us himself. He gives us his Holy Spirit so that we can know his will and make the right decisions. If our relationship with God is healthy and strong, we will feel no need to consult with people who are involved with dark powers. Witchcraft, magic, and fortune-telling are practices that are condemned by the Lord. Be careful of people who play with Ouija boards, who claim to tell fortunes by reading the tea leaves left in teacups, or who use cards to predict the future. Instead, let us trust the Lord to lead us through his Spirit and his Word.

W.W.J.

Jesus always prayed to his Father to find out what he should do.

March 23

David

Everyone is Equal

"All will share alike." (1 Samuel 30:24)

David and his army had to fight the Amalekites in a very tough battle that required all their strength and skill. Israel finally conquered the Amalekites, and then they took back all of the sheep and cattle that the Amalekites had previously taken from them. The Israelites also took all of the Amalekites' possessions as their loot.

While the battle was going on, there were two hundred men who were too exhausted to continue fighting alongside David. He left them behind at a stream in a ravine while he and the rest of the men continued to pursue the Amalekites in battle. After the Israelites had vanquished the Amalekites, David returned to these two hundred men and asked them how they were doing. However, some of the men who had gone with David said mean things about the men who had stayed behind. They told David that the men who did not fight the battle to the end should not be allowed to share in the spoils. Only those who were with David to the very end should be allowed to take some of the loot. David then told these soldiers that the Lord had given them the victory over the Amalekites. He then decreed that those men who had stayed behind in the ravine were to receive the same share of the spoils as those who fought the battle to the end.

David did not want to treat some men better than others. He wanted everyone to feel equally important, despite the fact that some were weaker than others. We too should always be fair in our dealings with others. We should not deprive others of their fair share just because we believe that we contributed more to the outcome of a project than they did. Let us rather be generous and share the glory with others.

W.W.J.

Jesus did not look down on those who were weaker than others.

David

HE CRIED

"I grieve for you, Jonathan my brother." (2 Samuel 1:26)

David received some very sad news. King Saul had been pursued by the Philistine army. Realizing that the Philistines would capture him and kill him, Saul decided to die first. He ordered his armor-bearer to kill him; but when the armor-bearer refused, Saul took his own sword and fell on it. During this same battle Jonathan, David's beloved friend, was also killed. When David received the news of Saul and Jonathan's deaths, he was very upset. He tore his clothes and wept.

David then wrote a lament for Saul and Jonathan. Of Jonathan he said, *"I grieve for you, Jonathan my brother; you were very dear to me. Your love for me was wonderful, more wonderful than that of women"* (2 Samuel 1:26). And so the friendship between David and Jonathan came to an end. David probably had many wonderful memories of the times that he and Jonathan had spent together. But now he would never see his friend again, at least not here on earth.

When our loved ones die, we are left behind to continue life without them. It is always very sad when this happens. Perhaps some of your loved ones have died. Keep the wonderful memories you have of these people close to your heart. But it is also good to weep and grieve, as David did. Perhaps you know someone else who has lost a loved one. Why don't you go out of your way to comfort that person today?

W.W.J.

When Jesus saw the grave of his friend Lazarus, he wept because his friend had died.

David

A Leader with a Purpose

And David knew that the Lord had established him as king over Israel ... for the sake of his people Israel. (2 Samuel 5:12)

David had to wait many years after the Lord had anointed him as king before King Saul died. Only then could David take over the leadership of Israel. He also spent many years fleeing for his life, because Saul was constantly trying to kill him. Furthermore, the Israelites were a little reluctant to accept their new king's leadership. For many years, there was a battle between the followers of David and the followers of Saul. And yet David went about the business of everyday life calmly and patiently because he knew that the Lord had already chosen him to be king over Israel. The Bible tells us that David's strength and power continued to increase and that the Lord Almighty was always with him. The king of another country even came to David and offered to build him a palace. When this happened, David realized that the Lord had confirmed his leadership of Israel, for the sake of Israel's future.

It sometimes takes years before you and I truly understand why we are alive and what God's plan for our lives is. All we can do is to be obedient and follow him, day after day. Then we will realize that our lives do have meaning and significance. Ask the Lord to help you to be patient as he prepares you for all that he will call you to do.

W.W.J.

When we walk with Jesus, our lives are meaningful and significant.

March 26

David

First Ask

So David inquired of the Lord. (2 Samuel 5:19)

One of David's best personal qualities was the fact that he consulted with the Lord regularly. Especially when he was a young man, David was very careful and always made sure that he was doing the will of the Lord. Before he set out on an important venture or before he made a big decision, he first prayed to the Lord and asked what his will was.

When the Philistines heard that David had been anointed as king, they set out in full force to make war on Israel. David had to prepare himself and his country for battle. He immediately conferred with the Lord and asked whether he should go out and attack the Philistines. He wanted to make sure that the Lord would give them the victory over the Philistines. The Lord answered David and gave him permission to attack. Later the Philistines again marched against the Israelites, and again David asked the Lord's advice. But this time the Lord told him not to attack the Philistines immediately, and he gave David another strategy for dealing with them.

There were probably people who said that David should have immediately attacked the Philistines despite the Lord's advice, because the Philistines did, after all, invade his country. Therefore he should have defended himself. However, David believed that he should not rely on his own understanding and judgment only. Perhaps David's success as leader, king, and commander of the Israelite army is to be ascribed to the fact that he always asked God to give him advice about his plans and strategies.

The Bible says that we should not rely on our own understanding. Instead, we should trust in the Lord. Before making a decision, first make sure that it is the will of the Lord. After all, the Lord knows what is best for us.

W.W.J.

Peter did not ask Jesus whether he should cut off Malchus's ear. He just went ahead and did it, which turned out to be a big mistake. (John 18:10-11)

March 27

David

"... the Lord has ..." (2 Samuel 5:20)

After David had consulted with the Lord and the Lord had given him permission to attack the Philistines, the Israelites defeated their enemies. After David and his army had vanquished the Philistines, he did not sing his own praises. He did not tell everyone how powerful he was or how wonderfully brave his men were. No, David took great care to avoid this kind of thing. He knew that one should never steal the glory belonging to someone else.

That is why David immediately said that it was the Lord who went before him and destroyed his enemies. He insisted on giving all the honor and glory for the victory to the Lord. He knew that it was the Lord who guided them in the battle against the Philistines, and he had no intention of pretending that it was his strength and wisdom that had gained them the victory over the Philistines. He praised the Lord and gave him all the glory for the victory.

When we read the psalms that David wrote, we see how often David exalted the name of the Lord because he believed that the Lord had given him success in his ventures. Just read Psalm 124:2-3, 6, 8: *"... if the Lord had not been on our side when men attacked us ... they would have swallowed us alive. ... Praise be to the Lord. ... Our help is in the name of the Lord, the Maker of heaven and earth."*

Let us always glorify the Lord for every small success or achievement in our lives. If we ask for the Lord's help in our anxiety, we should remember to give him all the praise and glory for his assistance. It rightfully belongs to him.

W.W.J.

Jesus never boasted about his miracles, but always pointed to his Father who had sent him.

March 28

David

HE DANCED WITH ALL HIS MIGHT

David and the whole house of Israel were celebrating with all their might before the LORD. (2 Samuel 6:5)

David's heart's desire was to return the ark of the Lord to Jerusalem. It had been removed years before. As the place where the Lord met with his people and spoke to them, David obviously wanted it back in its rightful place.

When the ark was carried into Jerusalem, the Israelites were very happy. David himself was exuberant with joy. He was so glad that he danced before the ark of the Lord with all his might, while the Israelites celebrated and praised the Lord with songs and with harps, lyres, tambourines, rattles, and cymbals. The Bible tells us that David danced before the Lord with complete abandonment.

In David's time, the Israelites loved to dance. They often used dancing as a way to praise the Lord. While the choirs were singing, people danced with joy. They wanted to show how happy they were that the Lord was their God and that they could know him. Today, there are still many Christians who want to dance for the Lord. They too want to show others that the Lord is in their hearts and that the Holy Spirit has filled them with joy. They dance to praise and honor the Lord. Perhaps you have seen people doing this. Maybe you too like dancing for the Lord and glorifying his name.

Regardless of whether we dance for the Lord, testify for him, or praise his name by singing songs, it is very important that we should use our bodies to show people that we belong to the Lord and love him. Use your mouth right now to tell him that you love him.

W.W.J.

When Jesus rode into Jerusalem on a donkey, the people danced and praised him. (Matthew 21:7-9)

March 29

Michal

What a Snob!

Michal daughter of Saul watched from a window. And when she saw King David leaping and dancing before the LORD, she despised him in her heart. (2 Samuel 6:16)

Not all people love the Lord. Not all people are excited about the things that the Lord does for us. Some people are very critical of the kingdom of God. Many of these people are actually members of the church. They read the Bible and pray to God, but their attitudes are always cold and critical.

Without judging such people, we should try to understand that people's feelings about things sometimes differ from ours. Perhaps we should just pray that the Lord will fill their hearts with love for him and that they too will become excited and enthusiastic about the things of the Lord. The Lord does not like cold hearts. Michal had a very cold heart.

Michal was Saul's daughter and David's wife. It doesn't seem as if she loved the Lord much. While everyone else was excited about the ark returning to Jerusalem, she despised David when she saw him joyfully leaping and dancing before the Lord. Later, she reproached him for being so happy and told him that he had behaved in a very undignified way by dancing with such abandonment in front of all the people of Israel. She was contemptuous and sarcastic. David was probably very hurt by her response. He was so happy about the Lord and about the ark returning to Jerusalem, and all his wife wanted to do was criticize him!

Even when people don't understand why we are so excited about Jesus, we should not cease to serve and follow him with all the enthusiasm that we can muster. Don't allow anyone to throw cold water on your fire and fervor for the Lord. The Lord loves people who serve him with all their hearts.

W.W.J.

Jesus reproached the church in Ephesus, because their fervent love for him had cooled. (Revelation 2:4)

March 30

Mephibosheth

HE WAS A CRIPPLE

"There is still a son of Jonathan; he is crippled in both feet." (2 Samuel 9:3)

David was a kind-hearted man. Even after he became king of Israel he never thought that he was more important than anyone else. He also often thought about his friendship with Jonathan, Saul's son. One day, while he was thinking about his good friend, he suddenly wondered if there was anyone left of Saul's family. He asked people, *"Is there no one still left of the house of Saul to whom I can show God's kindness?"* (2 Samuel 9:3).

One of David's servants told him that the only member of Jonathan's family who was still alive was Jonathan's crippled son, Mephibosheth. David immediately sent messengers to get him. Perhaps Mephibosheth thought that David wanted to do something hurtful to him, because Saul had treated David so badly and because Mephibosheth would have been in line to be king. But David told Mephibosheth that he need not worry, because he had decided to take him into his care for the sake of his vow to Jonathan. David also said that he would restore to him all the land that once belonged to Mephibosheth's grandfather Saul. Furthermore, David wanted Mephibosheth to live with him in the palace. Mephibosheth was very happy and more than a little surprised. David instructed his servants to look after Mephibosheth and to take care of his interests.

We can learn an important lesson from David's goodness. We should always look for opportunities to do good to other people. It doesn't matter what they have done to us or how badly they behave toward us. Let's try always to do good deeds for others.

W.W.J.

Jesus' entire life consisted of loving people and doing good to them.

David

SINNER AND KING

"... so he will be struck down and die." (2 Samuel 11:15)

The Bible is very honest about people and their lives. The Bible not only speaks about the attractive and pleasant aspects of people's lives, but also about the evil and sinful things. Many nice things are written about King David. He did many wonderful things, and he was a good man. And yet he was a flawed human being just as we are.

No one is perfect, and David was no exception. David's army went to war, but David did not accompany them. Perhaps things would have turned out much better had he gone with them and led his army. However, while he was at home, he one day saw a very beautiful woman bathing. Her name was Bathsheba. He immediately fell in love with the woman and decided that he wanted her for himself. When he found out that she was already married, he devised a really evil plan: he decided to have Bathsheba's husband killed. He used his power and authority as king to make sure that Uriah, Bathsheba's husband, would fight on the front line of the army. Everything happened exactly as planned, and Uriah was killed.

David married Bathsheba, but the Lord was not pleased with what David had done. He sent a prophet to David to tell him that he had committed a terrible sin. David was very sorry for what he had done, but by then it was too late, because Uriah was already dead.

Even though we are children of the Lord who try very hard to do his will, we are often disobedient. We often do things that we know are not right. All people sometimes do sinful things. It is terrible that it should be so, but that's just the way it is. Let's ask the Lord to help us make the right decisions. Let's try to do his will today. And if we do wrong, let's always be ready to seek God's forgiveness and to do better next time.

W.W.J.

Jesus died so that our sins could be forgiven. When we do wrong, we should confess our sin to Him and ask for His forgiveness.

April 1

Absalom

THE REBEL

"As soon as you hear the sound of the trumpets, then say, 'Absalom is king in Hebron.'" (2 Samuel 15:10)

David was a very successful king and the Lord loved him deeply. David had many children. One of his sons was Absalom. The Bible tells us that Absalom was a very handsome man. From head to toe, there seemed to be absolutely nothing wrong with him.

Unfortunately, it was only Absalom's outer appearance that was so appealing. His heart was not at all beautiful. He was the son of the king and believed himself to be much more important than anyone else. He even bought himself a fancy chariot and horses, and made fifty men run before him wherever he went. It wasn't long before Absalom decided that he wanted to be king in his father's place. He started making plans to get the people of Israel to side with him against his father. He wanted them to appoint him as king and get rid of his father. That was very wicked of him, don't you think?

Absalom decided to crown himself as king in Hebron. The great King David's son was a rebel. David was forced to flee from Jerusalem and the palace because his advisers told him that Absalom might be planning to kill him and the rest of his household. David's troops then tried to resolve the situation by attacking Absalom and his army. When Absalom tried to escape on his mule, his hair got caught in a tree and he was left hanging in midair. He was killed while hanging there. What a terrible end. David had not wanted his son to die, and so his heart almost broke.

Don't rebel against the authority figures in your life, not even in your heart. Respect your father and mother.

W . W . J .

Jesus taught us to be gentle of spirit.

Ahithophel

QUESTIONABLE ADVICE

For the LORD had determined to frustrate the good advice of Ahithophel in order to bring disaster on Absalom. (2 Samuel 17:14)

Ahithophel was an important advisor in David's government. He had to give counsel to the king whenever the king needed some good advice.

Absalom managed to win Ahithophel over to his side. When Ahithophel saw that the majority of the Israelites were on Absalom's side, he decided to help Absalom rather than David. Ahithophel poisoned Absalom's heart against David, giving Absalom advice on how to overthrow his father. In other words, he told Absalom how to go about becoming king in David's place. Ahithophel had all kinds of interesting bits of advice for Absalom and told him exactly what he should do. Together they devised many devious little plans. All David could do was to ask the Lord, *"O LORD, turn Ahithophel's counsel into foolishness"* (2 Samuel 15:31). The Lord answered David's prayer, and in the end, the advice brought ruin to Absalom.

There will always be people with dishonorable intentions who will want to give us advice. This advice is not always the best advice, and we should be careful of following it blindly. Sometimes our friends advise us to do things that are in their best interests instead of ours. We need wisdom to be able to distinguish between good and bad advice. We should also be careful not to follow just anyone's advice. Don't be gullible and simply believe what someone is saying. First ask the Lord for advice.

W.W.J.

Jesus is called our Counselor. Listen to his advice.

April 3

Hushai

A Secret Agent

"The advice of Hushai ... is better than that of Ahithophel." (2 Samuel 17:14)

David was in deep trouble. He was the king of Israel, but his son Absalom had decided to lead a rebellion against him. Not only did this act of betrayal make David very sad, it was also a very big threat to his rule as king.

David was forced to flee from Absalom because Absalom and his men wanted to kill him. David prayed to God and asked God to help him. Hushai was one of David's friends. He was just as sad and upset about everything that had happened. Hushai asked David how he could help him. David then asked a very big favor of Hushai. He asked Hushai to act as a secret agent for him.

Hushai had to return to Absalom and his men and tell them that he was on their side. Then he had to convince Absalom not to follow Ahithophel's advice.

Ahithophel was a very clever counselor of the king who had defected to Absalom's side. He advised Absalom to take his father's concubines and then to have his father killed. That would be the end of David's rule as king. The secret agent Hushai then risked his life and cleverly convinced Absalom not to follow Ahithophel's advice. Absalom decided not to kill David, and in this way David's life was saved.

Hushai was willing to risk his life for the sake of an important cause. Sometimes you and I also have to be willing to risk our lives for the Lord's cause. We should be brave enough to take a stand for God's kingdom. We should not shrink from taking a stand simply because we are afraid of what others will say or do.

W.W.J.

Jesus risked his life for the sake of God's kingdom and ultimately sacrificed his life so that you and I may have eternal life.

Solomon

WEALTH OR WISDOM?

"Ask for whatever you want me to give you." (1 Kings 3:5)

David's son Solomon became king of Israel after David died. The Bible tells us that Solomon was a very good king. He became even wealthier and more important than his father, David.

One night, the Lord appeared to Solomon in a dream and asked him what he wanted God to do for him. What a wonderful question, don't you think? Just think what you would do if the great God of heaven and earth asked you what you wanted him to do for you! What would your answer be? Perhaps you would say that you wanted to be a millionaire. Perhaps you would say that you wanted to be the most beautiful girl or the strongest guy in the entire world. What do you think Solomon answered?

Solomon probably thought very carefully about the Lord's question. Then he answered that he had seen how God had shown great kindness and faithfulness to his father David. He also said that he realized that God had chosen him to rule over Israel. He felt very young and much too inexperienced to rule over the people God had chosen as his own. Then he asked, *"So give your servant a discerning heart to govern your people and to distinguish between right and wrong"* (1 Kings 3:9). Solomon asked for wisdom, not for wealth or power or to be the most important person in the world!

The Lord was pleased with Solomon's answer and decided to give Solomon not only wisdom, but also wealth and glory, so that no one would be as great a king as he. Let us ask the Lord today to help us serve and follow him with wisdom. Who knows, he might give us much more than we asked for.

W.W.J.

Jesus taught us to seek his kingdom before anything else, for then we will receive everything else we need.

April 5

Solomon

ONLY THE BEST FOR THE TEMPLE

So he overlaid the whole interior with gold. He also overlaid with gold the altar. (1 Kings 6:22)

King David had really wanted to build a temple for the Lord, but the Lord did not allow him to do it. Instead, he planned for David's son, Solomon, to build the temple. The temple was a place where people could serve and worship the Lord.

The Bible tells us that Solomon procured the very best building materials for the temple. He wanted the house of the Lord to have only the best. He obtained the best wood, had the best stone cut into blocks, and had gold inlays created to be built everywhere into the temple. Only the best was good enough for Solomon. Only the best for the God of his life.

Today there is no longer a temple. God no longer lives in a temple or in buildings created by human hands. True, we do still have church buildings, but that is where we gather to collectively worship and praise the Lord. God's temple is now in the hearts of those who love him. Paul says that our bodies are temples of the Holy Spirit who lives inside us. Therefore, we should build his kingdom with the best materials to be found. We should not give the Lord our shabby hand-me-downs. This means that our bodies, which are God's temples, should be well looked after and treated with the utmost care. When we set out to do any task for the Lord, we should give our utmost to accomplish it successfully. For his kingdom only the best is good enough, just as only the best was good enough for the temple in Solomon's time.

W. W. J.

Jesus taught us that he would build a new temple – a spiritual temple – by dying on the cross for us and then being resurrected. (1 Corinthians 6:19)

The Queen of Sheba

AMAZED BY EVERYTHING SHE SAW

"But I did not believe these things until I came and saw with my own eyes."
(1 Kings 10:7)

The queen of Sheba was very curious about Solomon because she had heard many rumors about all the things that he had accomplished in the name of the Lord. People are always eager to find out more about the Lord. When the Lord's glory shines in people's lives, it always looks so beautiful and attractive that others are curious to know more.

This queen came to Jerusalem with a very large caravan of camels carrying expensive spices, large quantities of gold, and many precious stones. She decided to find out whether Solomon was really as wise as people said. When she finally met him, she spoke with him about all that she had on her mind, and Solomon had an answer to each one of her questions. She realized that Solomon was indeed a very wise king.

She also had the opportunity to see all of Solomon's wealth. She saw the temple that he had built; the fine, delectable dishes served at his table; the many attendants who served them; and the big procession that accompanied him whenever he went to the house of the Lord. The Bible says that she was completely overwhelmed by all of this.

However, the most important thing that we learn about the queen of Sheba is that she praised the Lord: *"Praise be to the LORD your God, who has delighted in you and placed you on the throne of Israel"* (1 Kings 10:9). She praised the Lord because she saw God's work in Solomon's life. May other people also praise and worship the Lord because they see that the Lord loves us and looks after us.

W.W.J.

The people were astonished when they saw how wise Jesus' disciples were. The disciples were wise because Jesus was the one who taught them.

April 7

Solomon

HIS WEAK SPOT

King Solomon, however, loved many foreign women. (1 Kings 11:1)

The Bible is very honest about the lives of God's children. It doesn't try to say only nice things about them. Without exception, people are imperfect creatures, and every single person has certain character flaws. The Lord knows this, and he wants to help us. He uses people as his instruments, but sometimes his instruments are stubborn and do just as they please.

Solomon was a very wise king, and the Lord worked through him in a very special way. And yet Solomon's character was not without flaws. Despite all his wonderful accomplishments and all his wisdom, he still did some really foolish things. One of Solomon's weaknesses was the fact that he loved foreign women. The Bible tells us that he had more than a thousand wives! He was not content with having one Israelite wife; instead, he took women from foreign nations to be his wives. And this he did in spite of the fact that the Lord had instructed the Israelites not to marry people from foreign nations. In an almost sorrowful tone, the Bible tells us, *"As Solomon grew old, his wives turned his heart after other gods, and his heart was not fully devoted to the LORD his God, as the heart of David his father had been"* (1 Kings 11:4). What a pity! Because of Solomon's weak spot, he dishonored the name of the Lord.

You and I also have our weak spots. We must ask the Lord to show us the things in our lives that cause us problems. Despite the fact that we are his children, we are not perfect. We should be very careful of those things in our lives that are problematic. Let us ask the Lord to help us not to yield to our weaknesses.

W.W.J.

Jesus taught us to keep watch and pray so that we would not succumb to temptation. (Matthew 26:41)

April 8

The Widow of Zarephath

She Gave Everything

"I don't have any bread – only a handful of flour in a jar." (1 Kings 17:12)

Elijah was a prophet of the Lord. This means that the Lord spoke to him and gave him messages to pass on to the people. In Elijah's time, a great drought came over the land. The Lord looked after Elijah and sent him to live in the Kerith Ravine, east of the Jordan. Here the Lord gave him water from the brook, and he also sent ravens to feed Elijah while he lived there.

After a while, the Lord instructed Elijah to go to a town named Zarephath. There, he saw a widow who was busy gathering sticks for firewood. He asked her if she could bring him some water and a little piece of bread to eat. She told him that she did not have any bread left, only a handful of flour in a jar and a little oil in a jug. She said that she was busy gathering a few sticks of firewood to take home so that she could make a last meal for herself and her young son, but she still offered some to Elijah. After this meal there would be no food left, and she was convinced that they would soon die of hunger.

Elijah had good news for her. He told her not to be worried and assured her that the Lord would not allow the flour in the jar to run out or the oil in the jug to lessen until such time as he sent rain to the land.

The woman then made food of the flour and the oil, and they all had something to eat. And truly, the flour did not run out and neither did the oil. They had enough food to eat every day until the Lord sent rain to the land. It was a miracle!

You and I should not be miserly in sharing what we have with others. The Lord is powerful and will always give us what we need, so that we will never lack for anything. You can trust the Lord to always meet your needs.

W.W.J.

Jesus fed an entire crowd with two fishes and five loaves of bread. There was enough for everyone to eat. (Mark 6:31-44)

Elijah

THE BIG SHOWDOWN

"Then you call on the name of your god, and I will call on the name of the LORD." (1 Kings 18:24)

In Elijah's time, a perpetual battle raged between the kingdom of light and the kingdom of darkness.

The Lord was going to send rain to the earth after a long period of drought. He sent Elijah to King Ahab. Ahab was angry with Elijah because he thought that the terrible drought was Elijah's fault. Elijah told Ahab that he was not the one to blame – the drought had come over the land because of the king and his family. King Ahab had been disobeying God and worshiping the idol Baal.

Elijah set out to prove, once and for all, who was Israel's true God. Elijah asked Ahab to summon all the people of Israel to Mount Carmel. The four hundred and fifty prophets of Baal and four hundred prophets of Asherah also had to be there. Elijah then challenged the other prophets. He told them to pray to their god while he prayed to his God, and then everyone would see who the true God was. Elijah built an altar, as did the other prophets. Elijah and the other prophets would each slaughter a bull and lay it on the altar. All the prophets should then pray, and the god who answered by fire would be the true God. Everyone was breathless with excitement and anticipation. The prophets of Baal prayed and prayed, but nothing happened. After they had prayed the entire day, no fire had come down from heaven.

Before Elijah started praying, he took four large jars of water and poured the water over the offering and the wood. He did this three times. Everything was soaking wet. When Elijah prayed to his God, the Lord answered, and the fire that came down from heaven burned up everything. It even licked up the water in the trench around the altar. Then the people knew that the almighty Lord was the true God. All the prophets of Baal were captured and killed.

Our God is great and powerful. Trust in him today.

W.W.J.

While walking with Jesus, the disciples witnessed God's miraculous deeds. (John 20:30-31)

April 10

Elijah

HE PRAYED FOR RAIN

"A cloud as small as a man's hand is rising from the sea." (1 Kings 18:44)

After a long time of drought, the Lord decided to send rain upon the land. Through his prophet Elijah, the Lord sent a message to the king and the Israelites. Elijah told Ahab and Jezebel that it was their fault that the drought had come over the land because they had sinned against God. He also told the people that God was much more powerful than the prophets of Baal and that they should serve the Lord God instead of worshiping the idol, Baal.

After God had sent down fire from heaven to consume Elijah's offering, Elijah went aside and prayed earnestly for rain to come upon the land. He prayed continually, and he repeatedly sent his servant to look and see if any clouds had appeared in the sky yet. Seven times Elijah sent his servant to see if there were any signs of rain clouds gathering. And Elijah simply continued praying. After the seventh time that he had been sent out, the servant returned and said that a cloud as small as a man's hand was rising from the sea. Soon, it started raining.

Elijah was merely human, just as we are, and yet he prayed for rain and the Lord answered him. The Lord answered Elijah's prayers because Elijah trusted in the Lord and continued praying until his prayer was answered. You and I should learn to trust as Elijah did and to always continue praying. Our prayers can make a huge difference to the world.

W.W.J.

Jesus taught his disciples to pray. (Luke 11:1-2)

Elijah

THE BRAVE MAN RAN AWAY

Elijah was afraid and ran for his life. (1 Kings 19:3)

God's servants are often very brave, and God can accomplish great miracles through them. However, at other times, they are overwhelmed by fear because they no longer trust in God as they should. This is what happened to Elijah, the great prophet.

After Elijah had single-handedly achieved a spiritual victory over 850 false prophets, something awful happened. Ahab's wicked wife, Jezebel, who did not believe in God but instead worshiped Baal, heard about Elijah's victory. She then sent a messenger to Elijah and threatened to have him killed.

Elijah was overwhelmed by fear and fled for his life. He ran away from Jezebel, and continued traveling until he had reached a remote spot deep in the desert. He felt terribly sorry for himself. He complained about his situation to the Lord and said that he felt completely worthless. Although he had just achieved a great victory in the name of the Lord, he was now trembling in fear and wishing to die! Exhausted, Elijah then fell asleep.

When Elijah awoke, the Lord sent an angel to bring him food. After eating, Elijah fell asleep again. He woke up completely refreshed, and then the Lord spoke to him and assured Elijah that he was with him always and that he need not fear anything.

Elijah was exhausted after the spiritual battle with the prophets of Baal. The Lord first gave him some time to rest and eat, and then he renewed Elijah's courage. You and I are also sometimes discouraged. When we are tired and hungry it is easy for us to lapse into negativity. Always make sure that you get enough rest. Make sure that your lifestyle is healthy. Once you have done this, hold on to God's Word and don't be afraid of people who threaten you.

W.W.J.

Jesus was often completely exhausted, and whenever he was tired he first rested, relaxed, and enjoyed a meal with his friends.

April 12

Ahab

He Wanted It!

"Let me have your vineyard to use for a vegetable garden." (1 Kings 21:2)

There was once a man named Naboth. He owned a vineyard that was located right next to King Ahab's palace. Ahab had more than enough money and possessions, but he longed to own Naboth's vineyard as well. Ahab went to Naboth and asked him to give his vineyard to the king. In exchange, the king would give him a better vineyard, or he would pay Naboth whatever the vineyard was worth. However, because Naboth had inherited this vineyard from his ancestors, he did not want to sell it. He attached great sentimental value to the vineyard, and God's law said that it should be kept in his family.

King Ahab then acted very childishly. He first became very angry, and then sullen. He lay on his bed sulking and refusing to eat. Everyone could see that he was unhappy about something. And all this just because he could not have his way.

Covetousness is a big problem. When we really want something that does not belong to us, we can become very unhappy if we don't get what we want. Some people go so far as to devise evil plans to get what they want. I hope you don't walk around sulking whenever you can't have things your way. Being sullen all the time is a very unappealing characteristic. Be content with what you have. If there is something that you really want, pray about it and ask your parents if you may have it. But always be content and thank God for what you do have.

W.W.J.

Jesus knows all our needs and will give us things that he knows are good for us. He knows best.

April 13

Jezebel

A Vicious Woman

"But seat two scoundrels opposite him and have them testify that he has cursed both God and the king." (1 Kings 21:10)

Jezebel did not serve the Lord God; she worshiped the false god, Baal. She was a wicked woman. She did not think twice about killing people who acted contrary to her wishes. For example, at one time, she made sure that all the prophets of the Lord that she could track down were killed. In their places, she appointed the prophets of Baal.

When Jezebel saw her husband lying on his bed and sulking because Naboth did not want to sell his vineyard to him, she devised an evil plan. She incited two men to bring false charges against Naboth. They lied and said that Naboth had cursed both God and the king. The people then seized Naboth and took him outside the city, where they stoned him to death. When Jezebel heard that Naboth was dead, she told Ahab that he was now free to take the vineyard for himself. Ahab took the vineyard without giving it a second thought.

Wicked people will always make evil plans to get what they want. You and I should ask the Lord to help us not to make evil plans or hurt other people just to get our own way.

W.W.J.

Jesus taught us to be content with that which we have. He knows what we need. We don't have to devise underhanded plans to get what we want.

Judas

The Backstabber

"What are you willing to give me if I hand him over to you?" (Matthew 26:15)

It is difficult to understand how one of the disciples who had lived with Jesus for three years could go so far as to stab Jesus in the back. We call someone a backstabber when we didn't expect that person to do us any harm – and yet he did. Attacking someone from behind and stabbing him in the back with a knife is a very cowardly act. The person doesn't even stand a chance to defend himself.

Judas decided that he had enough of Jesus and all his stories. He was probably not satisfied with all the things that Jesus did. In particular, Judas had a problem with money. He carried the disciples' money and handled any financial matters. Eventually, money became more important to him than Jesus' kingdom.

Judas secretly went to the chief priests and asked them how much money they would give him if he handed Jesus over to them. They then agreed that they would pay him thirty silver coins. This is how it came about that Jesus was arrested and eventually killed.

Later Judas was overwhelmed with regret over what he had done, and he returned the money. But by then it was too late. In his remorse, he did a terrible thing and killed himself.

Nothing in our lives should be more important to us than Jesus. Don't allow other things in your life to plant wrong ideas about Jesus in your mind.

W . W . J .

The Bible also tells us about the rich young man who decided that he loved the world more than he loved Jesus. (Luke 18:22-24)

Jesus

THE FIRST HOLY COMMUNION

While they were eating, Jesus took bread, gave thanks and broke it. (Matthew 26:26)

Jesus knew that his disciples would miss him very much. They loved him and had come to know him very well. For three years they had traveled with him, listening to all his sermons and witnessing all the miracles performed.

Jesus had also told them that he had to die for the sake of the world's sins. He said that he would be going away. He also knew that he would be killed. That is why he arranged to have a very special meal with his disciples one evening.

While they were busy eating, Jesus took some bread and asked the Lord's blessing. After that he broke the bread and gave it to his disciples. Then he said something very strange: *"Take and eat; this is my body"* (Matthew 26:26). He also took the cup with the wine and after giving thanks, he told his disciples to drink from it, for, he said, *"This is my blood ... which is poured out for many for the forgiveness of sins"* (Matthew 26:28). What did Jesus mean?

Jesus knew that it was important for his disciples to realize that he had come to earth to die for them so that their sins might be forgiven. His body was like the bread that was broken, and his blood was like the wine they drank. Food and liquids strengthen our bodies and keep us alive. In the same way, Jesus' body would be broken for us so that we might have eternal life with him.

The Holy Communion was instituted by Jesus. Every time we partake of it, we think about the wonderful fact that he died to save us.

W.W.J.

Holy Communion is a reminder to us of what Jesus did for us on the cross.

April 16

Peter

"I tell you the truth," Jesus answered, "this very night, before the rooster crows, you will disown me three times." (Matthew 26:34)

After Jesus had instituted Holy Communion, he told his disciples that they would all forsake him that very night. He told them again that he would be killed, but he also assured them that he would be resurrected. He then would go ahead of them to Galilee, and he would meet them there.

Peter was very indignant about Jesus' prediction that they would all desert him. He said that even if the other disciples forsook Jesus, he would never leave Jesus alone. Jesus had to give Peter some sad news. After all, he knew Peter's heart. He knew what would happen. Jesus told Peter that a rooster would crow, and when Peter heard that, he would know that he had disowned Jesus – not only once, but three times.

To disown someone is to tell a lie about your relationship with that person. For example, if you say that you were not in someone's company, even though you were, you are disowning that person. This is what happened to Peter. Two servant girls and a few men asked him if he was one of Jesus' disciples. This happened after Jesus had been arrested. Peter lied and said that he didn't even know Jesus. And after he did that three times, a rooster crowed.

You and I should not be ashamed to say that we know Jesus. We should not pretend that we don't belong to him. We should not be shy about our relationship with Jesus, and we should not be afraid to let people find out that we are Christians. Let's be proud of being Christians.

W.W.J.

When Peter realized that he had disowned Jesus he was filled with remorse and wept bitterly.

April 17

The Disciples

KEEP WATCH OR SLEEP?

"Could you men not keep watch with me for one hour?" (Matthew 26:40)

Jesus had entered the hour of his greatest distress. He realized that there was no turning back. This was a terrible thought, and it was very difficult for him to deal with it. He needed all the assistance and support that he could get. For three years, the disciples had lived with him. They knew him and understood him well. In this difficult time, they probably also did their best to encourage him. They believed in him. In Gethsemane, Jesus told them that his soul was overwhelmed with sorrow to the point of death, and he asked them to keep watch with him. This means that he wanted them to support him and pray with him. He then walked a small distance from them and started praying to his Father. When he later returned to his disciples, he was surprised and disappointed to find that they had all fallen asleep. Not one of them was willing to stay awake with him and support him in his personal struggle. He then told Peter that it was a pity that they were not able to stay awake for even one hour with him. Then he went away a second time to pray.

When he returned again later, he found the disciples fast asleep once again. They simply could not keep their eyes open. He left them and went away once more to pray. When he found them asleep for the third time, he woke them and told them that his hour had come and that he was about to be arrested.

The Lord sometimes tells us to keep watch and pray. He sometimes talks to us about important matters so that we may pray about them. We suddenly think about someone, and we realize that person might be in need of our prayers. We too should learn how to keep watch and pray. God expects us to intercede for others. He wants us to plead with the Father on behalf of other people. He wants us to keep praying that his kingdom will come soon.

W.W.J.

Jesus taught us to pray so that his kingdom would come.

April 18

Disciples of God

KEEP WATCH AND PRAY

"Are you still sleeping and resting? Look, the hour is near." (Matthew 26:45)

Jesus knew that he was about to be arrested and killed. He was certainly not looking forward to it. He knew that the only thing that could possibly help him was prayer. That is why he asked his disciples to go with him to a garden called Gethsemane.

When they arrived there, he told his disciples to sit and wait while he went aside to pray. He took Peter and two other disciples with him, and the disciples sat close by while he prayed. While Jesus was praying he became sorrowful and troubled and told them that he was overwhelmed by a deathly anguish. He then asked them to keep watch with him. But the disciples were so drowsy and tired that they fell asleep.

Jesus kneeled with his face to the ground and asked the Lord to let the cup of suffering pass him by. However, Jesus also said that he was willing to set aside his own will so that the will of God might be done. When he was done praying, he woke the disciples.

There are times when you and I must pray earnestly for and keep watch over the Lord's interests. We should not be lazy and fall asleep. We should do our share. Ask the Lord if there is anything specific that you should pray about today.

W. W. J.

Jesus said, "Watch and pray so that you will not fall into temptation". (Matthew 26:41)

The Soldiers

THEIR MOCKERY WAS THE TRUTH

They ... knelt in front of him and mocked him. "Hail, king of the Jews!" they said. (Matthew 27:29)

Jesus was arrested and taken to Pilate (the Roman governor) to be put on trial. Pilate believed that Jesus was innocent. At that time, there was another notorious prisoner in jail, called Barabbas. Pilate had always released a prisoner to the Jews during the Passover. Pilate thought that if he gave the people a choice between releasing Jesus and releasing Barabbas, they would surely choose Jesus, because Barabbas was a very evil man.

When Pilate asked the people which one of the prisoners they wanted released, however, everyone screamed that he should free Barabbas and have Jesus crucified. So Pilate ordered his soldiers to crucify Jesus. The soldiers stripped Jesus of his clothes and put a scarlet robe around his shoulders. They set a crown of thorns on his head and put a staff in his hand. Then they mocked him by pretending to kneel before him and greeting him as the King of the Jews. They spat on him and hit him on the head with the staff.

Without knowing it, the soldiers, even in their mockery, were telling the truth about Jesus. He was indeed the King of the Jews. But he is much more than merely the King of the Jews; he is also the King of the entire world and everything in it – including you and me.

W.W.J.

Jesus taught his disciples that he was more than just an earthly king. He is the King over earth, heaven, and all of creation – including us.

Simon

Bearer of Jesus' Cross

As they were going out, they met a man from Cyrene, named Simon, and they forced him to carry the cross. (Matthew 27:32)

In Jesus' time, there was a man named Simon, who lived in Cyrene. It is thought that he was a black man who came to Jerusalem during the Passover to bring a sacrifice of atonement for his sins.

It was during the time of Passover that Jesus Christ was put on trial before Pilate. In the end, Jesus was found guilty, despite the fact that he wasn't really guilty of any crime at all. Then the soldiers put a cross on Jesus' shoulders and ordered him to walk to Golgotha, where he and two other men would be crucified.

A large crowd of people shouted and booed while Jesus walked along the Via Dolorosa, the road of pain and suffering, toward Golgotha. People were jostling each other to get a good view of what was going on. Simon of Cyrene was among the people in the crowd.

When Jesus' strength gave out and he could no longer continue his walk, the soldiers pulled Simon out of the crowd and forced him to carry Jesus' cross. He probably didn't want to do it, but he had no choice but to be obedient. If he wasn't, he might have been thrown in prison. So he took the cross from Jesus' shoulders and set it upon his own.

This event probably changed his life. He was the one who had carried the cross of the Savior. Later we read that he was the father of Alexander and Rufus. They were both Christians (Mark 15:21). It was no coincidence that he was there to carry Jesus' cross. The cross changed his life.

W. W. J.

If Jesus had not been willing to die on the cross, our sins would never have been forgiven.

John

A Home for Mary

From that time on, this disciple took her into his home. (John 19:27)

Jesus suffered tremendous pain while hanging on the cross. He had been hanging on the cross since early morning, kept up by a few nails driven through his wrists and feet. Before he was crucified, he had been beaten and abused so badly that his pain must have been unbearable. And yet, while he was hanging on the cross, he did not think only about his own suffering. He also thought of the needs of other people, even at this terrible time.

There were people standing near the cross, watching everything that was happening. Some of these people mocked and cursed Jesus, but there were also a few who loved him and cared about him. Mary, Jesus' earthly mother, one of his disciples, and a few of his followers were among the people standing around the cross.

When Jesus saw Mary and John standing there, he told his mother to allow John to look after her from that time on. Jesus was dying and knew that he would no longer be able to take care of her. Therefore, he asked John to take care of his mother. The Bible says that from that time on John took Mary into his home, and she was like a mother to him and he like a son to her.

Even in his great suffering and distress, Jesus still cared about the earthly needs of people. In exactly the same way, he still cares about us today. He wants us to feel safe and happy in our relationships here on earth and to experience love and security. He wants those things for you today.

W.W.J.

Jesus taught people to live in peace and harmony with the members of their households and families.

April 22

Joseph

In a Rich Man's Tomb

As evening approached, there came a rich man from Arimathea, named Joseph. (Matthew 27:57)

On Good Friday, Jesus was crucified on Golgotha. This happened at nine o'clock in the morning. By three o'clock in the afternoon, Jesus was still hanging on the cross. At this time he called out, *"My God, my God, why have you forsaken me?"* (Matthew 27:46). A little later, Jesus again cried out, and then he died.

At the exact moment that Jesus died, the curtain of the temple was torn in two from top to bottom. The earth shook and tombs broke open. Many believers who had already died came back to life.

As evening approached, a rich man named Joseph arrived at the scene. He was also a follower of Jesus. He went to Pilate and asked if he could take Jesus' body so that he could bury it. Like all wealthy people, Joseph had his own tomb in a garden. Because he was a follower of Jesus and loved him very much, he decided to bury Jesus in his own tomb. He took Jesus' body, wrapped it in a clean linen cloth, and placed it in his own new tomb that he had cut out of the rock. There was a big stone in front of the entrance to the tomb. He rolled the stone in front of the entrance and then he went away.

Jesus was born in very simple surroundings: in the stable of an inn in Bethlehem. He lay in a manger from which animals ate their food. He lived a simple life, despite the fact that he was the Son of God. He died on a cross like a common criminal. But when he had finally completed his mission, he was placed in the tomb of a rich man. After this, he would be glorified by his resurrection, and he would sit at the right hand of his Father, from where he would reign as King of his kingdom.

Let us bring him praise and honor and tribute, because it is for us that he suffered and died.

W. W. J.

Many people have become followers of Jesus. Some are rich and some are poor. He lived and died for all of them.

April 23

The Angel of the Lord

THE STONE WAS ROLLED AWAY!

An angel of the Lord ... rolled back the stone and sat on it. (Matthew 28:2)

On the Friday of his crucifixion, Jesus was laid to rest in the tomb of Joseph of Arimathea. On the second day, the Jewish Sabbath day, he was still in the tomb. On the third day, Sunday, as day was starting to dawn, Mary Magdalene and another woman named Mary went to look at the tomb. Suddenly there was a violent earthquake and an angel of the Lord came down from heaven, went to the tomb, rolled away the stone, and sat on it. The angel's face was bright like lightning, and his clothes were white as snow. The Roman guards who were watching over the tomb had fainted with fear. The angel told the women not to be afraid. He knew that they were looking for Jesus Then he said that Jesus was not there because he had risen from the dead, just as he had said he would. The women just stood there in mute astonishment. Jesus was no longer in the tomb! The stone was rolled away from the entrance and the tomb was empty!

The angel told the women that they should go and tell the disciples that Jesus had risen from the dead. The women hurriedly ran from the tomb to give the disciples the news. Suddenly Jesus appeared before the women and greeted them. They went to him, clasped his feet and worshiped him. Jesus spoke kind words to them and told them not to be afraid, but to go and tell his disciples to go to Galilee, because there they would see him.

The greatest miracle is not only that Jesus died for our sins, but that he also conquered death through his resurrection. God's life was infused into his lifeless body anew, and his heart started beating again. In the same way, Jesus is alive for us right now, at this moment.

W.W.J.

Jesus predicted that he would die, but also that he would be resurrected. It happened just as he said. We worship a living God.

The Men of Emmaus

THEIR HEARTS WERE BURNING

"Were not our hearts burning within us while he talked with us on the road and opened the Scriptures to us?" (Luke 24:32)

Many of Jesus' followers were completely devastated when they heard that he had been crucified. How could it be? How could Jesus be dead? He spoke to them about his kingdom and said that he was the Son of God. They believed all he had told them. They witnessed all his miracles. Was it all in vain?

Two men who lived in a small town called Emmaus also felt this way. They were talking about everything that they had heard, and they were very upset. While they were walking along a road, talking to each other, Jesus himself came up behind them and started walking alongside them. However, the two men did not recognize him. Jesus asked them what they were talking about. With downcast faces, they started telling him everything that they had heard about Jesus. They spoke of how he was arrested and crucified, how he died and was buried, and how his body had disappeared from the tomb. Jesus listened very carefully to everything they had to say, and then he started teaching them and explaining to them what the prophets of long before had said about everything that would happen to Jesus.

When they arrived at their village, the two men invited Jesus to stay with them. While he was having a meal with them, he took the bread, gave thanks, broke it, and began to give it to them. Suddenly they realized that it was Jesus sitting at the table with them. Just as suddenly, Jesus disappeared. They were completely dumbfounded and said to each other that their hearts were burning within them while he was talking to them and explaining the Scriptures to them.

Even today, Jesus still speaks to us through his Word and his Spirit. If we hear and understand what he tells us about his life and his death, our hearts also burn warmly within us. Let us open up our ears to listen to what he says.

W. W. J.

While Jesus walked upon the earth, thousands of people followed him and listened to every word that he said.

April 25

Jesus

ANOINTED BY GOD

"I saw the Spirit come down from heaven as a dove and remain on him." (John 1:32)

One of the very important names that the Bible gives to the Lord Jesus is the name "Anointed One." This is the meaning of the name "Christ." But what does it really mean?

In the Old Testament, we read about kings and priests and prophets being anointed. When someone was anointed, fragrant oil was poured over his head. This was a way of acknowledging that a person had been chosen to perform an important task or play an important role. It also meant that God would help him to accomplish his task.

Jesus had the most important task of all. He had to deliver people from their sins. Although he is God, he had to come to earth as a man and pay the price for our sins. In order to accomplish his task, he needed to be equipped with tremendous spiritual strength. John saw the Holy Spirit descending from heaven like a dove. The Spirit came upon Jesus and remained on him. This was how Jesus became the Anointed One. God equipped him to do the work he was sent to do.

You and I have also been anointed by the Holy Spirit to do the Lord's work. If we give our lives to Jesus, we receive the Holy Spirit. He equips us to be good witnesses for Jesus.

W.W.J.

Jesus promised his disciples that the Holy Spirit would equip them to do his work – and the Holy Spirit did just that. (Acts 1:8)

April 26

Jesus

SENT BY THE FATHER

"As the Father has sent me, I am sending you." (John 20:21)

We will never be able to fully comprehend the extent of the Lord's love for us. He loves even the worst sinners, and he loves them so much that he was willing to die for them. John wrote that God loved the world so much that he was willing to send his Son to die on a cross so that our relationship with him might be restored and that we might be rescued from the devil's evil plans.

There are still billions of people who have not yet come to know the Lord as their Savior. They have not been reconciled with God. They are like people stumbling around in the darkness, falling over everything, and destroying themselves in the process. They have not yet arrived at a point where they discover that they need to have their sins forgiven and taken away. Looking down upon them every day, God's heart must be breaking. He probably thinks that he sent his Son to die for them so that they may be redeemed, and yet they continue to live in their self-inflicted darkness.

The Lord's heart passionately wants to bring all people to him. That is why Jesus told his disciples that he wants to send them into the world just as his Father sent him. The last thing that Jesus said to his disciples was that they should go to all the nations and teach everyone about Jesus.

You and I are also sent into the world; if we belong to Jesus, we have no choice but to follow his instructions. We must be willing to tell everyone about the wonderful message of Christ. Be a messenger of the Lord today.

W.W.J.

Jesus sends all people into the world as his messengers, regardless of whether they are old or young.

April 27

Thomas

BRING YOUR FINGER!

Then Jesus told him, "Because you have seen me, you have believed; blessed are those who have not seen and yet have believed." (John 20: 29)

It is very important to the Lord that we have faith in him. Unbelief comes easily and naturally to us, and it exists in our hearts of its own accord. It is not in our human nature to want to believe in God. We are actually born without faith. And if we do believe in something, we prefer to believe in ourselves, in our circumstances, or in that which we are taught by our parents.

True faith, according to the Bible, is faith in God through Jesus Christ, our Savior. To believe, or to have faith, is to listen to what God is saying and then to apply it in your life. It is to hear God's words and to take them to heart. In the same way, Jesus spoke many words to his disciples, and he expected them to believe what he said.

After Jesus was resurrected, just as he said he would be, he appeared to the disciples. However, Thomas was not with the other disciples when they first saw Jesus. When they told him that Jesus had been resurrected and that they had seen him, he refused to believe them. He said that he would not believe it unless he saw the nail marks in Jesus' hands and put his finger into the wounds where the nails were. Later, Jesus appeared to Thomas and told him to take a look at Jesus' hands and touch the holes the nails had made. Then he told Thomas to put his finger where the nails were. He also said that Thomas should stop doubting and believe.

We must not be skeptical of Jesus' words. Believe everything that is written in God's Word.

W.W.J.

Jesus was pleased when he realised that his disciples really believed in him. (John 16:31)

April 28

Peter

A Fresh Start

The third time he said to him, "Simon son of John, do you love me?" (John 21:17)

You probably remember how Peter had said that he would never forsake or deny Jesus. However, when Jesus was arrested and taken away, Peter was just as afraid as the other disciples, and he too ran away from Gethsemane. He later refused to acknowledge that he was one of Jesus' disciples in front of three witnesses. He disowned Jesus. He forsook his Lord.

When he heard the rooster crowing, Peter knew that he had forsaken Jesus, and he went outside and wept bitterly. He believed himself to be a complete failure. And Jesus was in jail, so Peter could not even tell him that he was sorry for denying him.

After Jesus was resurrected, he specifically called Simon Peter aside to speak with him. Three times Jesus asked Peter whether Peter loved him. Every time, Peter responded that he did. But he was a little bit ashamed at having disowned Jesus. Then Jesus asked Peter to take care of his sheep and to feed them. He also told Peter always to follow him.

In this way Peter was reinstated. He was given the opportunity to start afresh in his relationship with the Lord. You and I also often disappoint Jesus, but that doesn't mean that it's the end of our relationship with him. Apologize to him and continue to walk with him in faith.

W.W.J.

We are sometimes unfaithful, but Jesus always remains faithful to us.

April 29

Elisha

A Role Model

"The spirit of Elijah is resting on Elisha." (2 Kings 2:15)

For a long time, Elijah was Israel's foremost prophet. However, the time eventually came when the Lord decided that he wanted to take Elijah up to heaven to be with him. A new prophet would therefore have to be appointed in his place. The Lord chose a young man named Elisha to take Elijah's place.

Elisha knew that he had much to learn from Elijah. He was very young and did not have nearly as much experience as Elijah did. That is why he decided to go everywhere with Elijah. He watched Elijah very carefully and saw everything that Elijah did. He saw how Elijah spoke to the Lord and how the Lord worked through Elijah. Often Elijah told Elisha to stay at home while he went out to do God's work. But each time Elisha answered, *"As surely as the LORD lives and as you live, I will not leave you"* (2 Kings 2:2). He wanted to be with Elijah so that he could learn from him. Elijah was his role model.

Everywhere around us are people from whom we can learn. They can become our role models. Who do you look up to? Who can set an example for you? Always make sure that your role model lives according to the Lord's Word.

W.W.J.

Jesus is our most important role model.

A Young Jewish Girl

AN INSTRUMENT OF THE LORD

"If only my master would see the prophet who is in Samaria!" (2 Kings 5:3).

The brave soldier and commander of the king of Aram's army, Naaman, was ill with leprosy. Leprosy was a dangerous and deadly disease, and no one was able to help him – at least no one that he knew of.

During one of their raids on Israel, Naaman's army took captive a young girl from Israel. She became Naaman's wife's servant girl. This young girl saw how ill Naaman was. Then she told Naaman's wife all about Elisha, the prophet in Samaria, and recounted all the miracles he had done. She believed that if Naaman could only manage to get to Elisha, he would be healed. Because Naaman was desperate, he went to the king and told him about the prophet of Israel. The king felt very sorry for Naaman, and gave him permission to travel to Israel. The king also gave Naaman a letter to give to the king of Israel. In the letter, he asked the king of Israel to help Naaman find Elisha.

The Bible tells us that Naaman was healed. The prophet Elisha told him to go and wash himself in the Jordan. However, it was not the water of the Jordan that healed him, but the Lord God working through the river's water.

If the young Jewish girl had not told Naaman of Elisha, he would never have known where to go to be healed. He would also not have known God, who is the one who really healed him. Even today God still uses us to tell other people about redemption, healing, and hope. You and I can tell others about Jesus, our Savior. Even though you are still young, you can be the instruments that can lead even important people to the Lord. Don't be ashamed of being a witness for the Lord.

W.W.J.

Jesus said that we would be his instruments.

Naaman

He Had to Wash

"Go, wash yourself seven times in the Jordan, and your flesh will be restored and you will be cleansed." (2 Kings 5:10)

Naaman was the commander of a foreign nation's army. He was a very important man and a brave soldier. But then a terrible thing happened: he became ill with leprosy.

Naaman heard about the prophet Elisha who had the ability to heal people. He decided to journey to Israel to see Elisha because he was desperate to be healed. He traveled all the way to Israel and stopped at the door of Elisha's house with all his chariots and horses. Elisha sent a messenger to tell Naaman that he had to go to the Jordan and wash himself in its water seven times.

Naaman was annoyed with Elisha's response and went away angry. He had thought that Elisha would come out, call upon the name of the Lord, wave his hands over Naaman's leprous body, and thus cure him. When Elisha didn't do this, Naaman rode away in a rage. However, his servants spoke gently to him and convinced him that it would be best to do as Elisha told him. He went to the Jordan and washed himself in it seven times, just as Elisha had instructed him to do, and he was cured. The Bible says that his skin was restored like that of a young boy.

We sometimes think that the Lord should do his work in a way that would please us. However, God's plans are often different from ours. His ways are not like ours. We should simply do as the Lord tells us. When Naaman followed Elisha's strange instructions, he was cured.

W.W.J.

We can be spiritually healed only if we allow ourselves to be washed by the blood of Jesus.

Gehazi

He was Greedy

"I will run after him and get something from him." (2 Kings 5:20)

Gehazi was the servant of Elisha, the man of God. He witnessed all the wonderful things that the Lord did through the prophet Elisha. While he was with Elisha, he probably learned a lot about the Lord.

After Naaman had been cured of his leprosy, he decided to go back to Elisha to thank him. Naaman wanted to give Elisha a gift to show how grateful he was. However, Elisha felt that it would be wrong to accept gifts from Naaman. After all, it wasn't really Elisha who healed Naaman, but the Lord. Elisha wanted Naaman to give thanks to the Lord, so he refused Naaman's gifts. Naaman was very insistent, but Elisha refused.

Gehazi knew that Naaman was very wealthy. He didn't approve of the fact that Elisha refused to accept Naaman's gift. He decided that he would run after Naaman and ask him for a gift. He did as he planned and lied to Naaman by saying that Elisha had changed his mind and would like to receive a gift. Naaman was quite willing to give Gehazi some money and clothes to take back to Elisha. Gehazi took the gifts and hid them in his room.

Elisha realized that something was wrong, and knew that Gehazi had done something dishonest. Gehazi's sin quickly came to light, and then something terrible happened to him. The leprosy of which Naaman had suffered suddenly came upon Gehazi.

Gehazi's greediness caused him to tell a lie, thereby dishonoring God's name. Let's ask the Lord to help us not to be greedy.

W. W. J.

When we follow Jesus, we have to do what he expects of us.

Elisha

An Invisible Army

He looked and saw the hills full of horses and chariots of fire all around Elisha. (2 Kings 6:17)

The king of Aram declared war on Israel. However, every time the Arameans marched against the Israelites, the Lord showed the prophet Elisha where the army of Aram was about to advance on Israel. Elisha then warned the king of Israel, and in this way the Israelites were always prepared to fend off the attacks of the Aramean army.

The king of Aram found out that Elisha was behind all of his army's defeats, so he decided to have Elisha killed. He sent horses, chariots, and a strong troop of soldiers to the town where Elisha lived. Early one morning, when Elisha's servant got up and went outside, he saw that they were surrounded by horses and chariots. He was terrified and asked Elisha what they were going to do. Elisha answered, *"Don't be afraid ... Those who are with us are more than those who are with them"* (2 Kings 6:16).

Elisha's servant was puzzled, because he could see no one there to help them. Elisha then asked the Lord to open the eyes of his servant so that he could see what Elisha saw. Suddenly the servant was able to see invisible things. Elisha's house was surrounded by hills, and the hills were filled with horses and chariots of fire. God's angels were everywhere, ready to help Elisha.

When the Arameans rushed toward him, Elisha prayed to the Lord, and the Lord helped him. He struck the Arameans with blindness.

Sometimes we think that we are all alone. However, God's children are never alone. God sends his angels to help them. We can't always see his angels, but the Bible tells us that they are with us regardless. We should have faith and believe that the Lord is always on our side. We should do as Elisha did and pray to God, asking him to use his miraculous powers to help us.

W. W. J.

God the Father sent his angels to Jesus, so that they could help him. (Matthew 4:11)

May 4

Elisha

Repay Evil with Good

"Do not kill them. ... Set food and water before them so that they may eat and drink." (2 Kings 6:22)

When the Arameans rushed toward Elisha and his servant, Elisha prayed to God and asked him to strike the Arameans with temporary blindness. Everything happened just as Elisha asked. Elisha told the blinded Aramean army that he would lead them to the right city, where they would find the man they were looking for. Because they were blind they followed him, and he led them to Samaria, the capital of Israel!

When they arrived in Samaria, Elisha asked the Lord to open their eyes and restore their sight. When the Lord opened their eyes, they saw for the first time that they had been led right into the heart of the enemy city. The king of Israel wanted to kill them all, but Elisha said that they should not be killed. He gave the king much better advice, telling him to set food and water before them so that they could eat before returning to their own king. The king of Israel prepared a great feast for them. They ate their fill, and then he set them free to return to their own king.

The Arameans were so astonished by the wonderful treatment they received at the hands of the Israelites that they never again attacked them. Elisha's advice was the best advice the king could possibly have been given.

It is always best not to repay evil with evil. Rather, you should do good to those who want to harm you. In doing so you will make your enemies ashamed of their behavior, because they treat you badly and yet you treat them with kindness. Enemies sometimes become friends simply because you decide to treat them with kindness. Let's learn from Elisha to show only love toward those who want to harm us. Be kind to people who dislike you. Do or say something nice to someone with whom you don't usually get along.

W.W.J.

Jesus taught us to love our enemies and to conquer evil with good. (Matthew 5:44)

May 5

The Men Who Had Leprosy

Good News

"Let's go at once and report this." (2 Kings 7:9)

Terrible things were happening in the city of Samaria. A hostile king laid seige to the city, they surrounded it. No one was allowed to go out of the city; if anyone dared to come out they would surely be killed. This is how it came about that a great famine came upon Samaria. The enemy's siege of the city lasted so long that no one could go outside to gather food from the fields.

One day, four men who had leprosy were sitting at the entrance to the city gate. They were so hungry that they thought they would surely die. So they decided to go to the camp of the enemy and surrender themselves. They thought that their enemies would perhaps take pity on them and give them something to eat. In any case, if they stayed in the city, they were doomed.

When they arrived at the enemy camp, they were astonished. The entire army was gone. All the soldiers were gone, but all their possessions were still there. Even the food on the tables was still standing there, ready to be eaten. The four leprous men were overjoyed. They immediately sat down and ate and drank their fill. They also took some of the silver, gold, and clothes that belonged to the enemy. However, while they were busy eating, they suddenly remembered that their people in Samaria were dying of hunger. They decided to quickly return to Samaria and tell everyone that the enemy had fled.

God had caused the enemy army to retreat. He had caused them to hear the sounds of chariots and a great army the night before. Thinking that they were being attacked, they fled, and suddenly the city of Samaria was liberated.

You and I should also bring the good news to other people, just as the four men with leprosy did. Tell other people that Jesus came to be the bread of life, and that his death has given us the opportunity to have eternal life.

W.W.J.

Jesus said that he is the bread of life. (John 6:35)

May 6

Hezekiah

HE PLEADED

"Now, O LORD our God, deliver us from his hand." (2 Kings 19:19)

Hezekiah was the king of Judah. He always tried to serve the Lord with all his heart. He knew that the Lord was the only true God and that he was the only true source of deliverance in times of trouble.

The king of Assyria was very powerful, and he and his armies attacked the cities of Judah. Hezekiah knew that his army would never be able to defeat the Assyrians. When the king of Assyria was about to invade Jerusalem, he sent his field commander to Hezekiah with a message. He spoke to Hezekiah and insulted him as well as God. He said that they would never be able to defeat the Assyrians and that they would be much better off just surrendering without any fuss. But King Hezekiah went to the temple and spoke to God. He pleaded with God to help him so that Jerusalem would not fall into the hands of the enemy. The more insults and taunts his enemy hurled at him, the more fervently Hezekiah prayed to the Lord. Time and again he returned to the temple, and there he prayed and opened his heart to God.

The Lord then sent the prophet Isaiah to Hezekiah with a message. The Lord said that he had heard Hezekiah's prayers and that he would help the Israelites. That night, an angel of the Lord went into the Assyrian camp and killed 185,000 men. The Assyrians were so frightened that they immediately returned to Nineveh. God had answered Hezekiah's prayers.

When you and I are in dire straits, we should first speak to God about our problems and plead with him to help us. The Lord readily and joyfully answers our prayers, as long as we trust in him.

W.W.J.

Jesus invited us to pray in his name so that our hearts may be filled with joy. (John 16:24)

Hezekiah

An Ill Man Prayed

"I have heard your prayer and seen your tears; I will heal you." (2 Kings 20:5)

King Hezekiah was very ill. He was so ill that everyone knew he was at death's door. The prophet Isaiah also came to Hezekiah and told him that he would not recover from his illness, but would die soon. Hezekiah was very sad about this news.

He turned his face to the wall and prayed to the Lord. He pleaded with the Lord to give him another chance at life. He wept bitterly and reminded the Lord that he had always tried to do the will of the Lord during his reign as king.

God heard Hezekiah's prayer and granted his request. The prophet Isaiah had barely left the palace when the Lord instructed him to turn back and pass on a new message to Hezekiah. This time the message was a positive one. God said that he had heard Hezekiah's prayer and had seen his tears. As a consequence, he decided to heal Hezekiah. God spared Hezekiah for another fifteen years and continued to use him as king of Israel during that time.

There is tremendous power in prayer. When you and I plead with God, he always hears our prayers. However, God does not always give us everything we ask for. There are many ill people who pray for recovery – and still die. God always knows best. Nevertheless, you and I can always pray to the Lord for healing and recovery. Many people have asked the Lord to extend the duration of their life here on earth, as Hezekiah did. In response, the Lord has often granted their requests. You and I should never become so discouraged that we stop praying to and pleading with God.

W.W.J.

Jesus healed many sick people who came to him for help.

Jehosheba

SHE MADE THE RIGHT CHOICE

She hid the child from Athaliah so she could not kill him. (2 Chronicles 22:11)

Jehosheba grew up in a family that did not really serve the Lord. Her father, King Jehoram, was a wicked king because he did not rule according to the will of the Lord. His mother's name was Athaliah, and she too was a wicked woman who gave her son bad advice by telling him not to do God's will.

Jehoram died suddenly and tragically. When Athaliah heard about his death, she did a very evil thing. She had all the young princes killed so that she could take the throne. When Jehosheba heard what was going on, she quickly took one of the heirs to the throne, Joash, and quietly hid him. In this way, Jehosheba tried to ensure that a rightful king would one day reign over Israel again. She hid Joash for six years before he eventually became king.

Jehosheba came from an evil home environment. Her father was a wicked king, and Athaliah was full of treachery and murder. And yet Jehosheba decided to do the will of the Lord. She was also married to a priest. His name was Jehoiada. She knew the Lord and followed his instructions. Despite the fact that she grew up in a household in which no one wanted to do the will of the Lord, she made the choice to follow the Lord.

You have to decide for yourself whether you want to serve the Lord. Even if your parents don't really want to serve the Lord, you still have the opportunity to make your own decision and choose to follow the Lord. You can be obedient and faithful, like Jehosheba. God worked through her to ensure a good future for his people.

W.W.J.

Jesus' family did not always understand what his calling was, but he was faithful and obedient.

May 9

Joash

Lauded to the Skies

The officials of Judah came and paid homage to the king, and he listened to them. (2 Chronicles 24:17)

Joash was the king of Judah. His aunt had hidden him in the temple when Athaliah had killed all of his brothers so that she could take the throne.

Six years after he went into hiding, the leaders of Israel got rid of Athaliah and made Joash the rightful king. He was still very young – in fact, he was just seven years old when he was made king. His uncle, the priest Jehoiada, taught him to do the will of the Lord. Because he ruled according to the Lord's will, Joash was a very good king at that time. He restored the temple of God and encouraged the people to do the will of the Lord.

However, one day the priest Jehoiada died, and suddenly there was no one to give Joash the good advice that he needed. The Bible says that all the leaders of Judah then came to Joash and started to pay homage to him. This means that they came to him and told him how wonderful and fantastic he was. They tried to win his favor by buttering him up with all kinds of flattering words. They told him that there was no one in all the world who was quite as awesome as he was. Joash listened to their flattery, and this eventually led to his downfall. When Joash started believing all the things that the officials told him, he became arrogant. Because of his arrogance, Joash no longer listened to the Lord and began to make the wrong choices. He stopped serving the Lord and started following his own mind. In the end, the Lord allowed a tragic death to befall him.

It is always very dangerous to pretend that you are better than others. It is much better to be humble and grateful. Be on the lookout for the dangers of pride. Remember, pride will always lead to a fall.

W.W.J.

Jesus doesn't like proud and conceited people.

Huldah

The Minister's Wife

Huldah ... was the wife of Shallum ... She lived in Jerusalem. (2 Chronicles 34:22)

The Bible tells us about a very important woman of the Lord. We can almost call her a minister's wife. Her name was Huldah and she was married to Shallum. In a way, he was a minister, and he worked in the temple full-time. His wife lived with him in Jerusalem.

Shallum was well known, but his wife was even more famous. Everyone knew that Huldah had a very special gift. She was a prophetess. This means that God gave her a special kind of wisdom that helped her to know what would happen in the future. She could predict God's will as well as his deeds. The Lord showed her these things through the Holy Spirit.

In Huldah's time, there were many other important male prophets in Israel, like Jeremiah and Zephaniah. Nevertheless, the Bible tells us that when the Book of the Law of the Lord was found in the temple, the people went to her and asked her explain it to them. She then made the Lord's will known to them.

There are many women who act as leaders, minister's wives, pastor's wives, and many other kinds of spiritual guides. They listen very carefully to what the Lord tells them, and they lead many people along the Lord's path. We should thank the Lord for all these women. He uses them in a very special way. Pray for the women in your church who are spiritual leaders. Pray that the Lord will give them the wisdom and strength to teach others about his will. Pray that they will be filled with humility and love while they are doing the Lord's work.

W.W.J.

Jesus taught many women while he was here on earth. He taught them because he wanted to use them for his work.

May 11

Cyrus

COULD GOD USE HIM?

The Lord moved the heart of Cyrus king of Persia. (Ezra 1:1)

Sometimes we think that the Lord is interested in using only his own children. We think that we are God's favorites, and that he couldn't possibly be interested in using someone who doesn't even know him. But the Lord, the God of heaven and earth, decides for himself whom he wishes to use as instruments. He wants to accomplish his goals, and he can do so by using anyone he wishes.

Because Israel had been disobedient to the Lord, God decided that a foreign nation would conquer Israel and take the Israelites to Babylon as exiles. After many years had passed, the Lord decided that his people should return to Israel. He then moved the heart of the foreign king of Persia, named Cyrus, to let the people return to their land and rebuild their temple. This is how the Bible describes Cyrus's decision: *"The LORD, the God of heaven, has given me all the kingdoms of the earth and he has appointed me to build a temple for him at Jerusalem in Judah'"* (Ezra 1:2).

Don't look down on people who do not know the Lord. Sometimes God chooses these people to be his instruments and to do his will.

W . W . J .

Jesus said that if someone was not against him, that person was for him. (Luke 9:50)

Zerubbabel

HE RAN INTO DIFFICULTIES

Then the peoples around them set out to discourage the people of Judah and make them afraid to go on building. (Ezra 4:4)

King Cyrus instructed a man named Zerubbabel to build the temple in Jerusalem. After receiving their orders, Zerubbabel and his workers set out on the long journey to Jerusalem. After they had arrived there, they started laying the foundations of the temple. Everyone was overjoyed when the foundations were finally laid, and they praised and thanked the Lord.

However, because there is a perpetual battle between light and darkness, the devil is never happy when people do the Lord's will. That is why he made sure that the builders in Jerusalem ran into all kinds of difficulties. The devil planted seeds of unhappiness and anger in the hearts of some people who did not belong to the Israelite nation, and they became very angry about the building of the temple. They then started concocting plans to put a stop to the building process. Zerubbabel and his men had to persevere in their mission, and they had to act very wisely to make sure that the building of the temple could go ahead.

Whenever you and I are helping to build Jesus' kingdom, we are sure to run into resistance from some people. Be prepared to encounter others' negativity and opposition. Always act in love and be obedient to the Lord's instructions.

W.W.J.

Jesus encountered tremendous opposition when he was building his kingdom here on earth.

Ezra

A Stranger Provides

Praise be to the Lord ... who has extended his good favor to me before the king. (Ezra 7:27-28)

After the temple in Jerusalem had been rebuilt, the Lord sent Ezra to Jerusalem. Ezra was a highly educated man, and he knew everything that there was to know about the Law of Moses. His heart's desire was to teach the Israelites how to apply the Lord's laws in practice and to help them understand all of the Lord's instructions and decrees. After all, it is no use merely knowing what God wants you to do. You actually have to go out and do it. God chose Ezra to teach the Israelites how to do God's will and how to follow his instructions.

The Bible tells us that Ezra returned to Jerusalem along with a number of temple singers, priests, Levites, gatekeepers, and temple servants. However, this was possible only because the Lord worked in the heart of King Artaxerxes of Persia, who consequently decided to provide Ezra and his company with all the resources they needed for their long journey back to Jerusalem. They took silver and gold with them, and the king told them that he would provide them with anything else that they needed. He was even willing to give them all the riches collected in his treasury! Can you believe it? A king who did not even believe in the Lord was willing to donate generously to help the work of the Lord.

W.W.J.

Jesus will make sure we have everything we need to do his work.

Ezra

They Apologized

"But now, O our God, what can we say after this? For we have disregarded the commands you gave." (Ezra 9:10-11)

After the temple had been rebuilt, many of the Israelites returned to Jerusalem. Then Ezra started to teach the people from the Word of the Lord. They were deeply touched by what he taught them. After many years of exile, they were once again hearing exactly what the Lord expected of them and how they were supposed to live.

In their hearts, they also realized that their ancestors had made many bad decisions and that they had not followed the Lord as they should have. That is why the Lord decided to send them into exile in Babylon. The people then knew that they had to confess their sins. When you confess your sins you are completely honest about all the mistakes that you have made. However, the Israelites felt that they also had to confess and atone for the mistakes that their ancestors had made. And this is exactly what they did. They told God that they were sorry for all the things that had happened in the past and all the things they had done to hurt him.

When we look back on the history of the church, we have to admit that Christians have committed many grave errors. We too should tell the Lord that we are sorry for all the wrongs that we have committed. Once we have sincerely confessed our sins, we can be confident in the knowledge that we have been forgiven. Then we can continue our journey through life. Once we have accepted God's forgiveness, we can make a fresh start.

The same principle applies to your personal life. Confess your sins, apologize for all the wrongs that you have committed, and then look to the future with joy in your heart because you know that the Lord has forgiven you.

W.W.J.

Jesus taught us how to pray and how to ask for God's forgiveness.

Ezra

They Wept

While Ezra was praying and confessing, weeping and throwing himself down before the house of God, a large crowd of Israelites ... gathered around him. They too wept bitterly. (Ezra 10:1)

After the temple in Jerusalem had been restored and consecrated, God started a cleansing process in the hearts of his people. Ezra read to them from the Word of the Lord and in this way they heard exactly what the Lord expected of them. They realized that they and their ancestors had failed to comply with God's instructions. Therefore, they sincerely confessed all their sins and told God that they were very sorry for everything they had done wrong.

It is very easy to say that you are sorry for having done something, but do you really mean it? Superficial apologies don't have much value. If you really regret something you will feel sincerely sorry for what happened. One of the things that indicates true remorse is when you feel very sad about what you have done.

The Bible tells us that when the Israelites joined Ezra in confessing their sins, they were filled with sadness about everything that they had done wrong. While Ezra was kneeling in front of the house of the Lord and praying and confessing, a large number of Israelites gathered around him: men, women and children. Ezra wept and all the people wept with him. This intense kind of crying is perhaps the best kind of crying that there is. It is possible to cry because your pride has been injured, because you are angry, or because you feel ashamed. You can also cry for selfish reasons. However, when you cry because you are sorry for all the sins that you have committed, you are truly weeping, and this is the best kind of crying that there is. Your sorrow and remorse help to cleanse your heart.

When did you last really cry about your sin? If you truly regret some of the things that you have done, your heart will be so filled with sorrow that you will want to weep.

W. W. J.

Jesus wept for the sins of Jerusalem. (Matthew 25:37-38)

May 16

Nehemiah

Working Together

Next to him, the repairs were made by ... (Nehemiah 3:17)

After the Israelites were exiled to the distant land of Persia, the Lord inspired Cyrus to undertake the rebuilding of the temple in Jerusalem. Ezra arrived in Jerusalem to teach the people about the laws of the Lord. The next important thing to be done was the reconstruction of the city wall. This was a big job, and there was a lot of work to be done.

The Lord called a man named Nehemiah to be the leader of this project. He had to take the lead and organize the rebuilding of the city walls and the gates. Nehemiah encountered a great deal of resistance, but he did not allow this to deter him from his calling. He persevered with the work. However, he could not do all the building by himself. All the Israelites had to do their part so that the rebuilding could be completed. Even those who were not really skilled at building had to pitch in and help with the reconstruction. The Bible tells us that there were many people who each built a small piece of the wall. The religious teachers built, the farmers built, the government officials and the office workers built, the jewelers and goldsmiths built, and the Bible even mentions a couple of chemists who helped with the building. Men, women, boys, and girls all worked together to complete the building process.

We can learn a very important lesson from this. We must all do our part to complete God's building process. Sometimes we feel like sitting back so that others can do all the work, but it is important to realize that we all have to work together at building the Lord's kingdom. Are you willing to do your part?

W.W.J.

Jesus called ordinary people to build his kingdom.

Nehemiah

A Good Leader

... all I have done for these people. (Nehemiah 5:19)

Sometimes God sends special leaders to help people know how to live for him. Nehemiah was one such leader. He was a really good leader for his people. He did not seek to further his own interests, but only wanted to do the task that the Lord had given him to do.

Nehemiah was appointed as governor of Judah, and even though he was entitled to receive a salary because of his position, he did not make use of his salary for twelve years. He preferred to give his money to the people who really needed it, and especially to the builders of the wall. He never bossed the people around. Furthermore, he worked just as hard as everyone else at building the wall, and he never enriched himself by buying land. He encouraged his workers to give their all so that the work could be completed. He even went so far as to provide a hundred and fifty of the workers with food every single day. Every day he cooked an ox, six choice sheep, and some poultry, and he served it to the workers together with some wine.

We should pray for our leaders to be just as dedicated and honest as Nehemiah was. We should pray for leaders who are willing to serve others unselfishly and to live up to the calling that God has given them. If the Lord has chosen you to be a leader, you should do your best to follow Nehemiah's example. Pray for the leaders of your country, your congregation, and your city or town.

W. W. J.

Jesus said that if we want to be truly great in God's eyes, we will have to become servants. (Matthew 23:11)

May 18

Esther

The Beautiful Queen

Now the king was attracted to Esther more than to any of the other women. (Esther 2:17)

Every person consists of a body, a mind, and a spirit. All three of these elements are important. God created us with a body, a mind, and a spirit, and all three of these parts are equally important.

Because our bodies were created by God, we need to look after them and take care of them. We are not all equally attractive, and sometimes the Lord uses someone's beauty to fulfill his plan and purpose. King Saul, for example, was very attractive, and the Bible says that he stood head and shoulders above the other Israelite men. And what about Absalom? The Bible tells us that all of the Israelites were talking about how attractive he was.

Esther was a very beautiful woman. She lived in the time when the Israelites were in exile in Persia. She was a Jewish girl. In this time, an evil man named Haman devised a wicked plan to kill all the Israelites in Persia. However, God had a plan and he decided to use the beautiful Esther to carry it out.

Because Esther was such a beautiful woman and also had a lovely personality, King Xerxes was more attracted to her than to any of the other women. He decided to make her the queen of Persia. Esther's uncle, Mordecai, found out about Haman's evil plan. Esther had been placed in a perfect position to talk to the king and ask him to put a stop to Haman's evil plan, so Mordecai told her to speak up for her people. God used Esther to prevent the Israelites from being murdered.

Don't be jealous of all the beautiful people you know. Pray that they will allow themselves to be used as instruments of God and that they will love and follow the Lord. If you are very attractive or beautiful, thank the Lord for your beauty. Use your beauty in the service of the Lord.

W.W.J.

Many women became followers of Jesus and even his financial supporters. (Matthew 27:55)

May 19

Esther

WHY ARE YOU HERE?

"And who knows but that you have come to royal position for such a time as this?" (Esther 4:14)

The story of Esther is one of the most beautiful tales documented in the Bible. If you recall, the book of Esther tells the story of a beautiful young Jewish girl who became a queen. God had a plan for her life, and Esther allowed herself to be used by him.

After Esther became queen, a terrible thing happened. An evil man, Haman, who was an enemy of the Jews, wanted to destroy the entire Jewish population. When news of Haman's plot got around, Esther's uncle, Mordecai, became very worried. He asked Esther to plead with her husband, King Xerxes, to save the Jews' lives. Perhaps he would listen to her because he loved her. However, Esther knew that if she just went to the king without him summoning her, he could kill her right then and there. This was a law in that time. If he did not hold out his gold scepter to her when she approached him, she would be in deep trouble. But Mordecai told Esther that perhaps God had allowed her to become queen for a reason: so that she could intercede for her people with the king.

And then a miracle happened. When Esther approached the king, he held out his gold scepter to her and accepted her. He listened to her, and in a wonderful way the Jewish people were saved. God accomplished a miracle through Esther.

Why are you alive? Why are you here? Today there is still a great need for people who are willing to fulfill their calling and destiny. God wants to use you and me to build his kingdom. Esther realized what her calling was. In the same way, we should be aware of our calling and destiny. Perhaps we are placed here on earth precisely because God needs us here at this particular point in time. Ask God how he wants to use you.

W.W.J.

Jesus used ordinary people as his instruments so that he could accomplish God's plan and purpose.

May 20

Haman

The End of a Conceited Man

Calling together his friends ... Haman boasted to them about his vast wealth. (Esther 5:10-11).

King Xerxes decided to promote a man by the name of Haman to become the leader of all his other officials. They all had to honor him. Because of this Haman became very conceited and arrogant.

Everyone bowed and kneeled before him wherever he went, except Mordecai, a Jew who was also the uncle of Esther. When Haman saw that Mordecai refused to kneel before him, he was furious. He decided to do a very horrible thing. He went to the king and asked him to have all the Jews killed.

Because the king did not know that Esther and Mordecai were Jewish, he gave his consent for all the Jews to be killed in one day. When Haman heard that he had gotten his way, he became even more haughty and vain. He strutted around like a peacock and boasted about how important he was. He told everyone just how rich he was, how wonderful his sons were, how the king had honored him, and how the king had elevated him above all the other officials.

The Bible says that pride goes before a fall. This means that when you start becoming conceited, you quickly stumble over your own feet. And usually that leads to a very embarrassing and humiliating fall. This is exactly what happened to Haman. Esther asked the king to spare the Jews' lives, and the Lord also worked in the king's heart. Haman's plot came to light, and Haman was exposed as the one who wanted to kill Esther and her people. The king then ordered Haman to be hanged from the gallows that he had built for Mordecai.

Don't be quick to brag and boast about your achievements. Don't imagine that you are so terribly important. It is much better to be humble. People who put themselves up on pedestals quickly come to a fall – and then they fall very hard, as Haman did.

W.W.J.

Jesus was the Son of God, and yet he was always humble in word and deed.

May 21

Job

THE BET

"But stretch out your hand and strike everything he has, and he will surely curse you to your face." (Job 1:11)

Job was a very important and highly respected man. He was also very wealthy and prosperous. However, the most notable thing about Job was that he loved the Lord and lived his life according to the Lord's will. Then the devil devised a little plan.

Satan went to the Lord and said that the only reason why Job served the Lord was because his life was so prosperous and comfortable. Satan then challenged God to a bet. He said that if the Lord allowed him, the devil, to take away Job's happiness and prosperity, Job would certainly no longer follow the Lord. Instead, he would curse God for his misfortune. However, the Lord did not believe that Job would do such a thing. He had faith in Job. That is why he allowed Satan to cause all kinds of misfortunes to befall Job. He was sure that Job would still follow him, despite adversity and difficulty.

Satan allowed many afflictions to come upon Job and his family. First a gang of men robbed Job of many of his possessions and murdered his servants. Then lightning struck his livestock and killed all of them. Then Job was robbed again. But the worst was when his sons and daughters were all killed in an accident. Job was completely heartbroken. He simply could not understand why all these things had happened to him.

This was the start of a very long personal struggle for Job. During this time, he struggled with God and with his faith. But in the end, he emerged with his faith intact. Job continued to praise and worship God, even though he was enduring tremendous suffering.

We don't always understand why bad things happen to us. There are many reasons why these things happen. But the most important thing is to always have faith and praise the Lord – yes, even when we are suffering.

W. W. J.

Jesus said that we would experience much suffering in this world, but that we should never lose our faith and courage. (John 16:33)

Job

Be a Good Friend

Then they sat on the ground with him for seven days and seven nights. No one said a word to him, because they saw how great his suffering was. (Job 2:13)

Friends are very precious. The Lord gives us friends who provide us with support, compassion, and empathy. Our friends understand us. Our friends can bring us much joy, and when we are sad, they can help us carry the burden of our sorrow. A friend's love, encouragement, and support are very valuable.

When Job found himself in the midst of sorrow and trouble, he was completely overwhelmed by grief. He could not understand why all these terrible things were happening to him. When his children died, Job could no longer contain the extent of his grief. Three of Job's friends heard of all the disasters that had befallen him. They went to him to offer their support and consolation. The Bible says that when they saw Job, they started weeping. For seven days they sat with him without saying a word because they saw how great his suffering was. When someone is very sad it is perhaps best to do as Job's friends did. You shouldn't try saying all kinds of nice words to console the person. Simply sit quietly with him or her and show that you care. After seven days, Job started talking and opened his heart to his friends. He started to share all his feelings and problems with them and asked them for advice. They didn't always know all the answers to his questions, but they were always willing to talk things through with him.

Is there someone who needs your friendship? Perhaps you should go to that person and merely sit quietly beside him or her. Show him or her that you care. Show your love. Listen to your friend's sorrows. It is important to pray for your friend. You can pray out loud or you can just pray silently in your heart. Be a good friend to someone today.

W.W.J.

Jesus often spoke to his disciples about the matters that were close to his heart. However, when he was alone in Gethsemane, his friends disappointed him. (Matthew 26:40)

Job

HE STRUGGLED WITH GOD

"Does it please you to oppress me, to spurn the work of your hands, while you smile on the schemes of the wicked?" (Job 10:3)

The devil went to God and accused Job of being insincere in his faith. He said that Job would not serve the Lord if Job had to face pain and disaster. The Lord had so much faith in Job's sincerity that he allowed the devil to bring terrible calamities over Job.

While Job was enduring all these terrible sufferings, he started to ask all kinds of questions. There were so many things that he simply could not understand. After all, he had no inkling of the conversation between Satan and God. He didn't know that his faith was being tested. He could not understand why all these disasters were befalling him. That is why he asked so many questions. And what was just as terrible was that he could not seem to find any answers to his questions. The answers that his friends gave him seemed very unsatisfactory to him.

Job started struggling with God. He asked the Lord many questions. He said, *"Even today my complaint is bitter; his hand is heavy in spite of my groaning"* (Job 23:2).

The Lord did not take offense at Job for asking so many questions. I actually think that the Lord welcomed Job's questions. We often have many questions about all the suffering that we experience in life. Like Job, we also want answers. Terrible things happen to us because we are ordinary human beings living in a fallen world. We do not always understand these things. Go ahead and open your heart to the Lord. Tell him about everything that is happening in your life. Ask your questions, and perhaps the Lord will answer you. But like Job, you should always be faithful and never stop believing.

W.W.J.

The disciples asked Jesus many questions because there were many things that they did not understand.

Job

GOD ANSWERED

Then the LORD answered Job out of the storm. (Job 38:1)

A great deal of time had passed since Job had first been struck by misfortune. In this time, Job had asked many questions and had struggled with God continuously. He simply could not understand why all these things had happened to him. Despite his despair, he wanted answers to all his questions. So he ceaselessly talked to God about everything that had happened to him.

After Job had completely emptied his heart and thoughts to God, the Lord answered him by reminding Job of his divine greatness and omnipotence. God started speaking about creation and how wonderful everything in it is. The longer God spoke to Job, the smaller Job felt. He realized that God is infinitely great. The Lord spoke about all the animals of the fields, about the snow on the mountains, about the sea and everything in it, about the rain, the stars, and many other things. Job then realized that he was no match for God. He realized that God is so great that he always knows best. He then apologized to the Lord and said that he knew that God could do anything. He said that he was sorry for blaming God for what had happened to him. Job also prayed for his friends, because he had earlier blamed them for all the inappropriate advice that they had given him. And then the Lord changed Job's circumstances. The Lord made Job richer than he had ever been.

If you truly seek answers to your questions, the Lord will supply them, even though it might take some time.

W. W. J.

Jesus said that we should knock, because then the door will be opened for us; and we should seek, because then we will find. (Matthew 7:7)

May 25

God

They Call Him El-Elyon

I will sing praise to the name of the LORD Most High. (Psalm 7:17)

The names of God explain to us who he is. If we understand the different meanings of his names, we are better able to appreciate and worship him. One of the names of God that we read about in the Bible is El-Elyon. This name means "Most High God." The Bible uses this name to tell us that God is the greatest and most powerful being that exists.

We know that people have always worshiped idols. These idols were gods like Baal, Ashtoreth, Ra, all the Greek gods, and hundreds of other idols. The Bible makes it clear that these idols are small and insignificant. Paul tells us to remember that all these supposed gods are nothing but idols created by human beings.

There is only one true God. His name is El-Elyon, the Most High God. He is high above any human being or manmade idol. He is incredibly great, powerful, and wonderful.

Let us bow before this Most High God today. He is higher than the highest tree, higher than the topmost pinnacle of the highest mountain, higher than anything on earth. And he loves you.

W.W.J.

The disciples witnessed God's wonderful deeds and praised his greatness when Jesus showed it to them.

David

SING WHILE CRYING

To [the tune of] "The Death of the Son." (title of Psalm 9)

David is well known for all the songs that he wrote. Some of these songs are very joyful and many are about the majesty of God. However, David also wrote songs about sadness and sorrow. One of the most striking songs of David was written about the death of a son.

We don't know whose son it was who died, but this fact is not really important. What is important, however, is that David praised and worshiped the Lord even in his sorrow and his grief. This song begins with the words, *"I will praise you, O Lord, with all my heart; I will tell of all your wonders. I will be glad and rejoice in you; I will sing praise to your name, O Most High"* (Psalm 9:1–2).

Only people who know that God is in control of everything and that he wants only the best for them are able to praise and worship the Lord even when standing beside the grave of a loved one. I have met many bereaved people who were able to smile and keep the hope in their hearts alive despite their grief. In the same way, David praised the Lord with all his heart, even though he did not understand why someone he loved had to die.

Let us praise and worship the Lord, even when we are sad.

W.W.J.

Even in the most sorrowful hours of Jesus' persecution, he still praised and worshiped his Father.

David

Sing of Stars

The heavens declare the glory of God; the skies proclaim the work of his hands. (Psalm 19:1)

David looked up at the heavens and he could not help himself: he simply had to sing a song of wonder and amazement. When he saw all the beautiful stars in the heavens above, millions upon millions of them, he was filled with wonder.

Today, experts tell us that there are many galaxies. This means that there are many, many more stars, so far away that we cannot see them. Some stars are so far away that it would take us millions of years to reach them – if we could reach them at all! How great and majestic God is! This is exactly what David sings about in Psalm 19.

He also sings about the sun that rises early in the morning and shines brightly throughout the day. David sang about the wonder of God's creation. In Psalm 8, we read how excited David was about everything that the Lord had created. David says, *"When I consider your heavens, the work of your fingers, the moon and the stars, which you have set in place, what is man that you are mindful of him, the son of man that you care for him?"* (Psalm 8:3-4).

Take some time right now to thank and praise the Lord for the majesty of his creation.

W.W.J.

Jesus told his disciples all about the majesty of his Father and the splendor of creation.

May 28

David

SING ABOUT THE WORD

The law of the LORD is perfect, reviving the soul. (Psalm 19:7)

It is easy to sing about all the majestic and wonderful things that you can see with your eyes. It is also very easy and enjoyable to sing about the love that you feel for someone else. But what about singing about the Word of God? Can anyone really become thrilled and excited about the Word of the Lord?

David teaches us that we can really sing joyfully about the Word. He is so excited about the Word of the Lord that he simply cannot stop singing about it. So what exactly is he singing about?

He sings that the Word is trustworthy and reliable, that it gives wisdom to those who are still inexperienced, that it revives the soul, that it shows people which path to take, and that it makes people happy. He also sings that God's Word is steadfast and unchanging. He sings that the Lord's words are just and fair. He sings that the Word of the Lord is more precious than gold and much sweeter than honey to those who live their lives according to it.

I hope that you too can sing about the Bible. The Bible is precious because it is God's Word given to us. Those who follow the instructions given in his Word will find eternal life. Let us thank God for his Word and sing a joyful song to praise and glorify him.

W.W.J.

Jesus taught us some wonderful words. Even today we sing about how wonderful his words are.

David

SING ABOUT THE SHEPHERD

The LORD is my shepherd, I shall not be in want. (Psalm 23:1)

When David was a young boy, he was the shepherd who looked after his father's flock of sheep. As a shepherd, he knew that his flock needed his love, attention, and care. Sheep are easy targets for predators, who attack and devour them. Sheep need to be watched over. They should, furthermore, be led to places where they can graze and find abundant food. Sheep should always be kept together in a flock, because a single sheep can easily stray and get lost.

David started thinking that people were very much like sheep. People also need a shepherd. Someone has to take care of them. They have to be fed. They need water to drink. They should be guided on the right paths. They sometimes find themselves in dangerous situations, and then they need to be guided back to safety. In Psalm 23, David sings that the Lord is our Shepherd and that he ensures that we have everything we need. He makes us lie down in green pastures. He leads us to quiet waters. He strengthens our spirits. He guides us on the right paths so that his name may be honored. Even when we have to walk through the valley of the shadow of death and even when we have to face dangerous situations, we need not be afraid. The Lord is always with us, and in his hands we are safe.

While he was at it, David added another verse to the song. In this verse, he says that the Lord is truly wonderful because he gives us everything we need. It is almost as if the Lord has arranged a big party for us and given us many gifts. And this goodness and love of the Lord will be with us for all eternity.

What a beautiful song! Let's join David in singing a song of praise to our Lord. He is the Shepherd who always takes care of us.

W.W.J.

Jesus also said that he was the Good Shepherd who came to look after his sheep. (John 10:14)

May 30

David

SING ABOUT THE LORD'S PATHS

Show me your ways, O LORD, teach me your paths. (Psalm 25:4)

David traveled quite often. One day when he was young, he had to take some food to his brothers while they were away from home, fighting against the Philistines. For many years, he wandered in the wilderness as King Saul attempted to kill him. Because David traveled so often, his journeys took him on many different paths. I suppose he also sometimes got lost, just as you and I do! We all know how easy it is to choose the wrong path. And once you have done this, you inevitably end up at the wrong destination.

This also applies to our lives. You and I are like travelers. Every day brings new paths that we can walk. We can do new things. We can take a new direction. And all these choices will lead us to a particular place or destination. Some paths look like they are the right ones to take, but before we know it we have completely lost our bearings. We need wisdom and knowledge to be able to choose the right paths.

That is why David sings a song about paths and journeys. In his song, he asks the Lord to reveal his will to him and to teach him the right paths to take. When we live according to the Lord's will, we are following the right path. That is why David asks the Lord, "Teach me your paths." He also asks that the Lord's truth will guide him and that he will walk in the Lord's paths every single day. He goes on to sing that the Lord's paths are always characterized by love and faithfulness. God wants to guide us lovingly on his path, and he will always be faithful to us, no matter how long or difficult the journey. David also sings, *"Who, then, is the man that fears the LORD? He will instruct him in the way chosen for him. He will spend his days in prosperity ..."* (Psalm 25:12-13).

We need the Lord's wisdom and guidance if we are to choose the right path. Ask the Lord to lead you on the right path today.

W.W.J.

Jesus himself said that he was like a road. He said that he was the way to eternal life. (John 14:6)

May 31

David

Sing about Sin

I confess my iniquity; I am troubled by my sin. (Psalm 38:18)

Sin is probably not a very popular topic for a song. We much prefer to keep our sin secret. So why would one want to sing about it? Sometimes we even go so far as to pretend that we have no sin at all. But this is not true, because the Bible says that all human beings sin. The Bible also says that if we say we have no sin we are deceiving ourselves. In other words, if you say that you have no sin, you are definitely lying. We all sometimes commit sin.

In one of his letters, even the great apostle Paul complains about his sinfulness. He says that he never does all the good things that he intends doing. And at the same time, he just keeps on doing all the bad things that he knows he should not do. We also struggle with sin, just as Paul did.

What does it mean to sin? When we sin, we cannot attain God's goal for our lives. When we sin, we simply do as we please and do not bother about God's instructions. As a result, we totally overlook God's plan for our lives. If we sin, we can't live our lives to his honor, and therefore we can't really be happy.

David wrote many songs about his sin. He decided not to hide his sin, but to be honest about it. In his songs, he looks his sin straight in the eye and tells himself that the things he has done are wrong. He then apologizes to God for his sins. In Psalm 38, David sings that his sins trouble him and make him unhappy. He sings that he doesn't want to commit sin any more and that he wants to live according to the Lord's will.

Let us learn a lesson from David. If you want to, you can also sing a song to the Lord and tell him that you are sorry for all your sins and that you want to make amends. Singing a song like this is the same as praying to the Lord and asking him to forgive your sins.

W.W.J.

After Peter had sinned against Jesus, he was very remorseful. He asked for forgiveness, and the Lord forgave him and reinstated him. (John 21:15)

David

Sing about Doubt

Why are you downcast, O my soul? Why so disturbed within me? (Psalm 42:5)

We often encounter doubt in our lives. We doubt whether we did the right thing. We are filled with doubt whenever we have to make difficult decisions. We feel doubtful largely because we don't know what the future holds. This uncertainty causes us to doubt.

David also felt uncertain and restless about certain aspects of his life. That is why he yearned for guidance and wisdom so that he could decide on the correct course of action. In Psalm 42:2 he sings, *"As the deer pants for streams of water, so my soul pants for you, O God."* This song is about himself. He sings about his own feelings and all the questions that worry him. He was probably lying awake at night because of all his problems, and that is why he decided to write a song about them. In the song, David asks why his heart is so troubled and why his soul is so downcast. Then he goes on to tell himself that he should trust in God as his helper. Even in his despair, he sings and calls out to the Lord to help him. As he sings, he starts to feel better, and then he tells himself that he will soon be singing a song of praise again, instead of a song of doubt and despair.

When you are overwhelmed by your problems, or when your heart is filled with doubt, you should open your heart to the Lord, as David did. Talk to the Lord about your problems or sing a song about them. You will soon feel better. Then you'll be able to sing a song of praise to the Lord for helping you.

W.W.J.

The disciples probably sang very sad songs after Jesus died on the cross. But just think of the songs of praise that they sang after he was resurrected!

June 2

David

I'm Sorry!

Against you, you only, have I sinned and done what is evil in your sight. (Psalm 51:4)

After the prophet Nathan had convinced David of his sin, David was overcome with sorrow. He suddenly realized that he could not hide his sin any longer. David realized that the Lord knew all about his sinfulness. He knew that the Lord was very dissatisfied and unhappy with him. David was overcome with sorrow and realized that he was a terrible sinner. He realized that he had drifted away from the Lord. Sin always drives us away from God.

It is truly wonderful, and necessary, to realize that you are a sinful human being. If you have remorse over your sin and cry because you are sad about what you have done, the Lord will forgive you. However, if you are proud and arrogant and think that your sins aren't really all that bad, the Lord cannot forgive you. The Bible says that if we confess our sins and repent, the Lord will forgive us. This is what David did.

In Psalm 51, we read David's sorrowful words as he confesses his sin. He asks the Lord to be merciful and to blot out all his transgressions. He asks, *"Wash away all my iniquity and cleanse me from my sin"* (Psalm 51:2). He asks the Lord to restore him so that he may once again experience joy and happiness. He asks the Lord to cleanse him so that he may be whiter than snow. He asks to be steadfast in his faith. He asks the Spirit to lead him. God heard all his pleas and forgave his sins.

Is there sin in your life today? Why not confess your sin right now? Tell God that you are sorry for what you have done and ask him to forgive you. He promises that he will.

W.W.J.

The most wonderful thing of all is that Jesus paid the debt of our sin by dying on the cross for us.

June 3

Asaph

His Feet Slipped

My feet had almost slipped; I had nearly lost my foothold ... when I saw the prosperity of the wicked. (Psalm 73:2-3)

Asaph was a composer and a singer. One of his songs is about how doubt almost caused his feet to slip out from under him. Asaph looked at all the rich and important people around him, and he saw how wealthy and prosperous they were. Everything always seemed to go their way. It seemed as if they had no problems whatsoever. They were living in luxury, and from their wealthy positions they looked down on other people. However, the worst thing about these rich people was that they slandered God. They did not believe in God. Instead, they worshiped their money and wealth. They were very conceited and thought that they were better than everyone else.

Asaph tried to serve the Lord with all his heart. He was not nearly as rich as the people he saw every day, and this caused him to become a bit jealous of them. He started thinking that it wasn't really worthwhile to serve the Lord. After all, the evil people were the ones who prospered! One day, while he was walking the streets, filled with self-pity and complaining to himself, he decided to go into the temple. While he was there, the Lord spoke to him. Suddenly, he realized that those wicked people were actually living very dangerous lives. In a single moment, they could die or lose all their possessions. And then God would not even be there to help them. When he thought about this, Asaph was no longer jealous. The Lord took care of him every day and was with him every single minute. And the Lord would also be there when he died.

So Asaph sang a song about how foolish he had been to be jealous of people who lived their lives without God. Don't feel neglected just because you don't possess all the beautiful things that the world has to offer. The most important thing is to have Jesus Christ as the Lord of your life.

W.W.J.

Jesus asked what it would profit us to possess all the riches of the world if we did not have him in our life. (Mark 8:36)

June 4

David

He Wanted to Praise God

Praise the Lord, O my soul; all my inmost being, praise his holy name. (Psalm 103:1)

David had been taught to praise the Lord ever since he was a young boy. David played the harp and composed beautiful praise songs. Even when he became king, David continued to write songs to glorify the name of the Lord. I'm not sure that anyone before or since has praised the Lord quite as beautifully as David did.

David had a continual desire to praise the Lord. It was as if he could simply not stop talking about how wonderful the Lord was and how marvelous all his deeds were. Of course, David was also sometimes overcome with doubt when things started going wrong in his life. We know that he wrote many songs about sadness and suffering. He also wrote songs in which he questioned his faith in the Lord, and often his songs were born of sheer desperation. Nevertheless, David always tried to thank and praise the Lord for all the wonderful things that he received from the Lord's hands. That is why he writes in this psalm that he wants to praise the Lord with all his inmost being.

You and I should also cultivate the habit of worshiping and praising the Lord every single day. Sing songs in his honor. Why not create your own songs to praise him? Be the kind of person who praises the Lord every day.

W.W.J.

We could never praise Jesus enough for all that he has done for us.

David

Sing about Love

But from everlasting to everlasting the LORD's love is with those who fear him. (Psalm 103:17)

Innumerable songs have been written throughout the ages. Many of these songs are about love. People usually sing about their love for a man or a woman. We are bombarded with love songs every day. We hear them on the radio and we see music videos of love songs on television. Music stores are filled with CDs that contain love songs.

David probably also wrote ordinary love songs like these. However, in the Bible we find many love songs that he wrote for the Lord. He often says that he wants to love and praise the Lord. He also sings about God's love for him and for all people. David says that the love between people is something that passes very quickly. He says that a human being is like a blade of grass or like a flower. Today the flower blooms beautifully, but tomorrow, when the desert wind blows over it, it withers and dies, and then its place is empty.

People do not live forever, and therefore the love that they feel for one another also cannot last forever. However, God lives forever and will love us forever. He does not love us one day and then change his mind the next and stop loving us. The Lord will always love you. Now isn't that something to sing about?

W.W.J.

Even today we sing many songs about Jesus' indescribable love for us.

June 6

The Pilgrim

Just a Little Peace

Too long have I lived among those who hate peace. (Psalm 120:6)

Isn't it just wonderful to live among people with whom you have peace? When people are tolerant, understanding, and loving toward one another, it is truly enjoyable to be among them.

In Psalm 120, we read about a man who says that he had a terrible time living among a certain group of people. These were the people who lived in Meshech and Kedar. When he lived with them, he realized that they did not understand him at all, just as he did not understand them. All he wanted was a little bit of peace and love, but instead he only got quarrels, strife, and even hate. He says, *"I am a man of peace; but when I speak, they are for war"* (Psalm 120:7). Regardless of how hard he tried to maintain the peace, everyone always ended up fighting.

There are always people intent on stirring up trouble. They are always out to pick a fight with someone. These people don't have peace in their hearts, and that is why they want to make sure that there is also no peace among other people. Living harmoniously with these people is very difficult.

When you choose your friends, make sure that they are peacemakers. Be sure to have friends that are not constantly out to create discord among people, but who rather want to make peace. And you too should be a peacemaker. Don't argue with people all the time. Remember that it takes two people to argue. If you choose to step back from the argument, it will be much easier to keep the peace.

W.W.J.

Jesus taught us to turn the other cheek when someone mistreats us. (Luke 6:29)

June 7

David

SING ABOUT TRANQUILLITY

But I have stilled and quieted my soul; like a weaned child. (Psalm 131:2)

When you are in the company of someone who is constantly restless, you will soon find yourself becoming restless, too. Some people just have the ability to make you feel agitated and restless. This is usually the case when someone has no peace and tranquillity in his or her own heart.

A restless heart is like a lake with waves on the surface created by the wind blowing over it. A peaceful heart is like a lake with still, quiet water and little ducks swimming on the surface. I think that most people would prefer a tranquil heart to a restless one.

David saw that there were people around him who were very proud and liked to constantly prove that they could achieve better and higher things. Such people are always restless, because they are perpetually striving to achieve greater things. Their hearts are filled with discontent because they never quite manage to achieve everything they want to achieve. They try and try and try, but they never manage to be the best or the prettiest or the strongest. That is why they are always restless. David sings that he does not strive to achieve great things. He accepts himself for what he is, with his limitations as well as his wonderful abilities. And as for those things that elude his grasp – those things that he simply cannot manage to achieve or possess – he simply forgets about them and relaxes. He says that he has found peace and tranquility, like a child who lies quietly in the arms of his mother.

Never be too ambitious. Accept yourself just as you are. Make peace with who and what you are. Be content with your life. By all means strive to realize your dreams, but don't allow yourself to become restless when you don't immediately achieve your goals.

W . W . J .

Jesus invited us to come to him so that we may have peace in our hearts.

June 8

David

SING ABOUT FAMILY

How good and pleasant it is when brothers live together in unity! (Psalm 133:1)

It is a really terrible thing when family members are constantly arguing and fighting with one another. Our homes are supposed to be havens of love and peace. In our homes, we are supposed to be surrounded by people who are willing to understand, forgive, support, and help one another.

Because we live with our families every single day, we should always try to live together in peace and harmony. Of course, there are sometimes differences of opinion, and, of course, we sometimes feel misunderstood. We also sometimes fight with our brothers and sisters. Despite this, we should always try to find a solution for the problem as quickly as possible.

David saw how wonderful it is when brothers and sisters live together in peace and unity. In this song, he says that it is like a wonderful fragrance. He says that it is like a drop of dew glistening on a blade of grass somewhere on a beautiful mountain. Do you think that David is right? Would you like it if there were always peace between you and your brothers or sisters? Let's strive to live in peace with our families. Forgive one another, talk to one another, and love one another.

W.W.J.

Jesus taught his disciples that the most important commandment is to love one another. (John 13:34-35)

June 9

David

Cool Music

... praise him with the clash of cymbals, praise him with resounding cymbals. (Psalm 150:5)

Music is a gift from the Lord. There is probably not a single person who can say that he doesn't like music. Not everyone has a talent for music, and yet most people like listening to music or making music.

There are many different kinds of music. Every person has his own favorite style. I probably won't like the kind of music that you like listening to, and you probably won't like my music. This is perfectly natural, because every human being is unique. What kind of music do you like best?

Even though your definition of cool music might differ from mine, the Bible tells us that we can use all kinds of musical instruments to praise the Lord. In Psalm 150, we read about many different instruments that we can use to praise the Lord. An entire orchestra of instruments is mentioned here! There are stringed instruments, wind instruments, and percussion instruments. We are even told that we should dance before the Lord while making music on these instruments. Now doesn't that sound like cool music? We can use any instrument we want to praise and worship the Lord. Thank God for giving us music, and praise him with your music.

W.W.J.

Jesus praised and worshiped his Father with music. (Mark 14:26)

Solomon

ARE YOU WISE OR FOOLISH?

Trust in the LORD with all your heart and lean not on your own understanding. (Proverbs 3:5)

Solomon was a very wise man. He asked God to give him wisdom, and the Lord answered his prayer. Solomon then wrote an entire book filled with all his wise sayings. When we read this book, we are bound to find many wonderful guidelines for living our everyday lives according to God's will.

Because Solomon was very wise, he wrote a great deal on the topic of wisdom. The most important thing that Solomon says in this regard is that we should not follow our own minds. We should also not trust in our own understanding. Solomon knew that people make many mistakes, and when people trust only in themselves, they will inevitably make decisions and do things that will bring them nothing but sorrow. His advice is to trust in the Lord completely. This means that we should ask the Lord to give us wisdom. We should read his Word and ask his Holy Spirit to lead us in doing the right things. Solomon also says, *"... in all your ways acknowledge him, and he will make your paths straight"* (Proverbs 3:6).

A foolish person follows his own thoughts. The Bible tells us that a clever person asks the Lord what his will is – and then lives according to it.

W.W.J.

Jesus taught his disciples how to live.

Solomon

WHAT DOES IT MEAN TO BE CLEVER?

The fear of the LORD is the beginning of wisdom. (Proverbs 9:10)

How can we tell if someone is smart? And how do we know when someone is not? Some people are good at math, for example, while others are good when it comes to working with their hands. Others are good at art. However, it is more difficult to say whether someone is really smart or not.

In school, children are often tested to see how intelligent they are. Some children even feel very badly about themselves just because they can't seem to do some things as well as others. They start thinking that they are stupid. You should never feel bad if you aren't as good as someone else at something. The Lord has given you specific talents and abilities. You are unique. You are unlike anyone else. And because you are unique, the Lord can use you in a special way.

The Lord is not really concerned with whether we have an exceptionally sharp mind. Knowledge is not the most important thing to the Lord. Instead, the Lord most values wisdom. Having wisdom means understanding the things of the Lord and knowing how to live a meaningful life in accordance with God's will. That is why the Bible says that true wisdom only begins when we decide to serve the Lord. When we serve the Lord, he teaches us through his Holy Spirit how to live a good life and how to make the right decisions. Of course, we still make many mistakes, but the Lord is patient and willing to teach us the things we need to know. And in so doing, we grow wiser and wiser day by day.

W.W.J.

If we choose to serve Jesus, he will teach us how to live wisely.

June 12

Solomon

ARE YOUR WORDS LIKE SWORDS?

Reckless words pierce like a sword. (Proverbs 12:18)

The tongue is a very important part of our bodies. Not only does it enable us to taste delicious as well as unpleasant things, we also use it to speak. We can choose to say good or bad things with our tongues.

The Bible tells us that we should be very careful not to speak too hastily. Someone once said that we have two ears and one mouth, and therefore we should listen twice as much as we speak. You can do a lot of damage when you say something without thinking. The Bible says that such thoughtless words are like swords that can hurt people and ruin their lives. Only foolish people don't think before speaking.

Wise people think twice before saying something, and when they do speak, their words bring healing. The Bible says that we should use our words to encourage and inspire people. The words that our tongues speak should never be used to disparage or hurt someone. It is very easy to hurt people with our words. Using words in a positive and encouraging way – now that is a little more difficult.

May the words that you speak today not be like swords used to hurt others. Let your words rather be like a soothing ointment that heals people's wounds.

W.W.J.

Jesus said that we will one day be held accountable for every word that we have ever spoken. (Matthew 12:36)

June 13

Solomon

SEEK JOY!

All the days of the oppressed are wretched, but the cheerful heart has a continual feast. (Proverbs 15:15)

People who have spent a lot of time studying the human psyche say that constant depression is very harmful to people. Depressed people are unhappy people. Scientists tell us that constant unhappiness is also bad for the body. When you think and say depressing things, your body produces certain chemical substances that make you feel even worse.

However, when you are happy and joyful, your body also benefits. You feel good, and then (so the scientists say) your body starts to produce substances that contribute to your physical health and well-being. Perhaps this is why the Bible tells us to be cheerful. Listen to what Solomon says: *"A happy heart makes the face cheerful, but heartache crushes the spirit"* (Proverbs 15:13). We should make an effort to think positive thoughts so that we can be cheerful and happy. Paul says that we should think about things that are beautiful and lovely and wonderful.

Always make sure that you find yourself in the kind of company that is uplifting and has a positive effect on the spirit. Don't choose friends who have negative attitudes and continually complain about everything. Choose friends who have positive attitudes and cheerful spirits. If you can learn to be cheerful about everything that comes your way, every day will be so much fun – almost like going to a party every single day! Your life will be a continual feast. Ask the Lord right now to help you think only about beautiful and positive things so that your heart may be filled with joy and happiness.

W. W. J.

Jesus said that we could have his joy – joy that overflows.

Solomon

Don't Be a Tattletale

A gossip separates close friends. (Proverbs 16:28)

One of the nastiest things that a person can do is to say bad things about someone else behind his or her back. This is called gossiping. A tendency to gossip is a very unpleasant characteristic. As a matter of fact, gossip has been called the language of the devil.

Have you ever heard people saying horrible things about others? Perhaps you yourself have said something cruel about someone behind that person's back. I think we are all guilty of committing this sin occasionally. That is why we have to ask the Lord to keep us from saying negative things about other people.

Why do we speak ill of others? Perhaps because we are jealous of them. Or maybe we just don't like them. Or perhaps we want to draw some attention to ourselves. Maybe we just don't have anything better to do than walk around spreading ugly rumors. Regardless of the reason, gossiping is a very bad habit.

Unfortunately, the devil is so finely attuned to any kind of gossip that he can immediately seize that story and use it to hurt people. A rumor usually spreads like wildfire. Pretty soon everyone is talking about it and passing it on – despite the fact that it may not even be true!

We should ask the Lord to keep us from gossiping. If we have a problem with someone, we should not gossip about him or her behind his or her back. It is much better to go to that person and have a calm conversation to sort out the problem. And if someone gossips about another person in your presence, you should have enough courage to tell that person that what he or she is doing is wrong. Instead of gossiping, try to see how many nice things you can say about someone.

W.W.J.

We should follow Jesus' example and speak words that are gracious. (Luke 4:22)

Solomon

How Do You Deal With Anger?

A man's wisdom gives him patience; it is to his glory to overlook an offense. (Proverbs 19:11)

Every single one of us sometimes gives in to anger. Even the tiniest little baby loses his temper when he doesn't get what he wants. Have you ever seen a baby screaming so loudly that he turns red in the face? That's because he is really angry!

Anger is a part of being human. Even Jesus was angry at people on occasion, such as when he drove the merchants from the temple.

Being angry for the right reasons is not a sin. However, when you lose your temper (in other words, when you are no longer in control of yourself because of your anger), it is very easy to fall into the trap of sin. It is wrong to be angry for the wrong reasons. For example, anger is wrong if you are angry because of selfish reasons, not because the honor of the Lord is at stake.

The sooner we learn to keep our tempers in check, the better. We should learn to rein in our angry emotions. We put reins on a horse to lead and guide it. If a horse is guided by reins, it can't run wild and do whatever it pleases. The rider has the power to keep the horse under control. In the same way, you and I should be led and reined in by the Holy Spirit. This is the only way to keep our tempers under control. People who lose their tempers invariably do foolish things. They say things that should have remained unsaid, and in so doing, they hurt other people. Sometimes it is not only their words that hurt others, but also their deeds.

The Lord gives us a new attitude toward people. Because of this new attitude, we want to forgive people rather than hurt them. The Lord helps us to be sensible and wise. Even when we are angry, he helps us to rein in our anger so that we do not go overboard and hurt people. Let's ask the Lord to instill this attitude in our hearts.

W.W.J.

Jesus said that we should live in peace with all people because we are all his children.

June 16

Solomon

Do Not Abuse Alcohol

Wine is a mocker and beer a brawler; whoever is led astray by them is not wise. (Proverbs 20:1)

Have you ever seen a drunken person? It is definitely not an attractive sight, and many people do very strange things when they are under the influence of alcohol. Every person reacts differently to alcoholic drinks. Some people start making jokes, some start doing weird things, others just become plain silly, and still others become violent and aggressive. But all of them end up with exactly the same problem: they are no longer able to control themselves. That is why the Lord warns us against drunkenness. Solomon warns, *"Wine is a mocker and beer a brawler ..."* (Proverbs 20:1), and he goes on to say that you can simply not act sensibly and wisely if you are drunk.

You should be very careful not to abuse alcohol. If someone in your family has a drinking problem, you know very well just how much sorrow and heartache it can cause. If this is the case in your family, I pray that the problem will be solved. Fortunately, there are people who can help alcoholics recover from their problem. An alcoholic is someone who has a drinking problem, one who regularly consumes too much alcohol and becomes drunk because of it.

Ask the Lord to keep you from ever abusing alcohol. Remember that it simply isn't cool to be drunk.

W.W.J.

Jesus did turn water into wine, but he was never drunk. He definitely does not want people to abuse alcohol.

June 17

Solomon

Ouch!

As iron sharpens iron, so one man sharpens another. (Proverbs 27:17)

When you take two pieces of stone or iron and constantly grind them against each other, an amazing thing will eventually happen. One wouldn't really think that stones can change just because they are being rubbed together. After all, stones are as hard as stone! And iron, too, is a very hard and strong metal. And yet it is true that the stones will eventually start changing their appearance, and the iron will take on a different shape just because the pieces are being rubbed together.

This is the image that the wise Solomon uses to tell us that people, and especially friends, can change each other profoundly with the passage of time. This means that we are always influencing one another. When you spend a lot of time in someone's company, you eventually start thinking and even talking like that person. You also start behaving in a similar way. That is why it is so important to choose the right friends. We all change and influence one another.

Many people start doing bad things not because they are bad people, but because they keep company with bad people. Eventually, they start to imitate the bad example that their friends are setting. However, there are also people who used to live wicked lives, but when they made friends with good people, their lives changed for the better.

Choose friends who live beautiful Christian lives and be a good friend to others. In this way, you can shape your friends to live increasingly in line with the will of the Lord.

W.W.J.

The longer the disciples lived alongside Jesus, the more they started thinking and acting as he did. (Acts 4:13)

June 18

Solomon

A Noble Woman is Very Valuable

A wife of noble character who can find? She is worth far more than rubies. (Proverbs 31:10)

God saw that Adam was lonely, and that is why he decided to create a companion for him. The Bible tells us that God took one of Adam's ribs and from it made a wife for Adam. And yet women are unique and are very different from men. They are indeed a wonderful part of God's great and marvelous creation.

How would we ever be able to thank the Lord enough for women? Every one of us has a mother. From a child's earliest years, it is usually the mother who looks after the child and raises him or her to become an independent adult. Mothers are gifts from the Lord. We should not set aside only a special day to say thank you to and for our mothers; we should also make some time every day to thank the Lord for giving us our mothers.

The wise Solomon knew that a good woman is very valuable. In Proverbs 31, he writes that a wife of noble character is more valuable than precious jewels. And then he talks about what a woman of noble character is like. He also describes all the things that she does. He says that she is hardworking and diligent, that she has a good business sense, and that she takes good care of her family. He says that she is very skilled in all kinds of handicrafts, that she can do all kinds of household tasks, and that she is generous toward the poor and those in need. In short: she is a woman of good character. Solomon also mentions that all her actions are characterized by wisdom and love.

If you are a male, pray that the Lord will bless all the women in your life. If you are a female, pray that the Lord will help you grow to become a woman of noble character, like the woman described in Proverbs 31.

W.W.J.

While Jesus was hanging on the cross he asked John to take care of his earthly mother for the rest of her life. (John 19:27)

June 19

The Teacher

Just Do It!

Whoever watches the wind will not plant; whoever looks at the clouds will not reap. (Ecclesiastes 11:4)

The writer of the book Ecclesiastes was simply called the Teacher. He was a writer who spent a great deal of time pondering life. He asked many questions about the meaning and purpose of life. We don't really know who the Teacher was, but many people believe that it was Solomon.

The Teacher taught that we should simply go ahead and do whatever needs to be done. We can't always wait until everything is perfectly right before we act. We often doubt whether we should do something, and then our uncertainty causes us to become so embroiled in fear that we can't summon the courage to do anything at all. What if we make a mistake? What if we do the wrong thing? What if we fail?

The Teacher from Ecclesiastes tells us that a farmer cannot always wait until everything in nature is absolutely perfect before sowing his seeds. If you are always looking for everything to be perfect before you make a move, then you will never go anywhere. No, the Teacher says, go ahead and act. Trust in God and set out to do the things that you have to do.

If you are convinced that the Lord wants you to do a certain thing, if you are at peace with what you are about to do, and if other people advise you to go ahead, you should simply undertake your task with faith in your heart. Don't allow uncertainty to keep you from action.

W.W.J.

Jesus taught his disciples what true faith meant. True faith is to know God and to trust in him.

The Teacher

Sow your seed in the morning, and at evening let not your hands be idle. (Ecclesiastes 11:6)

Yesterday we learned that we should always act in faith. We never need to stay trapped by uncertainty. In addition to having faith, there is another thing that we need to do: we should work hard at the task assigned to us.

The Bible often tells us that we should not be lazy. Think back to what the Bible says about ants. It tells us to take a look at ants and to note how hardworking and diligent they are. We should be like the ants. We should simply roll up our sleeves and do whatever needs to be done. The Teacher also writes that we should sow our seed early in the morning, and in the afternoon and evening we should continue the sowing because we don't know which batch of seeds will eventually yield a harvest. The Teacher uses this image to say that a farmer should actually keep on sowing all the time, because then he will be assured of a harvest.

You and I should do exactly the same thing. We shouldn't complete one little task and then sit back contentedly. We should immediately set out to do even more things for the Lord. The greater the number of things we set out to do, the more possibilities for success we have, and the more fruit we will harvest from our labors.

What is there for you to do today? Do it to the best of your ability!

W.W.J.

Jesus was always busy with the things that he was called to do.

The Teacher

HE ASKED QUESTIONS

Now all has been heard; here is the conclusion of the matter. (Ecclesiastes 12:13)

The Teacher was constantly struggling with many questions about the purpose and meaning of life. Why am I here? What is the meaning of my life? Where am I going? Where did I come from? What role should the Lord play in my life? What is the secret of experiencing true happiness?

However, the Teacher didn't just sit around asking questions about all these things. He went out into the world and tried many things to test the truth and validity of his thoughts. He truly wanted to be happy and sought to find something that would bring him happiness. He read many books and studied very hard to see if this would perhaps bring him happiness. He also worked very hard and undertook many different projects, but this didn't really make him happy either. He became very wealthy and made a lot of money, but his riches did not bring him happiness. He built many houses for himself and planted many vineyards. He created lovely gardens and parks with all kinds of fruit trees in them. But none of this made him happy. Then he decided to try his hand at farming, and he eventually became a very wealthy farmer with large herds of cattle and other livestock. He also became quite well known and successful in the world of music. He dated many attractive girls to see if they would bring him happiness. But nothing made him truly happy.

Ultimately, the Teacher discovered only one thing that brought him true happiness. His final word of advice is that the way to true happiness is to serve God and to obey his commandments. The Teacher knew that doing this would assuredly bring true happiness. He sought happiness all his life, and he finally found it with God.

W.W.J.

Jesus said that we could find abundant life with him. (John 10:10)

June 22

Solomon

You have stolen my heart ... with one glance of your eyes. (Song of Songs 4:9)

The wise Solomon wrote a love story about a man and a woman who loved each other very much. It might even have been Solomon himself who fell madly in love with a girl who was so beautiful in his eyes that he simply could not stop talking and writing about her. This story is recounted for us in the book Song of Songs.

When Adam saw Eve for the very first time, she must have taken his breath away. Ever since that time, men and women have had special feelings for each other. Men and women fall in love and then want to spend all their time with each other. The love between a man and a woman is truly beautiful.

Perhaps there is someone whom you really like. There is nothing wrong with this. Ask the Lord to show you how to behave toward that person. Don't just be madly in love with someone; show the love of Jesus Christ to that person as well. You should always respect the person you care for. Pray with him or her. Wait for God's timing and God's guidance. He will guide you to the love of your life. As you enjoy life together, remember to always ensure that the Lord is the King of your relationship.

W.W.J.

If we walk with Jesus, our relationships with people of the opposite sex, and ultimately with the person we marry, will always be something beautiful.

June 23

Isaiah

HERE I AM!

Then I heard the voice of the LORD saying, "Whom shall I send?" And I said, "Here am I. Send me!" (Isaiah 6:8)

The Lord is always looking for people who are willing to do his work. This does not mean that we should all be preachers and prophets. It simply means that we should place ourselves, together with all our unique abilities and interests, at the Lord's disposal so that he can use us for his work. He can use you even though you are still just a student. The question is whether you are willing to allow him to use you.

The Lord once had a very special task that he needed someone to do. He needed someone to deliver a message to his people. He wanted to use Isaiah for this job. The Lord appeared to Isaiah and asked him to deliver the message to the Israelites. Isaiah heard the voice of the Lord asking whom he could send and who would be willing to be his messenger. Isaiah was so overwhelmed that he simply said, *"Here am I. Send me!"* (Isaiah 6:8).

I hope that you are also willing to be the Lord's messenger today.

W.W.J.

Jesus said, "As the Father has sent me, so I am sending you". (see John 20:21)

Isaiah

For to us a child is born, to us a son is given. (Isaiah 9:6)

Long before the birth of Jesus, Isaiah predicted the events of that first Christmas. How did he know? The Holy Spirit sent this message to the people through Isaiah. When the Holy Spirit speaks through someone in this way, we say that the person is prophesying.

Christmas is a wonderful time of year. However, Christmas isn't just all about the gifts we give and receive. Christmas is actually a celebration of the greatest gift of all: God's gift of his Son, Jesus. Listen to how Isaiah describes him. Isaiah says that the Son will be born and that he will govern or rule as King over everyone. He will be wonderful, and there will be no one like him. He will give people good advice because he is the Counselor. He will be the Mighty God, the Everlasting Father, and the Prince of Peace.

And so Isaiah goes on to describe the marvelous characteristics of Jesus. He also describes exactly how much Jesus would mean to humankind and how important he would be to us.

When we are in need of advice, Jesus will give it to us. When we lack strength, he will supply us with all the strength we need. He loves us as an earthly, mortal father loves his children – no, he actually loves us far more than that. And no one else can give us the peace that he can give us. And these are all the wonderful gifts that we receive because of Christmas!

Isaiah also says that Jesus' reign as King will be eternal and that his kingdom will never end. Actually, I think that Jesus wants to turn every single day of the year into a Christmas celebration!

W.W.J.

The disciples understood that Jesus was Immanuel, God with us.

God

The Flag is Up

In that day the Root of Jesse will stand as a banner for the peoples. (Isaiah 11:10)

In Exodus 17, we read of the Israelites' battle against the Amalekites. Moses was standing on top of a hill. As long as he held his hands up, the Israelites were winning the battle. But as soon as he lowered his hands, the Amalekites started winning. Then Aaron and Hur held Moses' arms up, and that is how the Israelites managed to be victorious. Moses then built an altar and called it *"The Lord is my Banner"* (Exodus 17:15).

The name that Moses gave to the Lord at that altar means banner, standard, or flag. Even today when we have a festival to celebrate something, we hoist flags into the sky where everyone can see them blowing in the wind. When we want to show that we are proud of our country or our athletes or our sports teams, we let them carry the national flag. A banner flutters in the wind and tells everyone that you belong to the one whose colors and name are on the banner. God is like a banner over his children, like a great flag. He is the one who gives us the victory. He is great and powerful, and we can and must be proud of him. That is why we carry him in our hearts, like a banner.

Isaiah also said that Jesus would be like a banner flying over all the nations. Of course, we are proud of our country's flag. But we are even prouder of Jesus, who is like a banner above us everywhere we go. We belong to him. And with him on our team we are always on the winning side.

That is why we can celebrate with flags and with banners. Let Jesus' flag be hoisted high in your heart.

W.W.J.

"Hosanna, hosanna!" the people cheered when Jesus rode into Jerusalem in a festive procession. (John 12:13)

June 26

God

The Righteous One

"The Lord Our Righteousness." (Jeremiah 33:16)

There are many things that are wrong in this world. Although there are laws and rules that tell people how they should behave so that everyone can be happy, safe, and prosperous, many people break these laws. Because of those lawbreakers, the world isn't always a wonderful place to live.

The reason why so many things are wrong with this world is simply that people do not have the right kind of relationship with God. God is fair and just, and he knows what is best for us. If we surrender the control of our lives to him and obey his commandments, our lives will take the right direction. Everything will start going better for us, and we will be able to make the right decisions. We will harvest the abundant fruits of a good relationship with God. However, this is not the way that things stand in our world. Most people won't be bothered with doing God's will. They simply do whatever they think is right.

One of the names of the Lord mentioned in the Bible is "The Lord Our Righteousness." This means that he is the One who puts things right, who brings justice and righteousness. In Hebrew, this name is Yahweh-tsidkenu. This name means that the Lord brings justice and righteousness into our lives. He judges with fairness and does what is right.

Jesus came to carry out God's justice. When he died for our sins, he opened the door for us to live in righteousness before God. He restored us in the sight of the Lord. He washed us clean and restored our relationship with God. Jesus enabled us to make things right with God by his sacrifice on the cross. Have you squared things with the Lord yet? Have you made things right with him?

W.W.J.

Jesus said that the Holy Spirit would make our hearts righteous. Jesus is on the side of justice and righteousness.

June 27

Isaiah

CHARGE YOUR BATTERIES

He gives strength to the weary. (Isaiah 40:29)

A car's battery sometimes goes dead and the car won't start. The only thing you can do when your car's battery has gone dead is to either recharge it or buy a new one.

People also need strength and energy to function properly. We don't have batteries like cars do, but our bodies provide us with the strength that we need to move and do things. But our "batteries" also sometimes go dead. Sometimes we just feel tired, weary, and discouraged, and then we simply don't feel up to doing anything. Even the strongest and youngest of men sometimes become tired and weary.

One's spirit can also go flat and powerless, usually because of discouragement or dejection. When this happens, we feel completely powerless to do anything about our situation. Our spirit needs to be recharged first, so that we can once again find the courage to tackle life with courage and enthusiasm.

The Bible knows that we need strength. Isaiah invites us to go to the Lord for the strength that we need for our everyday lives. The Lord never becomes tired and he never needs to sleep to regain his strength. God does not grow old as we do – he lives outside time and is ageless. God is like an eternal source of power, like a battery that never goes dead. And he wants to give some of his strength to us. Isaiah says that God does not grow weary; instead, he gives strength to the weary. So how do we go about drawing on this strength? The answer is this: *"... those who hope in the LORD will renew their strength ... "* (Isaiah 40:31).

If we wait for the Lord and remain in his presence, if we read his Word and talk to him and ask his advice, his strength will flow into our hearts. Then we can regain our strength and become vigorous enough to live every day to the fullest.

W.W.J.

Jesus promised that he would give us his Holy Spirit to strengthen us.

June 28

Isaiah

ARE YOU AFRAID?

But now, this is what the LORD says ... "Fear not, for I have redeemed you."
(Isaiah 43:1)

What are you afraid of? I'm sure you could make a list of things that make you afraid. Some people are afraid of the dark, others fear snakes or spiders, others are afraid of being poor, and some are even afraid of other people. Being afraid is a part of our everyday lives.

The Lord wants to liberate us from negative fear. Isaiah invites us to come close to the Lord because the Lord can help us to conquer all our fears. The Lord uses the voice of Isaiah to tell us that he knows us intimately because he created and formed us. He also tells Israel that they need not be afraid, because he wants to redeem them and save them. And then he says something very beautiful, *"I have summoned you by name; you are mine"* (Isaiah 43:1). Because we are God's children, we belong to him, and he does not want fear to spoil our lives.

The Lord assures us that he knows us, that he loves us, that he cares for us, and that he will help us. If there is something that you are afraid of today, tell the Lord about it and ask him to help you. You have to learn to trust in him more and more every single day. If you are a child of the Lord, you can rest assured that he is always beside you. He knows everything; he even knows what awaits you in the future. Talk to him, be steadfast in your faith, and always hold on to the Lord.

W.W.J.

When the disciples were afraid of the storm, Jesus calmed the storm for them. (Luke 8:23-25)

Isaiah

CAN GOD FORGET?

"The LORD has forsaken me, the LORD has forgotten me." (Isaiah 49:14)

When I was a little boy, we once went to a big city to do some shopping. My parents were so busy trying to find all the things they were looking for in the big store that they forgot all about me. The next thing I knew, I was completely lost. I couldn't see my mom or dad anywhere, and I was suddenly very scared. Fortunately, my mom finally found me.

It is definitely not a nice experience to be forgotten or abandoned. Can God forget about you? Isaiah says that it is impossible. Not only does God know everything about you, if you are his child he will also never forget you or forsake you. The Lord speaks through Isaiah and says, *"Can a mother forget the baby at her breast and have no compassion on the child she has borne? Though she may forget, I will not forget you!"* (Isaiah 49:15).

The Lord says that he has engraved our names on the palms of his hands and that he always keeps an eye on us. Because he loves us and cares about us, he is always with us. You don't have to be afraid that God will forget you. He knows everything and he is present everywhere. Wherever you go, he goes with you. Take a moment right now to thank him for always being with you.

W.W.J.

Jesus said, *"Remember that I am with you always, even to the very end of time"*. (see Matthew 28:20)

Isaiah

ARE YOU THIRSTY?

"Come, all you who are thirsty, come to the waters." (Isaiah 55:1)

You have probably had the experience of being really thirsty. Your body needs water, and without water you eventually become so thirsty that your tongue starts to cling to the roof of your mouth. Without water, you will ultimately die of dehydration. In the Bible, God's prophet Isaiah says that our hearts can also be thirsty. To satisfy this thirst, we also need water, but a special kind of water: spiritual water. We need water for our spirits and our hearts so that we can be refreshed and revitalized. Who do you think could give us this water?

Isaiah says that the Lord himself is the spiritual water that refreshes us and gives us life. He says that all we need to do when we are thirsty is come to the water and drink of it. How do we drink of God's water?

We drink of God's water whenever we enter into his presence, whenever we listen to him, whenever we focus all our attention on him, whenever we ask what his will is, whenever we call upon his name, and whenever we cast off our sinful ways and turn to him in repentance.

Jesus also said that he would give us water that will be like living streams inside of us. I think he was talking about the Holy Spirit that he would give to us. Jesus himself was also called the Living Water. The spiritual water that he gives us ensures that our hearts will never again be thirsty. Do you drink of this water every day?

W.W.J.

Jesus told the woman at the well of Sychar to drink of the living water. (John 4:13-14)

Isaiah

Seek the Lord

Seek the Lord while he may be found; call on him while he is near. (Isaiah 55:6)

You call out to someone when you want to catch that person's attention. When you are walking barefoot and you suddenly step on a thorn, you call a friend to come and help you take the thorn out of your foot. Someone who has fallen into a deep well will direct his calls for help up toward the opening so that someone can hear him and help him.

Isaiah says that we should call on the Lord. The Lord wants to help us, but you and I first have to call on him and ask him to help us. When your life is over and you pass away, it is much too late to call on the Lord and ask him to help you. You should call on him while he is still nearby. Jesus came to the earth and walked among us, and he gave us his Word and his Spirit. In this way, Jesus ensured that we could always have contact with the Father. But we have to call out to him. What should we say? We should call to the Lord to forgive our sins, to live inside our hearts, and to take us by the hand and lead us.

Calling out to the Lord goes hand in hand with asking: we should ask him about his will for our lives. We should ask him to show us how to live and what to do. And the Bible tells us that if we ask, he will answer.

Call out to the Lord and ask him what his will is for you today. I am sure that he will answer you. Then walk with Jesus today.

W.W.J.

Our Lord Jesus constantly called upon his Father and followed his will.

Isaiah

THIS IS HOW YOU GET GOD'S ATTENTION

"This is the one I esteem." (Isaiah 66:2)

There are many people who say that God doesn't really take much interest in people. Some think that he is just too busy to pay attention to us. Others say that he is much too far away to know about everything that happens to us here on earth. And yet others think that he is much too exalted and mighty to concern himself with the petty, trivial problems of ordinary human beings. But this is not what the Bible tells us.

Because the Lord created us, he loves us. He knows everything about us, and his attention is always focused on us. Every single human being is important to him. He knows about all our troubles, our fears, our dreams, and our desires. Indeed, he is always keeping watch over us.

Isaiah says that the Lord is particularly attentive when people are in distress. The Lord listens to people who repent of their sins. When we confess our sins, the Lord pays special attention to us. Isaiah also says that the Lord pays attention to people who fear and respect his Word. The Lord takes notice of us when we read his Word and take what is written in it seriously. It is almost as if the Lord has a very special place in his heart for people who love his Word.

Do you want to become God's friend? Confess your sins, call to him from within your distress, and read his Word every day.

W.W.J.

Jesus always helped people who called to him from their distress and despair.

July 3

Jeremiah

EVEN BEFORE HIS BIRTH, GOD KNEW HIM

"Before I formed you in the womb I knew you." (Jeremiah 1:5)

Jeremiah is another prophet we read about in the Old Testament. In the same way that he called Isaiah, the Lord called Jeremiah to give a message to his people, the Israelites. Jeremiah was an ordinary person, just like us, but he had a special assignment that he had to perform.

When the Lord called Jeremiah, he assured the would-be prophet that a plan for Jeremiah's life had been in place even before Jeremiah was born. Doesn't this thought excite you? Just think: even before you were born the Lord had already decided on a plan for your life. He knows why you are here on earth and what he wants to accomplish through you.

Sometimes you meet people who believe that their birth was nothing but an accident. The Bible tells us that the Lord did plan our birth. Jeremiah writes that God told him, *"... before you were born I set you apart; I appointed you as a prophet to the nations"* (Jeremiah 1:5).

You can live your life in the secure knowledge that the Lord has a plan for you. Commit yourself to him and ask him to fulfill his plan for your life. Even before you were born, the Lord knew what color your eyes would be, what color your hair would be, what your interests and talents would be. What a privilege to fulfill his plan!

W.W.J.

Jesus told Nathanael, "I saw you even before you had seen me" (read John 1:48). Jesus had had a plan for Nathanael's life all along.

July 4

Jeremiah

I Can't, Lord

"Ah, Sovereign Lord ... I do not know how to speak; I am only a child."
(Jeremiah 1:6)

Sometimes we think that the Lord can only use us if we are very clever, or have a great deal of knowledge about him, or have many talents, or are very religious. This is definitely not the truth.

The Lord called Jeremiah to be a prophet to Israel and all the other nations of the world. But like Moses, Jeremiah had many excuses. Do you remember how Moses said that he was no good at public speaking? Here Jeremiah offers exactly the same excuse to the Lord! In addition, Jeremiah also told the Lord that he was much too young to be a messenger of God.

Never think that you are too young to be used by the Lord. You can serve the Lord even when you are very young. As a matter of fact, younger people are quite often much more energetic and able to do some kinds of work for the Lord that older people cannot do. Paul wrote to the young man Timothy and assured him that he was not too young to do the Lord's work. In his letter, Paul says that youthfulness is not something to be scorned or despised. He goes on to tell Timothy that he should always set an example for all people, despite the fact that he is still so young.

In addition to feeling like he couldn't speak and that he was too young, Jeremiah was also a little bit scared of the responsibility. But the Lord told him that his excuses were unimportant and invalid. The Lord said that he would help Jeremiah, and he did. The Lord wants to use you today, even though you might still be very young.

W.W.J.

To Jesus, children and young people are just as important as grownups – and God can do great things through their faith.

July 5

Jeremiah

THE FOUNTAIN OF LIFE

... because they have forsaken the LORD, the spring of living water. (Jeremiah 17:13)

People who are planning on traveling through a desert should ensure that they have enough water with them before they set out on their journey. A desert has very little water and it is very hot in the daytime, so a person would become thirsty very quickly. In a desert, however, you will occasionally find an oasis or a fountain. These springs of water are the only real sources of fresh water in the desert. When you reach such an oasis, you can replenish your water supply so that you can survive the rest of your journey.

Jeremiah spoke to the Lord and said, *"O LORD, the hope of Israel, all who forsake you will be put to shame. Those who turn away from you will be written in the dust because they have forsaken the LORD, the spring of living water"* (Jeremiah 17:13).

Jeremiah says that if you do not have the Lord in your life, you have lost all hope of eternal life. If you do not have the Lord in your life, you are destined for disappointment. When you turn away from God, it is the same as saying yes to eternal death. A person who abandons the Lord, abandons the source, or fountain, or oasis of true life.

You and I should be very sure that we have accepted the Lord as our hope and our source of eternal life. Nothing and no one else can give us eternal life. No amount of money or power, no number of dreams or deeds can guarantee that we will one day receive eternal life. Only God gives eternal life. He is the Source of life.

W.W.J.

Jesus is like a fountain that gives us eternal life. When we find Jesus, we find the Source of eternal life.

Jeremiah

LET'S TALK ABOUT MATTERS OF THE HEART

The heart is deceitful above all things. (Jeremiah 17:9)

When the Bible talks about the "heart," it is usually referring to the essential core of your life and being. For example, the Bible says that you should give your "heart" to the Lord. The Lord is saying that when you put your heart into something, you commit everything you have and are to that cause. The attitudes and feelings that you carry in your heart determine how you act toward other people. Your heart contains everything that you feel, think, or decide.

It isn't always easy to know what is going on inside another person. No one can really look into another person's heart. Only God knows the contents of every human heart. Very often a person's outer appearance will give the impression that he or she does not have a good heart. But the better you get to know that person, the more you realize that he or she has a really good heart underneath a rough exterior. Or the opposite can be true. Someone can appear kind and sincere, but his or her heart is filled with evil.

However, the saddest thing of all about the heart is that a person can act in a certain way one day and a completely different way the next. This fact certainly makes it clear that the human heart is very deceptive. This is exactly what Jeremiah says in the Bible. He says that the heart is the most deceitful thing on earth and that its deceitfulness is incurable. He then goes on to ask the question, "Who can understand the heart?" We find the answer to this question in verse 10: *"I the LORD search the heart and examine the mind."* We cannot hide anything from God because he looks deep into our hearts and knows exactly what we think and feel and decide. The only way to repair our deceitful, wicked hearts is to give them to the Lord so that he can wash them clean and make his home in them.

W. W. J.

Jesus said that where your treasure is, there your heart will be also. (Matthew 6:21)

July 7

Jeremiah

Trouble

They were angry with Jeremiah and had him beaten and imprisoned. (Jeremiah 37:15)

God chose a very difficult time to send Jeremiah as his messenger to the Israelites. At that time, the Israelites did not want to listen to God at all, and they pretty much did whatever they pleased. At the same time, there were many false prophets and teachers who were deceiving the people. They were saying all kinds of things that definitely did not come from God's heart. Nevertheless, they pretended to speak in the name of the Lord. Jeremiah's task was to remedy this unacceptable situation.

Poor old Jeremiah was really misunderstood by the people of his time. Every single time he said something, they completely misinterpreted his words. They didn't want to hear bad news, so when Jeremiah brought them bad news from God, they would attack and hurt him. They even beat him and had him thrown in prison. Despite all this, the Lord always looked after Jeremiah. The Lord's hand on Jeremiah was so powerful that Jeremiah simply had to speak out about what was in God's heart.

If you want to serve the Lord, you have to be willing to stand up for what is right, and that may make you unpopular. Jesus' disciples were persecuted throughout their lives simply because they were his followers. Following Jesus is not always the popular thing to do, but in the end it is always worthwhile.

W.W.J.

Jesus said that our lives here on earth would not be easy, yet he asked us to follow him with dedication and commitment.

Ezekiel

THE SKELETONS CAME TO LIFE

"I will put my Spirit in you and you will live." (Ezekiel 37:14)

Ezekiel was one of the Lord's prophets, and the Lord often appeared to him in dreams and visions. One day Ezekiel had one such vision, a picture in his mind that left a lasting impression on him. It was the Holy Spirit who gave him this vision.

Ezekiel saw himself standing in the middle of a big valley. All across the valley, bones were scattered. The Lord then prompted Ezekiel to walk among the bones, and Ezekiel saw that there were so many bones that he couldn't even count them. The bones were also very dry. Then the Lord asked Ezekiel whether he thought that these bones could possibly come back to life. Ezekiel didn't think that they could.

Then the Lord told Ezekiel to speak to the bones. He had to tell the dry bones that God would send his spirit into them so that they could come to life: *"I will attach tendons to you and make flesh come upon you and cover you with skin; I will put breath in you, and you will come to life ..."* (Ezekiel 37:6).

This vision simply meant that the Lord wanted to give new life to his people, whose spiritual life was completely dead. He wanted to make them come back to life by giving them his Holy Spirit. God wants to give us his Holy Spirit to live within us so that we may truly live. Without the Holy Spirit, we are nothing but a pile of old, dead bones.

W.W.J.

On the day of Pentecost, the Holy Spirit came to live inside Jesus' followers. When we accept Jesus as Savior, the Holy Spirit fills our lives as well.

Ezekiel

God's River of Living Water

But now it was a river that I could not cross, because the water had risen. (Ezekiel 47:5)

One day, the Lord gave Ezekiel another vision. This time he dreamed that water suddenly started streaming out from underneath the temple. In his dream, Ezekiel was walking, accompanied by another man. The man told Ezekiel to walk through the water. The level of the water reached up to his ankles. Fifteen hundred feet further, the man again told Ezekiel to walk through the water, and this time the water reached to his knees. Yet another fifteen hundred feet further, the water was as high as his hip; another fifteen hundred feet, and the stream was so deep that he could no longer walk through it, but instead had to swim to the other side.

The man who was with Ezekiel told him that the water flowed all the way to the Dead Sea. The water of the Dead Sea sustains no life because it is extremely salty. There are no fish or plants in the water. But where the water flowed into the Dead Sea, its salty water suddenly became fresh and was filled with fish and plants.

Ezekiel was probably very curious to know exactly what this vision meant. The Lord was saying that although Israel was as spiritually dead as the Dead Sea, God would bring the nation back to life. That is why, in his vision, the stream of living water flowed from the temple. This stream became deeper and deeper, and it brought back to life everything that was dead. On both shores of the Dead Sea fruit trees would grow. Their leaves would not wither and they would never fail to bear fruit.

The Lord wants his children's hearts and lives to be filled with life, not death. You and I should draw our life and strength from the stream of life that God gives us through Jesus, the Living Water. Allow his water to flow into your heart.

W.W.J.

Jesus' life is like living water that nourishes us so that we can bear fruit.

God

He is Always There

"And the name of the city from that time on will be: THE LORD IS THERE." (Ezekiel 48:35)

Another one of God's names in the Bible is Yahweh-shammah. This name of God means that he is always there. Shammah means "there." This name tells us that the Lord is never absent from our lives. He never slumbers or sleeps. He never goes on vacation. He never hides from us. He never turns his back on us. God is always there. Whenever we need him, want to talk to him, or just want to feel his presence close to us, we can know that he is right there.

God is omnipresent. He is everywhere. He is always around, but his presence is especially strong wherever people allow him to be the God of their lives. If you are a believer, God promises to stay with you even when, at times, you turn away from him and go your own way. Even then, he is still with you. When you turn back to God, you can rest assured that he is always nearby. Allow God to be present in your home, in your room, in your friendships, in your heart. He will never leave you because he is always there with you and for you.

W.W.J.

Jesus' name was also Immanuel, which means "God is with us." (Matthew 1:23)

Daniel

Too Much Junk Food is Bad for You

At the end of the ten days they looked healthier and better nourished than any of the young men who ate the royal food. (Daniel 1:15)

If you were honest, you would probably say that you eat your share of "junk food." You know, the stuff that is really not very healthy to eat, but is usually the kind of food that we like best. It could be very fatty food, or very sweet food that is packed with sugar, or simply food that has no nutritional value. Eating too many hamburgers or sweets, or drinking too many milkshakes, is definitely not good for you. If you eat junk food like this every day, without eating healthy food too, you are bound to get sick.

Daniel and his friends lived in the time of King Nebuchadnezzar of Babylon. They had been taken there as slaves from Israel. The king took a number of young men into his employment. They had to attend a special royal school where they were taught all kinds of things. They were also given food and wine from the king's table every day. Their training period lasted for three years.

Daniel, Shadrach, Meshach, and Abednego were Jews. They knew that if they had to eat of the king's food every day, they would be going against the food laws that God had given his people. That is why they asked the king's chief official if they could please have other, healthier food to eat. After only ten days, it was clear that Daniel and his friends, who ate only fresh, healthy food, looked much healthier and better nourished than the other young men. Not only did they look much better, they also learned much faster than the others and surpassed all of the other young men in skill and knowledge.

You and I have a responsibility toward the Lord, and also toward ourselves, to eat a balanced, healthy diet of foods and to look after our bodies. Don't treat your body as if it were a piece of old junk – so stay away from too much junk food.

W.W.J.

I think Jesus often enjoyed meals with his disciples, but he would never have eaten food that was bad for his body.

July 12

Shadrach, Meshach, and Abednego

Whom Do You Worship?

"As soon as you hear the sound of the horn, flute, zither, lyre, harp, pipes and all kinds of music, you must fall down and worship the image of gold." (Daniel 3:5)

King Nebuchadnezzar had a golden statue made and commanded that whenever music started playing, everyone had to fall down and worship it. Almost everyone was quick in obeying the king's command because they feared him. The only people who refused to worship the statue were Shadrach, Meshach, and Abednego, who were Jewish.

When someone told the king that the three young men refused to worship the statue, King Nebuchadnezzar summoned them to appear before him. He was furious at their disobedience. He then said that he would let them off without punishment if they would fall down and worship the golden image the next time the sound of music was heard. The three friends then answered him, *"If we are thrown into the blazing furnace, the God we serve is able to save us from it. ... But even if he does not, we want you to know, O king, that we will not serve your gods or worship the image of gold ... "* (Daniel 3:17–18).

Do you agree that they were three very brave men? Their faith rested in God, and they did not want to disobey God by worshiping an idol. They believed that the Lord would help them. And even if he decided not to save them from the blazing furnace, they would still not be willing to worship a heathen god.

Are there perhaps things in your life, besides God, that you worship? Are there perhaps things that are more important to you than the Lord? Maybe some of your friends are encouraging you to do things that you know the Lord does not approve of. Be strong and resist the temptation, just as Shadrach, Meshach, and Abednego did.

W.W.J.

Jesus said that if we want to follow him we should take up our cross and be faithful to him. (Mark 8:34)

July 13

Shadrach, Meshach, and Abednego

WORSHIP THE STATUE OR BURN!

"Whoever does not fall down and worship will immediately be thrown into a blazing furnace." (Daniel 3:6)

Nebuchadnezzar erected a massive golden statue. Then he sent out a proclamation that ordered everyone to fall down and worship it whenever they heard the sound of music. Those who refused to worship the statue would be thrown into a blazing furnace.

All the people, regardless of their nationality or language, fell down before the statue and worshiped it whenever they heard the sound of music. Daniel's three friends were the only ones who refused. They would not worship the statue because they served only God. Someone reported to the king that the three friends refused to worship the golden image. The king was furious! But he gave them one more chance to worship the statue. They refused again.

The king became completely enraged and ordered his servants to make the furnace seven times hotter than it already was. He ordered some of his strongest soldiers to tie up the three friends and throw them into the furnace. The furnace was so hot that the soldiers burned to death when they came close to it. But Shadrach, Meshach, and Abednego, fell into the furnace, still tied up. All of a sudden another man appeared beside them in the furnace. The king saw this fourth man and was completely astonished. The fourth man looked just like an angel – and it was one! The Lord protected Shadrach, Meshach, and Abednego from harm. Then Nebuchadnezzar praised the God of Daniel and his friends.

God is powerful to protect and to help you, just as he protected and helped Shadrach, Meshach, and Abednego. But you need to be just as faithful as these three men.

W.W.J.

Jesus is beside us even when we pass through times of trouble. He is the only one who can save us from all our troubles.

July 14

Nebuchadnezzar

PRIDE GOES BEFORE A FALL

"... by my mighty power and for the glory of my majesty?" (Daniel 4:30)

King Nebuchadnezzar was a very proud king who did not believe in God. He was the ruler of a very large kingdom, and he prided himself on his many grand and magnificent achievements. Because Daniel was in his service, he heard about the God of Israel. He even praised this God of Israel upon occasion, after seeing the miracles that God could do – such as freeing Shadrach, Meshach, and Abednego from the fiery furnace.

One day, the Lord sent a message to Nebuchadnezzar in a dream. Daniel was called to explain the meaning of this dream. Through Daniel, God told Nebuchadnezzar, *"Renounce your sins by doing what is right, and your wickedness by being kind to the oppressed. It may be that then your prosperity will continue"* (Daniel 4:27).

Despite the message that the Lord sent to him, Nebuchadnezzar continued to live as he had always done. He did not serve God and lived only to glorify and exalt himself. He went around telling everyone how magnificent Babylon was, and that it was his power that made Babylon such a big and powerful royal city. He liked to heap honor upon himself and was constantly telling everyone how wonderful he was.

One day, while he was once again boasting about his wealth and power, a voice suddenly came down from heaven. The voice said that it had been decided that Nebuchadnezzar's royal authority would be taken away from him. He would lose his mind completely and be driven out of society to live with the wild animals in the fields. Everything happened just as the voice said.

Pride goes before a fall. People who are excessively proud are often brought back down to earth and taught a lesson about being humble. We should always be humble and never think too highly of ourselves, as Nebuchadnezzar did. Let us choose to serve the Lord instead.

W.W.J.

Jesus taught us the meaning of true humility.

Belshazzar

THE HAND AGAINST THE WALL

Suddenly the fingers of a human hand appeared and wrote on the plaster of the wall. (Daniel 5:5)

King Belshazzar was the successor of King Nebuchadnezzar. One day he was hosting a big feast for a thousand members of the nobility. They were all having a very good time at the party.

The party was in full swing, and everyone was drinking wine from the golden and silver cups that had been taken from the temple in Jerusalem when the Babylonians had sacked the city. These cups were supposed to have been set aside to be used in worship ceremonies for the Lord. They were holy objects, intended to be used only in the temple. But King Belshazzar and his guests used the cups to drink their wine. Eventually, they all became drunk. They were still drinking and praising their idols when a strange thing happened. A human hand appeared and started writing on the plaster of the wall.

The king's face turned as white as chalk. His legs were shaking and he was overwhelmed with fear. He called all his advisers and wise men and asked them to tell him what was written on the wall. No one could decipher the writing. Then they called Daniel, and God revealed to him what he had written. The words that were written on the wall were: *"mene, mene, tekel, parsin"* (Daniel 5:25). This means "numbered, numbered, weighed, divided." What was God trying to tell King Belshazzar? Daniel explained to the king that the Lord wanted to tell him that: (1) God had decided to end his reign as king. His days as king were numbered. (2) He had been weighed and found wanting, because he had lived only for himself. (3) His kingdom would be divided and given to other nations. That very same night, the city was overtaken by its enemies and King Belshazzar was murdered.

If we were to be weighed by the Lord, would he say that we have spiritual substance or that we were "wanting"?

W.W.J.

Jesus taught us that the value of our lives would one day be weighed before him.

July 16

Daniel

FLAWLESS WORK

They could find no corruption in him, because he was trustworthy and neither corrupt nor negligent. (Daniel 6:4)

After the death of King Belshazzar, Darius became the king of Babylon. He appointed Daniel as one of the most important ministers in his kingdom. Daniel was exceptionally competent, and he outshone all the other ministers. The king then decided to appoint him as minister over the entire kingdom.

When the other ministers, administrators, and officials heard about Darius's plan they were filled with jealousy. They knew that Daniel was a Jew, and they decided to devise a plan to make sure that he would no longer be so important. They tried to see if they could catch him doing something wrong so that they could charge him with negligence. They scrutinized his work very carefully to see if they could find an error or flaw that would give them grounds to charge him before the king. But they could find absolutely no fault with his work. Daniel was completely trustworthy and definitely not negligent in doing his work.

If you are asked to perform a task or to do something specific for your schoolwork, be sure to do it faithfully and meticulously, just as Daniel did. Do your work well and don't be lazy. Make sure that no one can point a finger at you for not doing your work properly. Honor God by doing your work well.

W.W.J.

Jesus used a parable to tell us that we should use our talents to the full and work hard every day. (Matthew 25:18-28)

Daniel

LION FOOD BECAUSE OF HIS FAITH

... and they brought Daniel and threw him into the lions' den. (Daniel 6:16)

When Daniel's co-workers saw that they could find nothing wrong with his work, they realized that they would have to find a different way of getting rid of him. They knew that Daniel was a very religious man whose faith in the Lord was absolutely unfaltering. So they decided to use this in their plan to make Daniel lose his position as the king's highest advisor.

They went to the king and told him to issue a decree that for the next thirty days, no one in the kingdom would be allowed to pray to anyone except King Darius. They knew that Daniel would never obey this decree. The king decided that it would be a good idea to issue such a decree, and he went ahead with it. Anyone who disobeyed would be thrown to the lions.

One day, while Daniel was busy worshiping, praising, and thanking the Lord, the wicked men rushed into his room and seized him. They dragged him before the king and told him that Daniel had disregarded the king's law by praying to the Lord. Daniel was then thrown into the lions' den.

However, we read that the Lord sent an angel to shut the mouths of the lions so they could not tear Daniel apart. Because Daniel was faithful to the Lord, the Lord was faithful to him. When King Darius saw what had happened, he ordered his people to worship and praise the God of Daniel.

Let us worship the Lord even though we might sometimes encounter opposition.

W.W.J.

Jesus said that we should honor God always.

Daniel

THE DREAM OF THE THRONE

"As I looked, thrones were set in place." (Daniel 7:9)

One night Daniel had a dream. This dream was actually a vision from the Lord about things that would happen in the future. Daniel recorded his dream in a book so that you and I can still read about it today.

In his dream, Daniel saw many thrones. God, who lives eternally, took his seat on his throne. His clothes were white as snow and his hair was white as wool. Thousands upon thousands of people stood before him, and millions of people served him. Then God opened a great book that contained all the accusations against all the people that had ever lived. This was followed by a big court session during which the accusations were heard.

All the wrong things that people had ever thought or done – even those things thought or done in secret – were written in the book. Every single person's life was judged.

Then Daniel also saw someone else at the court session. This One was given all authority, glory, and sovereign power, and all the nations served him. He was the greatest King of all. Who do you think this was? Of course – it was Jesus!

This is why you and I do not have to fear that day when we will have to stand before the great throne of God. If Jesus has washed us clean and if he is the King of our lives, he will help us on that day.

W.W.J.

Jesus said that he did not come to judge or condemn us, but to save us. (John 3:17)

Michael

THE DIVINE WARRIOR

"Then Michael, one of the chief princes, came to help me." (Daniel 10:13)

Michael is an important angel we read about in the Bible. The Bible tells us that he had the very special task of protecting and defending the Jewish people.

We read that Daniel was very troubled about what had happened to his people, and his heart was filled with sorrow. For three weeks, he fasted and prayed. Suddenly, a man dressed in linen and with a belt of the finest gold around his waist appeared before Daniel. His body glittered like a precious stone and his face was bright like lightning. His eyes were like flaming torches. His arms and legs gleamed like burnished bronze and his voice sounded like the rumble of thunder. Then the man spoke to Daniel and told him that he had been sent to Daniel to deliver a message to him. Actually, God had sent him on the very first day that Daniel started praying, but he could not come earlier because a strong evil spirit, called the prince of Persia, fought with him and kept him from coming to Daniel.

Michael then told Daniel that he should take courage and not be afraid. After he had spoken some encouraging words to Daniel he said, *"Soon I will return to fight against the prince of Persia, and when I go, the prince of Greece will come"* (Daniel 10:20). These princes that Michael spoke of were actually evil spirits, powers, and forces with whom he had to battle. They were the messengers of Satan.

Even today, the angels are still fighting in the spiritual realm. The good angels, like Michael, fight for us. Let us thank God for his angels, because he sends them out to fight on our behalf.

W.W.J.

An angel unlocked the prison doors when Peter was in jail for preaching about Jesus. (Acts 5:19)

Hosea

SHOW IT AND LIVE IT

"Go, take to yourself an adulterous wife and children of unfaithfulness." (Hosea 1:2)

So far, we have talked about several instances when the Lord wanted to send urgent messages to his people. In those days, people did not have Bibles as we do now, and the Holy Spirit was not yet living in people's hearts. Instead, the Lord sent prophets to tell people about God's will and word. One of these prophets was a man named Hosea.

The Lord gave Hosea a very strange order. He told Hosea to marry a wicked woman. Her name was Gomer, and she was a prostitute. Despite this, God asked Hosea to marry her. Why would he ask something like that?

The Lord didn't want Hosea merely to use words to give the Israelites his message; he wanted Hosea to show his message to the people by embodying it in his life. The Israelites had to see with their own eyes exactly how God felt about his people. Hosea had to marry the wicked woman Gomer and love her and take care of her even though she was constantly unfaithful to him. In the same way, the Lord was loving and caring for his people, even though they were wicked and unfaithful – constantly worshiping other gods.

Indeed, you and I are often unfaithful to the Lord when we disobey him. We are imperfect and often commit sin. Despite this, the Lord always loves us and always remains faithful to us.

W.W.J.

Jesus knew that his followers were sinful people. Despite this, he loved them and walked with them.

July 21

Joel

THE SPIRIT IS IN US

"And afterward, I will pour out my Spirit on all people." (Joel 2:28)

Joel was another one of the prophets sent by the Lord to give messages to his people. Joel also prophesied about what would happen in the future. Without understanding exactly what it meant, Joel prophesied about a wonderful event that we read about in the New Testament.

Through Joel, the Lord told his people, the Israelites, that they should return to him. He said that they should "tear" their hearts. In biblical times, people tore their clothes when they were very sad or unhappy. But God told his people that they should not only tear their clothes, but also (and especially) their hearts. Then the Lord would take them back and forgive them.

Then the Lord made another wonderful promise. The Lord said that he would pour out his Holy Spirit on all people and marvelous things would start happening. Young men and women would start prophesying about the Lord's will, and older people would have dreams of God's kingdom. Young people would see visions. And everyone who called on the name of the Lord would be saved.

Joel's prediction was actually about the day of Pentecost. This was the day when the Holy Spirit was poured out. Jesus promised that he would send his Holy Spirit and that all Christians would receive this Holy Spirit. In a very wonderful, mysterious way the Holy Spirit would come to live inside us. Then the Holy Spirit would tell us all about Jesus and lead us on the right path.

If you belong to Jesus, the Holy Spirit lives inside you. He is your Helper and your Comforter, and he uses the Bible, along with your conscience, to tell you how to live to the glory of the Lord. Take a moment right now to thank the Holy Spirit for living in you.

W.W.J.

Jesus promised that when he left, he would send the Holy Spirit to us in his place.

July 22

Amos

A Farmer Who Became a Prophet

"I was a shepherd, and I also took care of sycamore-fig trees." (Amos 7:14)

Amos was a farmer and a shepherd. He also had an orchard of wild fig trees. This was during a time when things were going really well in the northern parts of Israel. The people were very wealthy and prosperous, and it seemed as if the Israelites' relationship with God was strong and healthy. However, this was very far from the truth. Often when people become very rich and start living comfortable lives, they also start thinking that they do not need the Lord, and then they gradually drift away from him.

The Lord called Amos to be his prophet. Amos was just an ordinary farmer, but the Lord needed someone to give his message to his people, who had become spiritually cold. Amos obeyed God's call and started to tell the Israelites about God's will for his people. He told them that the Lord wanted them to return to him and that they should dedicate their spiritual and everyday lives to the Lord. The Lord also made many promises to his people through Amos. He said that if they lived according to his will he would give them abundant prosperity. He said that they would have even more than they already had. Just listen to what the Lord said: *"New wine will drip from the mountains and flow from all the hills"* (Amos 9:13).

The Lord still calls people to leave their everyday jobs and enter into his ministry. Many people decide to change their careers, and they dedicate their lives to preaching the gospel. However, such a drastic change is not always necessary. Every Christian, regardless of where he works or what he does for a living, is supposed to preach the Lord's message. Even if you are still in school preparing yourself for the job you want to do when you grow up, you are already an instrument of God. Let him use you today.

W.W.J.

Jesus wants everybody – not just ministers and preachers – to be his witnesses.

July 23

Jonah

But Jonah ran away from the LORD and headed for Tarshish. (Jonah 1:3)

Jonah was another person called by the Lord to be a prophet. The Lord told Jonah to go to Nineveh, but Jonah did not want to go. He was stubborn and decided that he would run away from God. Nineveh was a very large city and was the capital of Assyria. Jonah did not like the people who lived in Assyria because they were cruel and evil, and they were not of his nation and people. He had no interest whatsoever in the Lord saving them, but the Lord did.

Quite often, we find that there are certain people we do not like. We may find their language and culture strange. However, we have to remember that the Lord's view of people is very different from ours. The Lord does not find anyone's language or culture strange. He is interested in all people and loves every single person on the planet. That is why he has compassion upon all people, including those in Nineveh.

Jonah was very disgruntled because God had decided to have mercy upon the people of Nineveh. That is why he did not want to be God's messenger. We all know the story of Jonah being swallowed by the big fish. Jonah first had to learn his lesson before he was willing to obey God's instructions to go to Nineveh. When he arrived there, he told the people that Nineveh would be destroyed in forty days' time if they did not repent of their sins and turn to the Lord. When the people heard this, they repented and believed in God. They dedicated their lives to the Lord. Even the king of Nineveh confessed and apologized for the sins of his people. He made a law that all the people had to call on God, give up their evil ways, and repent. When the Lord saw all this, he had compassion on them and decided not to destroy the city.

Jonah wasn't very happy with this, but God had accomplished his goal. Even though there are people we don't like, we should still love them and tell them about the Lord. God loves all people.

W.W.J.

Jesus often spoke to Samaritans, despite the fact that the Jews did not like the Samaritans.

July 24

Jonah

Fish-food

Then they took Jonah and threw him overboard. (Jonah 1:15)

In the Bible, we read the story of a man named Jonah. The Lord visited Jonah and spoke to him because he had a job for Jonah to do.

The Lord asked Jonah to go to the big city of Nineveh and tell the inhabitants of the city about God. Jonah did not feel like following the Lord's instructions, and he ran away from the Lord. One can hardly believe that Jonah was that foolish. After all, we know that there is no person on earth who can run away from God or hide from him. The Lord is everywhere and he knows everything!

Jonah boarded a ship on its way to Tarshish. It wasn't long before a terrible storm came up. The storm was so severe that it threatened to sink the ship. Jonah knew very well that it was because of him that the Lord sent the storm. He told the sailors that if they threw him overboard, the sea would grow calm once again. When Jonah was thrown into the water, a big fish came and swallowed him. While he was sitting inside the fish, Jonah prayed to God. He told God that he was sorry for being disobedient and running away. He asked the Lord to save him, and the Lord did. Then the Lord once again told Jonah to go to Nineveh. This time, Jonah was probably too afraid to refuse, and he went to Nineveh.

We should listen carefully when the Lord asks us to do his will. Remember that his will is always what is best for us. It might not seem like it initially, but when we do as he instructs us, we will realize that we are happiest when we are obedient. Let us take the lesson that Jonah learned to heart. If we are stubborn and insist on doing things our way, we are sure to run into trouble.

W.W.J.

Jesus said that if we love him, we will also obey his commandments and do what he asks of us.

Micah

He Saw a Child

"But ... out of you will come for me one who will be ruler over Israel." (Micah 5:2)

The Bible often tells us about occasions when God asked his prophets to give messages to his people. At the same time, and often without knowing it, the prophets said something that turned out to be a prophecy of something that would happen in the future. In this passage, we read about one such prophet, Micah, who prophesied about Bethlehem, the small town where Jesus would be born.

Micah knew that Bethlehem was a very small and almost insignificant town. Nevertheless, he prophesied that from this small town someone important would come to rule over Israel. This One would stand before the nation and lead the people by the power that the Lord would give to him. He would ensure that peace would reign all over the world.

Bethlehem was the town of Jesus' birth. Actually, Jesus should not even have been born there, because his parents were from Nazareth. But because Joseph was of the house and line of David, they had to go to Bethlehem for a census. While they were staying in Bethlehem, Jesus was born. And in this way Micah's prophecy was fulfilled. Jesus, the Prince of Peace, was born.

The Old Testament contains many prophecies and many of these prophecies have been fulfilled. This fact helps to strengthen our faith in the truth of God's Word and in his promises for the future.

W.W.J.

Everything that Jesus taught his disciples about his kingdom, his life, his death and his resurrection was fulfilled.

July 26

Micah

How Deep is Your Love?

You will tread our sins underfoot and hurl all our iniquities into the depths of the sea. (Micah 7:19)

One of the most wonderful things that the Bible teaches us is that God is always willing to forgive people's sins. It would have been very easy for the Lord to push us away from him because we are sinners who repeatedly fail to do his will. However, he never pushes us away from him. The Lord wants to forgive us our sins. That is why he went so far as to send his Son to earth. Jesus came to earth to pay the debt of our sins.

Micah was a prophet of the Lord. The Lord instructed him to tell the Israelites that he truly wanted to forgive them for their sins. Micah was so excited about this that he said, *"Who is a God like you, who pardons sin ...? You do not stay angry forever but delight to show mercy"* (Micah 7:18).

Micah then continues to say that when God forgives us our sins, it is as if he takes all our sins and casts them into the depths of the ocean. His love is as deep as the ocean. He takes our sins out to sea and throws them into the water where they sink to the floor of the ocean. That means that no one can see our sins or bring them back up to the surface again. The Lord regards our sins as gone and buried. He no longer thinks about our sins, and he wants us also to stop thinking about our past sins as well.

Have you confessed your sins to the Lord yet? If you have, you must also accept that God loves you so much that he has taken all your sins away from you. It is as if he threw them into the deepest ocean. He no longer thinks about your sins, and neither should you.

W.W.J.

Jesus told the adulterous woman that he did not judge or condemn her, but that she should stop committing sin. (John 8:11)

Habakkuk

Just Look at This Mess!

Why do you make me look at injustice? Why do you tolerate wrong?
(Habakkuk 1:3)

Habakkuk was another prophet. Habakkuk spent nights lying awake and worrying about all the things that were happening around him. He was so concerned that he decided to speak to the Lord about it all. So what were the things that worried him?

Habakkuk wanted to know why the Lord didn't do something about all the terrible acts of violence that took place every day. He asked the Lord why there had to be so much injustice and so much suffering in the world. Wherever he turned, he could see only destruction, oppression, violence, strife, and conflict. People broke the law without thinking twice about it, and then they were not even prosecuted and punished for their crimes. It was as if there was no longer any justice in the world. It seemed as if the evil people had gained the upper hand over the good people, and therefore they did just as they pleased.

When we look around us today, as Habakkuk did so long ago, we have reason to be as unhappy as he was. Every single day, we hear about violence, injustice, murder, strife, and conflict. There are people who steal others' possessions and who think nothing of killing people in order to do so. How can God allow such terrible things to happen? Why doesn't he do something about it? These are the questions that Habakkuk asked and that we still ask today.

Perhaps the Lord wants to use us to improve the situation. He is always looking for instruments who are willing to carry his Word into the world and to administer his justice wherever they go. There is one thing of which we can be certain: we are not yet in heaven. This means that we will encounter many problems every single day. All we can really do is to stay in step with the Lord as we journey with him through life.

W.W.J.

Jesus was also moved by all the injustice that he saw around him.

Habakkuk

HE STOOD WATCH AND WAITED

I will stand at my watch and station myself on the ramparts; I will look to see what he will say to me. (Habakkuk 2:1)

Habakkuk was struggling with many difficult questions. Everywhere he turned, he saw only violence, injustice, and conflict. He wanted answers to his questions and decided to turn to God for answers. That is why he made time to be still and quiet and to ask the Lord about his opinion on everything.

This is exactly what you and I should do. We should consult with God and ask him what he thinks about all the injustice, the violence, the suffering, and the lawlessness that surround us. Let us learn a lesson from Habakkuk. He went and stood on a watchtower and waited for the Lord. This means that he went somewhere secluded to talk to the Lord. He asked the Lord to answer all his questions about the violence that he saw around him. We don't really have to go stand on a watchtower, but we should find a quiet place where we can talk to the Lord about our biggest questions and concerns. What does God think about all these things? What is his will regarding these matters? The Lord very much wants for us to talk to him about our problems. The Bible tells us what happened after Habakkuk had spoken to God, *"Then the LORD replied ..."* (Habakkuk 2:2). Yes, the Lord answered Habakkuk and he suddenly understood many things. We will also receive answers to our questions if we are willing to ask the Lord's opinion and wait patiently for his answer.

W. W. J.

The disciples often asked Jesus questions, and he always answered them.

July 29

Zephaniah

The Lord is Crazy about You

"The Lord your God is with you. ... He will take great delight in you, ... he will rejoice over you with singing." (Zephaniah 3:17)

There once was a man named Zephaniah. He was also one of the Lord's prophets. He said that God was going to make an end to everything on earth. Then a new day would dawn and people would be able to live with God eternally. Those who trust in the name of the Lord would one day live in the new Jerusalem.

Zephaniah writes that the Israelites ought to rejoice and be happy. They should be happy because the Lord is planning on giving them a bright new future. They would no longer have to fear any disaster. They would no longer have to be discouraged and dejected. They could simply rest assured that the Lord their God was with them and that he would take great delight in them. God loves all his children and wants to quiet them with his love.

We should never doubt that God loves his children. His heart brims over with joy whenever he thinks of us. The Bible wants to tell us that God is absolutely crazy about you and me. No wonder he gave his Son to help us. It just goes to show how much he really loves us.

Never think that you are not good enough for the Lord. Remember that he is absolutely crazy about you.

W.W.J.

Jesus always showed people that he did not want to push them aside. Instead, he wanted to embrace them with his love.

Zechariah

HE SAW A DIRTY PRIEST

Now Joshua was dressed in filthy clothes ... (Zechariah 3:3)

The Lord gave a vision to Zechariah. This means that Zechariah saw and experienced something in his mind. It was almost like dreaming. However, the vision that the Lord brought before Zechariah's eyes was very unpleasant. The Lord showed Zechariah the sins of his people. Everyone was committing sin, even the priests.

In his vision, Zechariah saw Joshua, the high priest, standing before the Lord. Satan was also there, accusing Joshua before God. But God rejected Satan's accusations. He told an angel to take off Joshua's filthy clothes (representing his sinfulness) and to dress him in clean, white clothes. Then the Lord promised the priest that if he did the will of the Lord, he would have a prosperous life and a good relationship with the Lord.

Ordinary people aren't the only ones who commit sin. Ministers and spiritual leaders also sometimes have sin in their lives. That is why we should pray for them. However, the most important thing is to make sure that we aren't the ones standing before the Lord in our filthy clothes. Let's ask him right now to forgive us for our wrongdoing and to wash us clean from all our sins.

W. W. J.

Jesus died on the cross so that we could receive the new, clean clothes of forgiveness and redemption.

Zechariah

SMALL THINGS

"Who despises the day of small things?" (Zechariah 4:10)

The Lord put it into the heart of Zerubbabel to rebuild the temple after the Israelites had been released from captivity in Babylon. Zechariah saw this plan of God in a dream or vision. An angel appeared to Zechariah and gave him a message to pass on to Zerubbabel.

This message to Zerubbabel was that he would not be able to rebuild the temple in his own strength and power alone. He would only be able to complete this task by drawing on the strength of the Holy Spirit. Zerubbabel felt that the rebuilding of the temple was like a great mountain that he had to climb and conquer. The Lord assured Zerubbabel that this great mountain would become level ground before him if he would allow the Lord to help him. It would still be Zerubbabel's hands and the hands of his workers that did the actual building, but in reality it would be the Holy Spirit guiding them and giving them the strength to complete the job. And then the Lord said a very important thing through Zechariah: *"Do not despise the day of small things."* In other words, the Lord wanted to tell Zerubbabel that he should start with the small things. God would bless each of these small efforts and ultimately the big project would be completed successfully.

We are often reluctant to start with something small. We feel that our efforts are too insignificant and could never lead to something bigger. However, the Bible teaches us that we should start by using all of the small things that we have, and eventually they will grow into great accomplishments.

W.W.J.

When the boy gave Jesus two fish and five loaves of bread everybody thought that it was far too little to make any difference. However, Jesus increased this little bit of food into a feast for a multitude.

Malachi

Is Divorce Okay?

"I hate divorce," says the LORD God. (Malachi 2:16)

The prophet Malachi often spoke about the sins that the Israelites were committing. In this passage, he mentions a whole list of things that are wrong and sinful. The people were doing just as they pleased and refused to follow the Lord's instructions. As a result, they found themselves in severe spiritual trouble.

One of the things that Malachi mentions in this passage is that many men left their wives to be with other women. These men simply decided that they wanted a divorce. They were not being faithful to their marriage vows. The Lord used Malachi to tell the Israelites that they should repent of their sins and should be faithful to their spouses. Malachi says that the Lord hates divorce.

If a man and a woman have promised each other before God that they will always stay together and help each other as long as they live here on earth, God expects them to keep their promise. There is no perfect marriage on this earth because there are no perfect people on earth. We all have our faults. However, we should love each other and be willing to live together despite our faults and weaknesses. Once you have said yes to sharing the rest of your life with someone, you should keep your word. This is what the Lord says.

Perhaps people are too quick to divorce. Today there are many people who have gone through a divorce. It might even be that your parents are divorced. Divorce is not so terrible a sin that God will not forgive it, but he much prefers to help people be happy together.

Even though you are still young, you should already start praying that the Lord will give you the right marriage partner. Also pray that the Lord will make you willing to live with your marriage partner for the rest of your life.

W.W.J.

Jesus also taught us that we should not divorce our marriage partners, but should work through problems together.

August 2

Malachi

ONE TENTH OF YOUR POSSESSIONS

"Bring the whole tithe into the storehouse." (Malachi 3:10)

The Lord gives us many guidelines. A guideline is something that tells us what we ought to do. The Lord gives us such guidelines and expects us to follow them because he knows what is best for us.

One of the guidelines that the Lord gives us in his Word is that we should voluntarily and lovingly give a portion of everything we own to him. This is called a tithe. Not that the Lord needs it! The Lord is not poor, and we don't have to give him a portion of everything we own because he needs our money or possessions. After all, the entire earth belongs to him, including all its riches. So why would the Lord ask us to give a portion of our money or possessions to him?

God wants us to do this to show that we understand that everything we have comes from his hand and not from our own efforts. We give a portion of our money and possessions to him to show our gratitude and to acknowledge that everything we have comes from him. In this way, we are constantly reminded that our strength is in the Lord, not in ourselves. What we give also helps advance the Lord's work in the world.

The guideline that the Lord gives us says that we should give one tenth of our income to the Lord. When you receive your allowance from your parents, you should give a little portion, perhaps a tenth, for the work of the Lord. You can give your contribution to the church, or you can give it directly to someone who needs it. This will help you to remember that, in reality, everything you have belongs to the Lord – yourself included. That is why you should be willing to make a contribution to the advancement of the kingdom of God. Your hands should always be open and ready to bless others.

W.W.J.

When a woman gave the last money she had as a temple offering, Jesus noticed the sacrifice that she had made. He praised her for her willingness to give. (Mark 12:44)

August 3

Malachi

LEAP LIKE A CALF

"And you will go out and leap like calves released from the stall." (Malachi 4:2)

Malachi is the last book of the Old Testament. It was written by the prophet Malachi, a preacher in the time after the temple had been rebuilt. Malachi preaches about the sins of Israel, but he also says that the Lord wants to bestow his grace and mercy upon his people, and he wants to forgive them.

Malachi speaks about a very important day that would come sometime in the future. This is the day of God's judgment, or the day when his court will be in session to judge all people. On that day, all people will have to stand before the Lord and answer for everything that they have done here on earth. Malachi says, *"Surely the day is coming; it will burn like a furnace ..."* (Malachi 4:1).

Malachi didn't know about Jesus, but he knew that his people needed to be saved from God's judgment. Malachi's vision of joyous redemption was ultimately fulfilled in Jesus Christ. We know that people who have sinned against the Lord and have not received God's forgiveness through Jesus Christ will be like straw or chaff that will be burned to ashes in the furnace. However, those who have been redeemed by the Lord will see the sun of redemption and righteousness rise. They will be free and will jump with joy, like calves released from their stall. A calf that has been tied up in a stall is very happy when it is released into the open fields. To show its joy, it jumps up and down. Malachi uses this image to show us what it is like to be truly free once we have received God's forgiveness through Jesus Christ. I hope that you have just as much joy in your heart because you no longer have to fear the day of judgment. You have been redeemed by Jesus, your Savior!

W.W.J.

Jesus redeemed us so that our joy could be complete.

John the Baptist

WHAT A BULLDOZER!

In those days John the Baptist came, preaching in the Desert of Judea. (Matthew 3:1)

When Jesus was thirty years old, the time had come for him to start telling people about his kingdom and how he would have to die for humanity's burden of sin. It was during this time that God the Father began to use a very special man to prepare people for Jesus' work here on earth.

This man's name was John the Baptist. His appearance and his behavior were like that of an Old Testament prophet. He lived in the desert and his clothes were made of camel's hair. He wore a leather belt around his waist, and his food was locusts and wild honey. The words that he spoke came directly from God, and more and more people started listening to the words of John the Baptist. They came in great crowds from Jerusalem and from all over Judea to listen to what he was saying. John the Baptist's message was that they should confess their sins and allow themselves to be baptized. Many people heeded his advice.

In this way, John the Baptist prepared the way for the Lord, making the paths level and straight before him. This is how the Bible describes the work of John the Baptist. One could almost say that he was like a bulldozer. A bulldozer levels the ground and makes it even so that it is ready to build a road. Jesus followed in the footsteps of John the Baptist and also started preaching. By this time, people's hearts were ready to receive Jesus' message because John the Baptist had prepared them for it.

You and I should also be like John the Baptist. Our words and deeds should make it easier for people to believe in Jesus. We should prepare the path for him, so that he can use us to accomplish his goals with people's lives.

W.W.J.

Jesus lived such a good life that people who saw him wanted to know more about God.

August 5

Simon and Andrew

THE FIRST DISCIPLES

"Come, follow me," Jesus said. (Matthew 4:19)

When Jesus set out on his earthly ministry, he decided to ask a few people to live with him, travel with him, and learn from him – these were the twelve disciples. However, before he actually chose these twelve men, he first spoke to his Father about it at length. He wanted to be sure that he would choose the right people to be his disciples.

One day, Jesus was walking beside the Sea of Galilee. There he saw two brothers: Simon (also called Peter) and his brother Andrew. They were ordinary fishermen. Every morning, at the break of day, they would get up, prepare their nets, and then set out in their boats to catch fish. This is how they made a living. They sold the fish, and the next day they would do exactly the same thing all over again.

When Jesus saw these two men, he said to them, *"Come, follow me ... and I will make you fishers of men"* (Matthew 4:19). The Bible tells us that they immediately left their nets and followed Jesus. They probably knew in their hearts that they simply had to follow him and that this was God's will for their lives.

Today, the Lord still calls people to follow him and walk with him in the journey of faith. In this way, you and I can also become part of the team that works for his kingdom. Have you answered yes to his call to discipleship yet? Do it right now!

W.W.J.

Jesus invited many ordinary people to be his followers.

Mammon

MORE MONEY!

"You cannot serve both God and Money [Mammon]." (Matthew 6:24)

Jesus used a very strange word while talking to his followers. This word is "Mammon." It comes from the Aramaic language, which is the language that Jesus spoke. What does the word "Mammon" mean?

In Jesus' time, when people spoke of Mammon, everybody knew that they were referring to money. However, the word refers to more than just money or wealth. It actually refers to greed. When you are greedy, you are never satisfied with the money that you have and you always want more and more.

Jesus said that it is impossible to serve both God and Mammon, or Money. If you serve God with all your heart, money becomes less and less important to you. God is your source of money and wealth, and because you serve him, you also believe that he will provide for you. Consequently, you no longer feel the urge to devise your own little plans and schemes to make more money. You prefer to make plans to live closer to the Lord so that he can give you what you need as he sees fit. You cannot serve two masters. If you are greedy, money becomes the god in front of whom you kneel.

Let us put the Lord first and not money and possessions. Dedicate yourself to the matters of the Lord, rather than to just making money.

W.W.J.

Jesus was very angry when the merchants in the temple enriched themselves by exploiting religion. He chased them out of the temple. (John 2: 15-16)

The Centurion

FAITH IN JESUS' WORDS

The centurion replied, "But just say the word, and my servant will be healed." (Matthew 8:8)

During the time when Jesus was here on earth, there were many Roman soldiers and officers living in the area where Jesus lived. The country where Jesus lived was a province of the Roman Empire.

One day, a Roman officer (also called a centurion) came to Jesus. He needed Jesus' help. He told Jesus that one of his servants was lying at home, completely paralyzed and in terrible pain. Jesus replied that he would come and heal the servant. The centurion then said a very interesting thing.

The centurion was very humble and said that he was not worthy to have Jesus come under his roof. He said that Jesus merely needed to say the word and the servant would be healed. Because he was an officer in the Roman army, he knew that if he gave an instruction, his soldiers would immediately obey his command. Jesus Christ was the Lord, and therefore whatever he said would be done. Jesus was amazed at the centurion's faith, and said to him, *"Go! It will be done just as you believed it would"* (Matthew 8:13). At that exact moment, the servant was healed.

We should have just as much faith in Christ's words as the centurion did. Allow God to speak his words in your life today. Have faith in him and he will never disappoint you.

W.W.J.

When Jesus said that something would happen, it always did. He never lied about anything.

August 8

Peter's Mother-in-Law

JESUS HEALED HER

He touched her hand and the fever left her. (Matthew 8:15)

Jesus had no home of his own here on earth. He grew up in the home of Joseph and Mary of Nazareth, and he often visited or stayed at the homes of friends and disciples. After all, he wasn't here to stay, but was merely passing through on his way home to his Father. One day, Jesus and his disciples went to visit Peter's home. When he arrived, Jesus saw that Peter's mother-in-law was very ill and running a very high fever.

Jesus loved Peter dearly. He also loved Peter's mother-in-law. She probably had often prepared nice meals for him, or offered him something to drink, or made a bed for him to sleep in. Because he loved her, he touched her hand, and suddenly a miracle happened. The fever left her completely and she was well again. She felt so much better that she immediately got up and prepared some food for her guests.

Jesus performed many miracles. He touched ill people or spoke to them, and they were healed. Today we still believe that the Lord can heal people who are sick. That is why we often ask the Lord to heal people. We pray that the Lord will perform a miracle in the lives of people who are terribly ill. Despite this, not everyone is healed, just as in Jesus' time there were many sick people whom he did not heal. When it comes to important decisions about our lives, God knows best. The Lord performed many special miracles during the time that Jesus was here on earth. He did this because he wanted people to take notice of Jesus, to believe in him, and to understand why he had to die on the cross.

If you are sick, you should ask the Lord to heal you. However, God also uses the hands and the knowledge of human doctors to help you heal. The most important thing is always to trust in the Lord, even when you are ill.

W.W.J.

Jesus made God's miracles visible for people to see here on earth.

August 9

The Gadarenes

DEMON-POSSESSED

"If you drive us out, send us into the herd of pigs." (Matthew 8:31)

In Jesus' time, there were many people who were harassed by the devil or were actually demon-possessed. This means that the devil and his demons lived inside them and made life very difficult and painful for them. The demons sometimes threw these poor people on the ground, so that they injured themselves. Possessed people often ran around screaming and yelling all kinds of strange things. People who are demon-possessed are not a pretty sight.

When Jesus arrived in the region of the Gadarenes, two demon-possessed men came to him. They lived in the graveyards. They were very dangerous and violent; no one dared to come anywhere near them. Suddenly the demons inside them screamed that Jesus should not torment them. The demons knew that Jesus was the Son of God. They also knew that the Lord Jesus loved people and wanted to free them from the power of the devil. They knew that Jesus was going to drive them out of the men, and they begged him to send them into a nearby herd of pigs so that they would at least have a home to live in. Jesus then commanded the demons to go into the pigs. The herd of pigs immediately went crazy and rushed down a steep bank into the lake of Galilee, where they all drowned.

Jesus wanted to liberate people from the power of the devil. Even today, he wants to free us from the power of the devil so that we can serve the Lord wholeheartedly. Only the almighty name of the Lord has the power to save people.

W.W.J.

Jesus said that he came to earth to undo and destroy the evil works of the devil.

August 10

Matthew

THE BUSINESSMAN WHO TURNED TO JESUS

Jesus saw a man named Matthew sitting at the tax collector's booth. "Follow me," he told him. (Matthew 9:9)

In Jesus' time, tax collectors were very unpopular people. The tax collectors collected taxes from the people; they acted as agents for the Roman authorities. A certain amount of the money they collected had to be given to the Roman authorities, and the rest they could keep for themselves. This made it very easy for the tax collectors to exploit the Jewish people in order to enrich themselves, and they often demanded much more money from the people than they were supposed to.

The Jewish people regarded the tax collectors as traitors to their people, and the tax collectors were spurned and excluded from the social life of the other Jews. They did not want to eat with them or be seen with them.

It is therefore truly wonderful that Jesus asked a tax collector to be one of his closest disciples. This tax collector's name was Matthew. One day, while Matthew was sitting at his tax collector's booth, Jesus approached him and simply said, "Follow me." Matthew immediately left his tax-collecting business and followed Jesus. Then Jesus did another strange thing. He went with Matthew to his house and there they had dinner together. Many other tax collectors and sinners also joined Jesus and his disciples there for a meal.

Jesus loved all people, and did not care who they were or what they did for a living. He simply wanted to help them. When the Pharisees complained about Jesus sitting down to eat with tax collectors and sinners, Jesus answered, *"It is not the healthy who need a doctor, but the sick"* (Matthew 9:12).

We also often think that we would rather not be seen with certain kinds of people. But when we do this we are not living according to Jesus' instructions. Jesus taught us to love everyone and to be friends with all people so that we can tell them about Jesus.

W.W.J.

Jesus said that he did not come to call people who think they are righteous. Instead, he came to call sinners.

August 11

Jairus's Daughter

Jesus Restored Her to Life

"My daughter has just died." (Matthew 9:18)

Jairus, one of the important rulers of the synagogue, came and kneeled before Jesus. He probably would never even have thought of doing such a thing, but because something terrible had happened in his family, he was so desperate that he sought Jesus' help.

Kneeling before the Lord, Jairus said that his daughter had just died. Can you imagine the grief, sorrow, and desperation that this man must have felt? His beloved daughter was dead.

The man then asked Jesus to come and lay his hands on the little girl so that she could be restored to life. In his desperation, this man called to Jesus to help him, fully believing that Jesus could perform a miracle. Jesus and his disciples went with the man to his house.

On their way, they encountered a woman who had suffered from bleeding for twelve years. She was also desperate to be healed, and when Jesus passed by her, she quickly and furtively touched the edge of his cloak. She believed that if she could only touch him, she would be healed. Jesus turned around, saw the woman, and told her that her faith had healed her. From that moment on, the woman was completely healed.

When Jesus arrived at Jairus's house, there were many people weeping and wailing to show their sorrow and grief over the little girl's death. Jesus took the girl's hand and she was immediately restored to life. The people couldn't believe their eyes. Everyone was talking about this miracle.

I don't know what your needs for this day are, but tell Jesus about them and trust that he will help you. Who knows, perhaps a miracle will take place in your life.

W.W.J.

Jesus never turned away anyone who came to him for help. He always ministered to people who were in distress.

August 12

John the Baptist

A Frank Question

"Are you the one who was to come, or should we expect someone else?" (Matthew 11:3)

The Bible tells us that John prepared the way for Jesus; people were ready to listen to Jesus when he told them about his kingdom. John the Baptist was a very brave, bold, and honest man. He was not afraid to admonish the Pharisees, King Herod, and other people in important positions whenever they did something wrong. We would be quite justified in saying that John the Baptist was a spiritual giant.

However, even spiritual giants or heroes of faith sometimes experience doubt. When John the Baptist was imprisoned, he probably had quite a bit of time to think about whether everything he had done was really worthwhile. While he was in prison, John heard about everything that Christ was doing, and he sent some of his followers to Jesus with a message. John wanted to know whether Christ was the One that they had been expecting for so long, or whether they should be waiting for someone else.

This was the same man who once said that he was not worthy to tie Jesus' sandals! And yet he succumbed to doubt. What if Jesus wasn't the Messiah? What if he was just an ordinary man? Jesus then sent an answer back to John, saying that the blind received sight, the lame walked, and those who had leprosy were cured. Jesus was trying to tell John that he should look and see for himself the miracles that Jesus was performing. After all, an ordinary human being could not perform such miracles, and all of his miracles were fulfilling Old Testament prophecies. And then Jesus said, *"Blessed is the man who does not fall away on account of me"* (Matthew 11:6).

Sometimes the devil causes us to doubt the Lord. When this happens, turn to the Bible. Read about his miracles. Talk to people whose lives he has changed. In doing so, your faith will be fully restored. You should never lose your faith in Jesus.

W.W.J.

The Word tells us that through faith we will conquer this world, and therefore we must have faith to the end.

August 13

Korazin and Bethsaida

CITIES REFUSING TO BELIEVE

Then Jesus began to denounce the cities in which most of his miracles had been performed. (Matthew 11:20)

Jesus performed most of his miracles in two towns: Korazin and Bethsaida. The people of these towns saw many strange and wonderful things happen right before their very eyes. People who were ill were healed, the blind regained their sight, and the lame started to walk. Everywhere one turned, people were talking about these miracles. And yet many people still refused to believe in Jesus. They did not believe that he was the Son of God. They did not give their hearts to him and did not become his followers. They made up all kinds of excuses for not believing in him and said that he was nothing but an ordinary man who had been raised in a small town nearby.

Jesus denounced the people of these cities for not believing in him. And then he said a terrible thing, *"But I tell you that it will be more bearable for Sodom on the day of judgment than for you"* (Matthew 11:24). Because the people of these two towns refused to believe in Jesus, they would endure terrible suffering on the day of God's judgment.

Let us not be like the inhabitants of these two towns. Let's have faith. Let's accept Jesus' words as they are given to us in the Bible. Let's take note of his work in other people's lives and let's praise and worship him for his wonderful deeds. Don't be a skeptic, and don't refuse to believe in Jesus.

W.W.J.

Jesus told us to believe in God and to believe in him.

The Man with the Deformed Hand

The Law of Moses or the Law of Love?

"Is it lawful to heal on the Sabbath?" (Matthew 12:10)

Jesus often ran into trouble with the spiritual leaders of his time. They wanted people to live strictly according to the Law of Moses. However, Jesus came to teach people a new law, and his life exemplified this new law. This new law was the law of love, the law of caring.

There was a man in the synagogue who had a deformed hand. The Pharisees pointed out this man to Jesus and asked Jesus whether it would be right to heal the man on the Sabbath or not. They wanted to trick Jesus. The Law of Moses stated that one was not allowed to do any work on the Sabbath, and the Pharisees thought that this should include healing someone. Jesus responded to the Pharisees' question in an interesting way.

He said that when a farmer has a sheep that falls into a pit on the Sabbath, he would undoubtedly rescue the sheep from the pit. Why? Because the sheep is in distress. And then Jesus said: *"How much more valuable is a man than a sheep!"* (Matthew 12:12). To prove his point, Jesus told the man with the deformed hand to put out his hand so that it might be healed.

The Lord never regarded a law as more important than a human being. Today, there are still many people who are very pious and devout when it comes to keeping all kinds of religious rules and regulations, but they don't really love people. Being a Christian is not about rules and laws and regulations. Being a Christian is all about loving God and loving people. We should love God wholeheartedly, and we should also love all people. As long as we follow this guideline, we will never be in the wrong.

W.W.J.

Jesus always regarded people as more important than things or laws.

August 15

The Parable of the Sower

WHEN DOES THE WORD PRODUCE FRUIT?

"But the one who received the seed that fell on good soil is the man who hears the word and understands it." (Matthew 13:23)

Jesus once told a story about a farmer who went out to sow his seed. In those days, a farmer who was sowing would put his hand into the seed bag, take a handful of seed, and scatter them across the ground. In the story that Jesus told, the farmer was scattering his seed, and some fell along the path, where the soil was hard, and the birds came and ate it. Some of the seeds fell on rocky places, where there wasn't much soil. These seeds sprang up quickly because the soil was so shallow. But once the sun started to warm the earth, the little plants withered because their roots were too weak. Some seeds also fell among the thorny weeds, which choked the little plants to death. Fortunately, there were also some seeds that fell on good soil, and produced a good crop.

What did this story mean? Jesus explained it as follows. The seeds that were eaten by the birds represent those people who hear the word of the Lord, but then the evil one comes and takes the word away from them. The seeds that fell on the rocky places represent those people who hear the word and rejoice in it, but who fail to live according to the Lord's words. Consequently, the word does not really take root in their lives. The seeds that fell among the thorny weeds represent those people who hear the word, but who are so worried about all of life's little concerns and are so desperate to become rich and wealthy that the word suffocates and does not yield fruit. The seeds that were sown in good soil represent those who hear the word, understand it, and live according to it.

God uses many different ways to sow his seed in people's lives. I hope that you are like good soil. I hope that you hear, understand, and live according to God's words – and that your life produces much fruit as a result.

W.W.J.

Jesus said that everyone who has ears should listen to what the Holy Spirit has to say.

August 16

The Enemy

SECRETLY SOWING WEEDS

"'An enemy did this,' he replied." (Matthew 13:28)

Jesus told another story, this time about a very devious enemy. This enemy did his utmost to thwart and undermine the hard work of a farmer who was busy sowing seed in his field. The man sowed good, healthy seed in his field, but one night, while everybody was asleep, his enemy came and secretly sowed weeds among the wheat.

When the young shoots of wheat started appearing, the farmer was very upset to see weeds appearing alongside the wheat. The farmer's workers then asked him why there were weeds among the wheat. Didn't he sow good seed in his fields? Where did the weeds come from? The farmer replied that it was most certainly the work of an enemy.

The workers asked the farmer if he wanted them to pull out the weeds. The farmer replied that they should not pull out the weeds because, in doing so, they would probably pull up the young shoots of wheat as well. He told them to leave the weeds and the wheat to grow together until the time came to bring in the harvest. Only at that time would he separate the weeds from the wheat.

This parable is actually about good and bad people. God's good seeds grow in people's hearts and produce good, healthy wheat. However, the devil also sows his seeds of evil and wickedness in other people's hearts. Consequently, these people do bad things, and become more like weeds. It is difficult for us, living here on earth, to know which people are wheat and which are weeds. We should therefore not simply start accusing people and pushing them away when we suspect them of carrying the devil's seeds in their hearts. The Lord will destroy these people on the day of judgment. All you need to do is to get rid of all the weeds that you can see in your own life.

W.W.J.

Jesus said that people are sometimes like whitewashed tombs: nice, clean, and attractive from the outside, but filled with corruption and wickedness on the inside. (Matthew 23:27)

August 17

The Jeweler

SEEKING PRECIOUS PEARLS

"Again, the kingdom of heaven is like a merchant looking for fine pearls."
(Matthew 13:45)

Another one of the stories that Jesus told was about a jeweler, or merchant, who was looking for the finest pearls. You have probably seen a pearl necklace. Pearls are very precious jewels and people are willing to pay a great deal of money to possess some of these fine jewels.

The jeweler in Jesus' story sought to find the very finest pearl that was available, and one day he actually found it. I'm sure that he was very happy and excited finally to have found this pearl. Because he was an expert on pearls, the man knew that it was very, very valuable. And because he so much wanted to own this pearl, he went and sold everything he had: his house and all his possessions so that he could raise the money to buy it. After he bought the pearl, he knew he was a richer man than he had ever been before.

The kingdom of the Lord is based on exactly the same principle. When you receive Jesus and his kingdom, you are receiving the most valuable thing in the entire world. No amount of money can buy what Jesus gives us: forgiveness, redemption, and eternal life. Giving up everything that you have in return for this wonderful gift will make you richer by far. Have you welcomed Jesus and his kingdom into your heart? If you have, you are very wealthy indeed!

W.W.J.

Without Jesus in our lives, we are spiritually poor.

Fishermen

CATCH THE FISH!

"The kingdom of heaven is like a net that was let down into the lake and caught all kinds of fish." (Matthew 13:47)

Jesus liked telling stories that had a deeper meaning. Once he told a story about fishermen. Jesus really loved fishermen, and the first people he called to be his disciples were fishermen, like Simon and Andrew. Jesus was very familiar with the life of a fisherman, and he probably spent many days sitting on the shore of the Sea of Galilee, watching the fishermen out in their boats.

Fishermen usually take a net and then let it down into the sea. After a while, they pull the net out of the water, and then they can see how much fish they have caught. They usually sort the fish, and put all the fish that are good enough to sell into baskets. The small and useless fish are usually thrown back into the sea.

In this story, Jesus tells us that the day of judgment will be exactly like this. All people will be gathered together, just as fish are pulled out of the water in a net. Then the angels will go out and separate the good people from the bad.

Are you a good fish? Have you been washed clean? Have all your sins been removed? Have you accepted Jesus' forgiveness? If so, you need not fear the day of judgment.

W.W.J.

Jesus told his disciples that we would all one day have to stand before God's throne. He will then separate the good people from the bad.

August 19

The Townspeople Who Did Not Honor Jesus

HE IS JUST JOSEPH'S SON!

And they took offense at him. (Matthew 13:57)

When Jesus lived here on earth, his hometown was the small village of Nazareth. He was raised as the son of a carpenter. His earthly father, Joseph, made a living from working with wood, and Jesus worked as a carpenter until he was about thirty years old. Then Jesus started to preach.

One day, Jesus was in the synagogue, or church, in Nazareth. He was busy teaching people about God, and they were amazed at his wisdom. They asked one another where he could possibly have gained his wisdom, knowledge, and miraculous powers. Then they said to one another that he was the carpenter Joseph's son. They knew that his mother, brothers, and sisters lived in Nazareth. Because they knew him and his family, they refused to accept him as an extraordinary person. The Bible says that they took offense at him. They said that they grew up with him and played with him. How could he then be the Son of God?

A prophet is seldom honored in his hometown or among his own people. Perhaps your family also doesn't want to accept or understand that you love Jesus. If so, just remember that Jesus was also scorned by his own people.

W.W.J.

Jesus wasn't always popular among all people. At first, even some of his family members did not believe in him.

John the Baptist

A Prophet of God Murdered

"Give me here on a platter the head of John the Baptist." (Matthew 14:8)

Just before Jesus began his ministry here on earth, John the Baptist started preparing the way for him. John the Baptist told people that they should repent of their sins, ask for forgiveness, and devote their lives to God. He was also not afraid to tell people when they did something wrong. He was even brave enough to challenge King Herod about all the wrongdoing in his life.

Herod was in love with his brother's wife, Herodias, and had taken her from his brother and was living with her. John told Herod that it had been wrong to take Herodias as his wife. Herod wanted to kill John for saying this, but he was afraid of how the people would react, because they regarded John as a prophet.

When Herod's birthday came around, he held a big party. The daughter of Herodias danced for all the guests. Herod was so pleased with her beautiful dancing that he swore to give her anything she asked for. Her mother, Herodias, then told her to ask for the head of John the Baptist. Herodias wanted to see John the Baptist dead because she hated him. The devil was working in her heart and prompted her to instruct her daughter to ask for the head of John the Baptist.

This is how it came about that John was beheaded in prison. When Jesus heard what had happened, he was very sorrowful. He knew that a prophet of the Lord had been killed. It must have been a terrible time for him, and yet he continued his task here so that you and I could ultimately receive God's forgiveness for our sins.

Let's thank the Lord for being willing to suffer for our sakes. And even when we are misunderstood or when we have to suffer for the sake of his name, we should not become discouraged.

W.W.J.

Jesus carried the cross on which he would be crucified all the way to Golgotha so that you and I could be redeemed.

August 21

Peter

He Walked on Water

Immediately Jesus reached out his hand and caught him. (Matthew 14:31)

One day, when Jesus had finished teaching the people, he went up into the mountains to pray. He stayed there until nightfall.

He told his disciples to take a boat and go on ahead of him to the other side of the lake. He would meet them there. At daybreak, while the disciples were trying to keep the boat from sinking under heavy waves, they suddenly saw someone walking toward them on the water. They were shocked and scared because, after all, this man was walking on water! They had never seen anything like it. They were very frightened and thought that it could only be a ghost that was walking toward them. They were so terrified that they cried out in fear.

Then Jesus spoke to them. He told them to take courage and not to be afraid, because it was he who was walking toward them. Peter called out to him, saying that if it really was Jesus walking on the water, he should prove it by giving Peter the power to also walk on the water. So Jesus invited Peter to go ahead and walk on the water. What a miracle! But when Peter came closer to Jesus, he suddenly realized just how strong the wind was, and he became afraid. Immediately he started sinking. He called to Jesus to save him, and Jesus reached out his hand and caught Peter. Then Jesus said to Peter, *"You of little faith ... why did you doubt?"* (Matthew 14:31).

When Peter had faith, a miracle happened and he was able to walk on the water. When we are certain that God has spoken to us, we should not allow doubt to set in, as Peter did. Remember, you are not walking on water, but on the words of God. When he says that we can do something, we must have faith that it is possible.

W.W.J.

Jesus said that if we had faith the size of a tiny little mustard seed, we would be able to tell a mountain to move, and it would happen.

Jesus

A Clean Heart Produces Beautiful Things

"What goes into a man's mouth does not make him 'unclean.'" (Matthew 15:11)

When you eat something that is harmful, you ingest it by putting it in your mouth and swallowing it, and then it usually makes your entire body feel ill. However, Jesus says that this is not how it works with sin. With sin, he says, it is exactly the other way around. It is not what goes into us that makes us unclean and sinful. The things that make us sinful and unclean are already inside us, and from there they spread into the outside world. You see, without Jesus, our hearts are so dirty and sinful that we are completely unable to do anything good. This means that we cannot do good deeds or think good thoughts because our hearts are so sinful and wicked inside us. Our sinful hearts thus cause us to do things that are wrong. Ultimately, therefore, it is not things from outside that make us do wrong things, but our hearts inside us that are filled with wickedness. Before we can fix our behavior we first have to fix our hearts.

Jesus says, *"... but what comes out of his mouth, that is what makes him 'unclean'"* (Matthew 15:11). Jesus wants to clean our hearts. The heart is the source of all life and from it springs everything we do. If our hearts are clean, we will be able to do and say only good things. Give your heart to the Lord today. He will wash your heart clean because of the sacrifice that Jesus made on the cross.

W.W.J.

Jesus is like a wonderful Surgeon who removes your sick, dirty heart and replaces it with a new, clean heart.

August 23

The Canaanite Woman

CRUMBS FROM JESUS' TABLE

"I was sent only to the lost sheep of Israel." (Matthew 15:24)

In Jesus' time, Jews tried to have as little contact as possible with Samaritans or other non-Jewish people. Jesus' calling, given to him by his Father, was to preach God's message about his kingdom to the Jewish people. This he did just about everywhere: in Jerusalem, in Galilee, and in all the surrounding regions. However, every now and then, he would also speak to people of other nationalities.

One day, Jesus was in the vicinity of Sidon. A Canaanite woman who lived in that area came to him and begged him to have mercy on her and to help her. Her daughter was suffering terribly from demon-possession. At first, Jesus did not answer her, and his disciples asked him to please send her away. Jesus then told the woman that he only worked among the Israelite people. However, the woman continued begging and pleading with Jesus. She kneeled before him and pleaded with him to help her. Jesus replied that he could not possibly take the children's bread and toss it to their dogs. He used this image to say that his work was like bread that he had to share among the Israelites. The woman then came up with a clever answer, and said that the dogs at least got to eat some of the crumbs that fell from their master's table. Jesus was amazed by her faith and told her that her request would be granted. At that exact moment, her daughter was healed.

The reason for this was simply the fact that the woman continued to have faith that Jesus would help her. We too should continually pray to the Lord, asking and pleading for his help. Doing this is the best way of showing him that we truly have faith in him.

W.W.J.

Jesus told a parable about a man who continually knocked on his neighbor's door asking for bread. Eventually, the neighbor got up and gave the man some bread. (Luke 11:5-8)

Peter

A ROCK FOR GOD'S CHURCH

"... and on this rock I will build my church." (Matthew 16:18)

One day, Jesus asked his disciples a question. He wanted to know who people were saying he was. After the disciples had thought his question over, they answered that some people said that he was John the Baptist, others said that he was Elijah, and yet others said that he was Jeremiah or one of the prophets. Then Jesus asked them who they thought he was.

After a while, Simon Peter answered him, *"You are the Christ, the Son of the living God"* (Matthew 16:16). Jesus was pleased with Peter's answer, and he said that Peter was truly blessed for believing that. Jesus said that Simon Peter was a very blessed man for knowing this, because that knowledge was not revealed to him by man, but by the Father in heaven. It is impossible to realize that Jesus is the Son of God and to believe in him, unless the Lord himself has worked that faith in your heart. And this is precisely what happened to Peter.

Peter's words of faith would become the foundation of Jesus' church. Every time someone acknowledges the truth of Simon Peter's words, he is laying the foundation for God's kingdom.

Do you believe that Jesus is truly the Son of God? Do you believe that he is your Savior? If you do, you are part of the church of Jesus Christ, which he is busy building.

W.W.J.

When Jesus lived here on earth, many people doubted whether he was truly the Son of God. However, others knew and believed that he was.

Peter

FROM ROCK TO SATAN

"Get behind me, Satan! You are a stumbling block to me." (Matthew 16:23)

When Jesus asked his disciples who he was, Simon Peter gave the right answer. He said that Jesus was the Son of the living God. The name "Peter" actually means "rock," and Jesus said that Peter's words were like a rock upon which one could build a house. This house was the kingdom of God.

Right after Peter uttered these words of faith, Jesus said that he would have to suffer and be killed so that people's sins could be forgiven. Peter was very upset, and said, *"Never, Lord! ... This shall never happen to you!"* (Matthew 16:22). Jesus then scolded Peter and told him that he was not allowed to speak such words. Just moments before, Peter had spoken words of faith, and now he was uttering the words of a man who did not understand the meaning of Jesus' work here on earth. Jesus admonished Peter and said that Peter should get out of his way because he was nothing but a stumbling block to him. Peter was thinking of what he and the other disciples wanted and did not consider what God wanted.

One moment he spoke words of faith, and the next his words were like stumbling blocks. The one moment Peter was the rock upon which the church would be built, and the next Jesus called him Satan.

You and I should not speak words of faith and words of disbelief from the same mouth. We should not speak about faith while at the same time saying things that indicate our unwillingness to have faith. Let's learn this lesson from Peter.

W.W.J.

Jesus is pleased when we speak words of faith, and consider what God wants.

August 26

Peter

His face shone like the sun, and his clothes became as white as the light.
(Matthew 17:2)

One day, Jesus took Peter, James, and John with him to a high mountain, where they were all alone. While they were standing on the mountain, Jesus' face began to shine like the sun and his clothes became as white as the light. Something wonderful was happening to him. Jesus was being filled with glory. Suddenly, Moses and Elijah, who were long dead, appeared and started talking to Jesus. The disciples almost felt as if they were in heaven with Jesus.

Peter was completely bewildered, and he offered to build three shelters: one for Jesus, one for Moses, and one for Elijah. Clearly, he did not understand the purpose of this privilege to see Jesus' glory. While he was still speaking, a bright cloud enveloped them, and a voice said, *"This is my Son, whom I love; with him I am well pleased. Listen to him!"* (Matthew 17:5). It was almost as if God the Father wanted to put Peter in his place by telling him to be quiet and respectful and to simply listen to what would happen next.

Sometimes when the Lord shows his glory, strange and inexplicable things happen. When this happens we should not be too quick to find a handy explanation for events or to provide an earthly solution for the strange things we have seen. Instead, we should be still and listen to what God wants to say to us. When we read the Bible and pray and our hearts are filled with the glory of the Lord, we should keep quiet and listen.

W.W.J.

Jesus' kingdom is not of this world. We should ask God to show us how we can be part of his kingdom.

The Disciples

So Little Faith

Then the disciples came to Jesus in private and asked, "Why couldn't we drive it out?" (Matthew 17:19)

A man kneeled before Jesus and asked him to have mercy on his son who was mentally disturbed and suffered terribly. The son often had seizures that caused him to fall into the fire or the water. The man said that he had already brought his son to Jesus' disciples so that they could heal him, but they had been unsuccessful.

Jesus was very unhappy when he heard this. After all, he had taught his disciples everything about the strength and power of God. So why was their faith insufficient to heal this man's son? It was clear that the man's son was possessed by a demon.

Jesus rebuked the demon, and the demon left the boy. The boy was completely healed. Then the disciples asked Jesus why they had been unable to drive the demon out of the boy. Jesus' answer was this: *"Because you have so little faith"* (Matthew 17:20).

The Lord wants us, his children, to act in faith, never forgetting that we possess the skills and the wisdom that Jesus gave to us. We are Jesus' agents in this world, and he wants to use us. We should learn from Jesus so that we can be good instruments in his service.

W.W.J.

Jesus said that we, as his followers, would be able to do greater deeds than even he did because his Holy Spirit would be present in all believers all over the world. (John 14:12)

August 28

The Tax Collectors

Jesus Paid Tax, and We Should Too!

"Doesn't your teacher pay the temple tax?" (Matthew 17:24)

In Jesus' time, the temple officials had the duty of collecting a temple tax from people so that the temple could be kept in good repair. One day, a few of these tax collectors went to Peter and asked him whether Jesus actually paid the tax. They appeared to be irate, and they were convinced that Jesus would not be interested in paying a tax for the upkeep of the temple. But Peter answered that Jesus would, of course, pay the required temple tax.

Jesus then spoke to Peter about the temple tax. He tried to tell Peter that he, as the Son of God, was not really required to pay the tax. Despite this, he told Peter to go to the sea and throw a fishing line into the water. He was then to pull out the first fish that took the bait. Inside the mouth of the fish, he would find a silver coin. Peter was to take the coin and use it to pay the tax for both Jesus and himself.

Jesus did this so that people would not be able to point a finger at him and say that he did not want to pay his taxes. In the same way, you and I should comply with our country's laws and regulations. We too have to pay our taxes.

W.W.J.

Jesus said that we should pay the emperor what is due to the emperor – meaning we should give the government what we are required to give. (Mark 12:17)

The Children

WE SHOULD BE LIKE CHILDREN

"I tell you the truth, unless you change and become like little children, you will never enter the kingdom of heaven." (Matthew 18:3)

Jesus loved children very much. On one occasion, he laid his hands on a group of children and blessed them. He did this after their mothers brought them to him to be blessed so that the children would be happy, healthy, and prosperous.

At one time, the disciples asked Jesus who were the most important people in the kingdom of heaven. They were probably thinking of the likes of the great prophets. Perhaps they thought that the most important person in heaven would be Moses, or King David, or Abraham. Maybe they hoped they would be the most important – after all, they were Jesus' closest friends. Jesus' answer caught them completely by surprise.

Jesus said that he who humbles himself like a child is the most important in the kingdom of heaven. He continued by saying that if we did not become like little children, we would never be allowed to enter the kingdom of heaven.

Small children usually don't have an overly high opinion of themselves. They don't think that they are somehow more important or better than the other children. A very young child never looks down on others. Young children are usually still innocent, and they find it easy to have faith. That is why Jesus said that we should become like little children. Only with such humility will we be able to enter into his kingdom.

W.W.J.

The most important people in the kingdom of God are those who have the faith of a child.

Your Brother in Jesus

Talk to Him When He Makes You Angry

"If your brother sins against you, go and show him his fault." (Matthew 18:15)

Most of us have a very bad habit in common. Whenever we are angry with someone, we run to someone else and talk to that person about how we feel. We prefer to go to someone else and indignantly gossip and complain about the person who has angered us. However, the Bible tells us that this is the wrong way to handle our anger.

The Bible says that if someone sins against you, you should not talk to other people about the problem. Instead, you should speak to the person who committed the sin against you. You should take him aside and privately talk to him about what he has done to you. Perhaps he will listen to you, and then the problem will be solved with no fuss at all. If he doesn't want to listen, you can ask someone else to come with you and talk to that person a second time.

If he still does not want to listen, even when two or three people have spoken to him about the problem, you can even go so far as to tell the entire congregation about it. Then the congregation must decide what to do about the problem.

If we follow Jesus' advice in this regard, the conflict between people is sure to lessen. Talking about someone behind his back gives the devil a wonderful opportunity to get us into all kinds of mischief that can cause a great deal of unhappiness. Gossip spreads like a wildfire, and more often than not, gossip is made up of nothing but lies. Let us rather do as Jesus tells us. Speak first to the person who has sinned against you before you run off and talk to other people.

Is there someone that you need to have a talk with about things that make you unhappy? Do it with a loving heart and an open mind.

W.W.J.

The Bible tells us that Jesus always spoke to people if he was troubled by something that they did.

August 31

Jesus

TWO OR MORE GATHERED IN HIS NAME

"For where two or three come together in my name, there am I with them."
(Matthew 18:20)

It's not good for people to isolate themselves from others. People need other people. That is probably why having a good relationship with our families is so important. When we are among people who love us and understand us, we feel safe. We can also talk about all the things that worry us, and perhaps we can get answers to some of our questions.

Jesus chose twelve disciples to accompany him. He knew that he would need them to help build his kingdom. He also needed them to keep him company and to talk to him, so that he would not be too lonely here on earth. Jesus was also a very good friend to the disciples. He taught them many things, and he understood them.

If you believe in Jesus and know that you need him, he is always with you. When you tell Jesus that you are completely dependent on him, he replies by assuring you that he is always with you. In this passage, Jesus says that when two or three of his children gather together in his name, he is with them in a very special way. It is almost as if people's faith grows stronger when they are not alone, but are among people who also have faith in Jesus. It is almost like being in a team of faith. Jesus says that when people are together in his name and when they are in agreement in their prayers, the Father will give them whatever they ask.

It is important for you to have Christian friends. Pray with them and talk about your faith with them. Make sure that you are in agreement about important matters. Whenever we are together with others in this way, the Lord's presence is with us in a very special way.

W.W.J.

Jesus is also called Immanuel, "God with us." We experience his presence especially when we are among other Christians.

September 1

Peter

HOW MANY TIMES SHOULD I FORGIVE?

"Lord, how many times shall I forgive my brother when he sins against me?" (Matthew 18:21)

We often make mistakes in our relationships with other people. And because we make mistakes, we hurt people. We are all guilty of doing this because none of us is perfect.

When someone has done something bad to us, we can either become bitter and angry, or we can decide to forgive the person. The Lord's way is the way of forgiveness. If you can forgive someone for the wrong he or she has done to you, your own heart will be filled with peace and you will feel so much better.

Peter once asked Jesus how many times he should forgive his brother for sinning against him. Then he asked, *"Up to seven times?"* (Matthew 18:21). Jesus replied that he should not only be willing to forgive someone seven times, but actually seventy times seven times. That's a lot of times to forgive someone for the same sin, don't you think?

What Jesus was actually trying to tell Peter is that we should forgive other people without keeping count of how many times we have forgiven them. Jesus' forgiveness is unlimited. It doesn't matter how many times someone has sinned against us, we should be willing to forgive him or her every single time. If you are the kind of person who is willing to forgive and forget, the Lord will perhaps find it much easier to forgive you for your sins. After all, we sin against the Lord more times than we could ever count.

If there is someone who hurt you or did something to make you unhappy, why not decide right now to forgive that person? If you forgive him or her, you will immediately be liberated from the burden and weight of negative feelings.

W.W.J.

Jesus taught us to pray to forgive those who sin against us just as God forgives us our sins.

The Rich Man

WHAT IS MOST IMPORTANT TO YOU?

"Teacher, what good thing must I do to get eternal life?" (Matthew 19:16)

Being wealthy is definitely not a sin. It is a good thing to have enough possessions and money to be able to serve others and use to help build the kingdom of God. In Jesus' time, as in ours, there were many wealthy people.

A rich young man once came to Jesus and asked him a very honest question. He wanted to know what he had to do to get eternal life. In response, Jesus asked him if he knew the commandments of the Lord. All he needed to do was to follow the commandments. The young man replied that he tried to follow the commandments, and that he was a very devout man. Because Jesus knew everything, he also knew that this young man's real problem was money. He did try to live according to the will of the Lord, but he was so attached to his money that it was almost more important to him than the Lord. Jesus wanted to test the young man's faith to see if he would really be willing to follow Jesus with all his heart.

Jesus told the young man that if he truly wanted to be perfect, he had to sell all his possessions and give the money to the poor. Then he had to come back and make following Jesus his full-time occupation. The young man was very unhappy about this because he had many possessions. He left very dejected. He thought that Jesus' requirements were just too difficult to follow.

The Lord doesn't really expect us to sell all our possessions, except when he specifically asks us to do so. But he knew that this young man was overly attached to his money, and that is why he wanted to test him. You and I should always be sure that nothing is more important to us than the Lord, and that includes our money and our possessions. We should also be sure to use our money and possessions in the service of the Lord and his kingdom.

W.W.J.

Jesus said that it was very difficult for a rich man to enter the kingdom of God. However, he also said that the Lord has the power to change even rich people's hearts.

September 3

Mrs. Zebedee

She Wanted Preferential Treatment

"Grant that one of these two sons of mine may sit at your right and the other at your left in your kingdom." (Matthew 20:21)

Because we are sometimes uncertain of ourselves or just want some recognition, we occasionally do foolish things. We sing our own praises. We try to convince others that we should be receiving preferential treatment because we are so special. We try to use our achievements to persuade people to heap praise on us. And we absolutely love it when someone shows us that we are very special.

Perhaps you sometimes do things to show your teacher just how cute or clever you are. We all like to be the teacher's pet because it makes us feel that we are just that – a little bit better than everyone else.

Zebedee had two sons, James and John, who were both disciples of Jesus. Zebedee's wife came to Jesus with a special request. She wanted to know whether her two sons could have the two most important seats when Jesus one day took his place on his throne in heaven. She wanted Jesus to give her sons preferential treatment. She wanted one of her sons to sit on Jesus' right-hand side and the other on his left-hand side. Mrs. Zebedee didn't really understand what she was asking for. Jesus answered that decisions like these were not up to him, but were at the Father's discretion.

In reality, her request was born from a negative attitude that she was harboring in her heart. She was a little bit selfish. She thought about heaven in earthly terms. We should not serve the Lord merely so that other people can admire us or so that we may one day occupy an important place in heaven. We should serve the Lord simply because we love him, even when we are right at the back of the line as far as importance is concerned.

W.W.J.

Jesus taught us that the most important people in heaven are those who are the most humble.

The Crowd

THEY YELLED "HOSANNA!" AND "KILL HIM!"

The crowds that went ahead of him and those that followed shouted ...
(Matthew 21:9)

When Jesus arrived in Jerusalem shortly before he was arrested, the people of Jerusalem were very excited about him. The disciples brought Jesus a young donkey and put their cloaks on it so that Jesus could sit on it. This is how Jesus went into Jerusalem. The people were very excited and the crowd was in an uproar. Some people cut branches from the trees and spread them on the road before Jesus. Others took off their cloaks and spread them before him. And while Jesus was riding into Jerusalem on the donkey, the people shouted, *"Hosanna to the Son of David! Blessed is he who comes in the name of the Lord!"* (Matthew 21:9). Why were the people so excited?

At that time, the Jews were ruled by the Roman Empire, and they didn't like it at all. They were being oppressed, and they believed that an earthly king would come to free them from the oppression of the Roman Empire. When Jesus arrived in Jerusalem, after he had performed many miracles, many people thought that he was this king who had come to free them from the Romans. That is why they shouted "Hosanna!" They praised his name and were very excited.

They did not understand that Jesus had not come to establish an earthly kingdom, but a heavenly one. His purpose was, first and foremost, to redeem people from their sins. That is why the same people who shouted "Hosanna!" were later so disappointed in him that they changed their cry to "Crucify him!"

Sometimes we praise God only because we have certain expectations that we want him to fulfill. When these expectations are not fulfilled, we turn our back on him. Choose today whether you want to praise him or crucify him.

W.W.J.

While Jesus was preaching, many disciples turned against him because they did not like what he was saying.

September 5

The Pharisees

BE HONEST

"Tell us then, what is your opinion?" (Matthew 22:17)

The church leaders of Jesus' time were the scribes, or the teachers of the law. They could be divided into two main groups: the Pharisees and the Sadducees. These people taught others all about the Law of Moses. After they had acquired as much knowledge as they could about everything the Jews believed regarding the Law of Moses, they taught other people how to obey the laws of the Lord.

Because Jesus started teaching people about his kingdom and about the Law of Moses in a whole new way, the teachers of the law were very skeptical. They were particularly upset about the fact that so many people came to listen to Jesus. And what was more, it appeared that Jesus loved everyone – even sinners – and he didn't teach people to obey all of the traditional commands and regulations. Instead, he taught them that all they needed to do was make sure that they had the right kind of relationship with God. Jesus loved sinners. Jesus wanted to teach sinful people how to live good lives, but the scribes did not understand this at all.

They wanted to entrap Jesus by driving him into a corner with a trick question. So they asked him all kinds of questions to try and prove that he was transgressing God's law. But Jesus saw right through their little plans. He knew that they were not really seeking answers to their questions. All they wanted was to find fault with him. That is why he said to them, *"You hypocrites, why are you trying to trap me?"* (Matthew 22:18).

We should be like Jesus and always express our opinions honestly. We should always be willing to be faithful to the truth and to make the will of God known to everyone. We should not be like the Pharisees, who where trying to be saved by keeping all the laws instead of by having a relationship with God.

W.W.J.

Jesus never tried to please people. He always tried to please his Father, and he was always honest and straightforward.

September 6

The Sadducees

THEY ASKED QUESTIONS ABOUT HEAVEN

"Now then, at the resurrection, whose wife will she be of the seven, since all of them were married to her?" (Matthew 22:28)

The Sadducees were a group of teachers of the law who did not believe that people could be resurrected after death and given eternal life. They asked Jesus a trick question. They reminded Jesus that the Law of Moses said that if a man died, his brother should marry his widow, so that she could have a family and bear children. They then asked the following question: Suppose there were seven brothers, and a woman married all seven brothers because all her husbands died. Who would be her true husband after the resurrection? After all, all seven were her husbands! Would she then have seven husbands in heaven?

Jesus candidly answered them that they were in error because they did not know the Scriptures and neither did they know the power of God. He said that people would no longer get married after the resurrection because they would be like the angels in heaven. And yes, God's power would give eternal life to every person who had faith in him, and they would live with him eternally in heaven.

Here on earth we do get married, but in heaven we won't. We will all know one another and love one another, but we will no longer live together in couples as man and wife. Even though we don't really understand what heaven will be like, we know that it is a time and a place that we can look forward to. Everyone in heaven will be perfect, and there will no longer be any sorrow.

W.W.J.

Jesus said that all earthly things would pass, but his kingdom would last forever. This also applies to our relationships with other people.

The Pharisees

WHAT IS THE MOST IMPORTANT?

"Teacher, which is the greatest commandment in the Law?" (Matthew 22:36)

One of the teachers of the law again tried to trap Jesus with a trick question. God gave Moses many laws and commandments that he had to teach to the Israelites. The Pharisee wanted to know which commandment was the most important one of all.

Jesus' answer to the Pharisee's question was, *"'Love the Lord your God with all your heart and with all your soul and with all your mind.' This is the first and greatest commandment. And the second is like it: 'Love your neighbor as yourself'"* (Matthew 22:37-39).

Jesus was trying to say that rules and laws and regulations are of lesser importance to God. The attitudes we harbor in our hearts and our relationship with him are much more important to God. Jesus came to teach us that we should love the Lord wholeheartedly. We should worship him. We should want to serve him. We should try to make him happy. We should show him that we love him – but not only him. One way of showing our love for him is to love other people as we love him. We should love all the people we know and who live with us every day. We should even love people we only meet occasionally. We should care for them, show them that they are important to us, and love them in word and in deed.

Try to show love to everyone you meet today.

W.W.J.

Jesus taught us how to love people in practice.

The Pharisees
and Sadducees

Notice Us!

"Everything they do is done for men to see." (Matthew 23:5)

One day Jesus spoke to his disciples about the teachers of the law, or the Pharisees and the Sadducees. He warned them to follow every one of the Pharisees' instructions regarding the Law of Moses, but he also said that they should not follow the Pharisees' example.

Unfortunately, the Pharisees did not practice what they preached. They pretended to be very pious and gave the people all kinds of religious instructions to follow, but they themselves did not adhere to these instructions. It was almost as if they delighted in placing unbearably heavy burdens on the shoulders of other people, but they did not lift a finger to carry these burdens.

Many of the Pharisees were spiritual snobs. The only real reason some of them did their jobs was to be seen by people. They thought that they were much more important than everyone else. They dressed themselves in their religious robes and made sure that everyone saw them parading around. They reserved the most important seats in the synagogues for themselves and made sure that no one else had the opportunity to sit in their place. They were also very pleased whenever they walked down the street and someone greeted them by their title.

We should be careful not to serve the Lord merely to be seen or praised by people. We should also not ask other people to do things for Jesus that we are not willing to do ourselves. Let's be servants, and let's never forget to be humble. Let's use our lives and our love to show other people that the Lord dwells in our hearts.

W.W.J.

Jesus was never pretentious and never pretended to be better than anyone else.

September 9

The Teachers of the Law

REAL SNAKES

"You snakes! You brood of vipers! How will you escape being condemned to hell?" (Matthew 23:33)

One of the things that really upset Jesus was the hypocrisy of the Pharisees. People who are hypocrites are deceitful. They say one thing and do something completely different. Jesus didn't like hypocrisy at all and, in no uncertain terms, he admonished the teachers of the law about it.

He told them that utter and complete misery awaited them. They were supposed to help people find God, but instead they closed the door to the kingdom in people's faces. Jesus said that they pretended to be spiritual leaders to other people, but they were spiritually blind themselves. And then he said a terrible thing. He said that they were snakes. Jesus knew that these men would eventually have him killed because they were so concerned with protecting their own interests and positions. He compared them to religious leaders in the past who had killed other prophets and preachers of the Lord. They would be punished because they were guilty of shedding the blood of the men of God.

We should pray for our spiritual leaders. Pray that they will be humble and that they will always do the will of the Lord with love in their hearts. As followers of the Lord, we should also be sure never to become like the Pharisees. We should never think that we are some-how better than everyone else, and we should never do evil things in the name of the Lord.

W.W.J.

Jesus wants us to be honest and sincere in our words and actions.

Jesus

No One Knows When He Will Return

"No one knows about that day or hour." (Matthew 24:36)

Jesus taught us that one day the world will come to an end. To explain this, he used the fig tree as an example. In the summer, the fig tree's twigs become tender and start sprouting young green leaves. Then small figs start to form on the branches. Everyone who sees this knows that it is summer.

In the same way, people will know when the time is near for the world to come to an end. Certain things will happen that will convince people that the day of the Lord's coming is at hand. Jesus also taught that the lives of the Lord's children would become increasingly difficult as the end of time drew near. Some Christians will suffer terribly because they will be oppressed and persecuted. Many false christs and prophets will appear on the scene, and they will perform all kinds of signs and wonders. Many people will believe that they are real prophets of the Lord, and they will follow them and believe in them.

When Jesus returns to the earth, all the nations will mourn. They will see him appearing on the clouds of the sky, with power and great glory. A loud trumpet call will resound, and his angels will come down and gather all his children from all corners of the world.

When will all this take place? We will be able to see the signs, but we don't know exactly when Jesus will return. Only the Father knows when he will send his Son back to the earth. And for this reason, there is no point in believing all kinds of predictions about Jesus' second coming. All we can do is be sure that we are ready for that day, every day of our lives.

What would you do if the Lord returned tomorrow? Would you be ready to go with him? You are only ready if he has forgiven your sins and if you belong to him and live to glorify his name. If we are the Lord's children, we need not fear the second coming of Christ.

W. W. J.

Jesus promised that he would return and take us with him so that we may live with him for all eternity.

September 11

Ten Girls

Is Your Lamp Filled with Oil?

"... but did not take any oil with them." (Matthew 25:3)

Jesus once told a parable to teach his disciples that they should always be ready and prepared for his second coming. He told a story about a wedding, which was attended by five wise girls and five foolish girls. They were waiting for the bridegroom to arrive, but he was very late. Eventually night fell. The five wise girls had brought enough oil to keep their lamps burning, but the foolish girls had forgotten to bring enough oil. Back then, people didn't have flashlights or electrical power. All the lamps needed oil to work. When the oil was gone, the lamp went out.

After a long time of waiting for the bridegroom, the ten girls fell asleep. When the bridegroom eventually arrived, the foolish girls could not get their lamps to work because there was no more oil in the lamps. They then wanted to borrow some oil from the wise girls, but the wise girls answered, *"No ... there may not be enough for both us and you. Instead, go to those who sell oil and buy some for yourselves"* (Matthew 25:9). However, while they were on their way to buy the oil, the bridegroom arrived, the wedding started, and the doors were locked so that no one else could get in. The foolish girls could do nothing but stand outside, and they missed out on all the festivity and celebration.

In the same way, we should always be prepared and have enough spiritual "oil" to keep our hearts burning. In other words, we should always be filled with the Lord. Then we won't be caught unaware when Jesus returns. We should always be filled with the Holy Spirit and live according to his will every day – regardless of whether we are in school, on the sports field, or having fun with our friends. Be prepared!

W.W.J.

Jesus said that we should be spiritually awake and ready at all times.

The Businessman

Make the Most of Your Talents

"It will be like a man going on a journey, who called his servants and entrusted his property to them." (Matthew 25:14)

Jesus told a story about a businessman who had to go away on a long journey. Because he would be gone for a very long time, he instructed his servants to take care of his property. They knew that his property was very valuable to him, and therefore they would have to look after it very carefully. To one servant, the businessman gave five golden coins; to another servant, he gave two golden coins; to a third servant, he gave one golden coin.

While the man was away, the servant with the five coins thought that it would be a good idea to make some profit with the money he was given. After all, he knew how the businessman felt about money matters. He was a businessman and wanted to see his money increase. The servant then put his money to work and made a profit of five more golden coins. The one who received two coins did the same thing, and he gained another two coins. But the man who received only one coin was afraid that he would lose the money. So he went off, dug a hole in the ground, and hid his master's money in it.

When the businessman returned from his journey, he saw the first two servants' hard work and the profits that they had made. He was very pleased with them and said, *"Well done, good and faithful servant! You have been faithful with a few things; I will put you in charge of many things. Come and share your master's happiness!"* (Matthew 25:21). However, he was not at all pleased with the servant who had buried his one coin, and he called him a wicked and lazy servant.

Jesus told this story to teach us that we should make the most of the talents that we have received. We should improve and develop the talents that we were given so that the Lord's name may be glorified. Make the most of your God-given talents today.

W.W.J.

God has given each of us special abilities and talents that we can use for His kingdom.

September 13

The Judge
THIS IS WHAT HIS SHEEP DO

"I needed clothes and you clothed me, I was sick and you looked after me."
(Matthew 25:36)

On that day when Jesus returns to earth in all his majesty, he will sit on his throne in heavenly glory. All the nations will be gathered before him, and he will separate the people into two groups, as a shepherd separates the sheep from the goats. He will put the sheep on his right and the goats on his left.

Jesus will sit on his throne of majesty and judge all the people. The sheep standing on his right are his children. They include all those people who chose him as their Savior and who therefore belong to him. They are all the people who have received forgiveness for their sins. But even more importantly, throughout their lives their lifestyles showed that they belong to him. In this passage, Jesus says that they are the people who gave food to the hungry, who gave those who were thirsty something to drink, who visited prisoners, who gave clothes to those who needed clothing, who looked after those who were ill. All in all, they are the people who always did God's will.

Every time you and I do something for someone else with love in our hearts, it is as if we are doing it for the Lord himself. This is what God expects of his sheep. Ultimately, this will also be the proof that we belong to him. And on the day of judgment, everything that you and I did in his name will come to light.

The goats are those who do not belong to God. They stand on the opposite side. They never loved God personally. They never tried to help other people from the love of their hearts. They never wanted to give people clothes, food, or water, or to care for them and nurse them. They lived only for themselves.

Let us do what is good because we love Jesus. Let us show our love for other people. After all, we are his sheep.

W.W.J.

Jesus' deeds showed people that he was the Son of God.

The Generous Woman

Perfume for the Hair?

A woman came to him with an alabaster jar of very expensive perfume, which she poured on his head. (Matthew 26:7)

Jesus and his disciples were having a meal in the house of Simon in the small town of Bethany. While they were enjoying the meal and one another's company, a woman suddenly came to Jesus with an alabaster jar of very expensive perfume.

The woman opened this jar of perfume and poured it on Jesus' head. In those days, people did this when they wanted to show their reverence for someone. It was a very big compliment. When the disciples, specifically Judas, saw what the woman had done they were completely astonished – and also a little bit indignant. They thought that it was a terrible waste of money. Judas said that it would have been much better to sell the perfume and to give the money to the poor.

However, Jesus told them to stop bothering the woman. She had done a good deed. The poor would always be with them, but Jesus would not. All she wanted to do was to honor and glorify him.

The woman poured the perfume over Jesus' head to show how much she loved him. What kind of perfume do we give to the Lord? Our praise? Our obedience? Our words of love? Our worship? Our hearts? Our lives? Yes, all these, and everything else we can do to show people that Jesus is our Lord.

W. W. J.

Jesus spent only a few years walking the earth. Today we can walk with him in faith. Give him all the glory that is his due.

Boanerges

It Means Thunder!

... (to them he gave the name Boanerges, which means Sons of Thunder) (Mark 3:17).

People often have very interesting nicknames. When someone is not very tall, he is sometimes called "Shorty." One guy was nicknamed "Smiley" because he was always smiling. Some men call their wife "Darling" or "Angel" or some other pet name. Some guys also have rather shocking nicknames, but we won't get into that here!

Jesus also gave a nickname to two of his disciples: James and John, the sons of Zebedee. Jesus called them "Boanerges," which means "Sons of Thunder." Why would Jesus have picked this nickname for them? They were probably called by this name because they were very bad-tempered. Perhaps they were easily angered and quick to get involved in a fight. Maybe they liked arguing with people. Perhaps that is why they sounded like thunder.

But a wonderful thing happened to them. When they got to know Jesus and gave their hearts and lives to him, they underwent a complete change of personality. The same John who was called "Son of Thunder" later became the disciple of love. His hardened heart changed and became gentle and kind. He no longer thundered and raged, but spoke only words of love. Go ahead and read 1, 2, and 3 John. In these letters, John writes time and again that we should love one another and show our love to one another. Isn't it wonderful how the Lord can change a person's heart?

W.W.J.

Through the power of Jesus, many hearts will be changed.

Jesus

Son of Man

"The Son of Man is going to be betrayed into the hands of men." (Mark 9:31)

Isn't it wonderful that God, who is almighty and all-powerful, decided to become a human being? The Bible tells us how God decided to send his Son to earth to become human. And then Jesus was born as a tiny little baby in a manger in Bethlehem. What a marvelous miracle!

Human beings are broken, fallen creatures. We are all born as beautiful, brand-new beings, but we also all have a yearning and a longing for better things. We crave true happiness. We want to be healed of our pain. We want to have peace. We would do anything to be happier than we are. The reason for all this is that we are full of sin.

The Bible often refers to Jesus as the Son of Man. This name means that he came to earth and became a human because he loves people. When Jesus was born, the angels sang that God wished only peace for all men. He loves us and wants the best for us. That is why Jesus is sometimes called the Son of Man. He is not only God's Son, but also our Friend and Savior.

Jesus experienced the same emotions as all people. He knows our dreams and he understands our pain. He too was cast aside and misunderstood by people. He suffered, just as people do. He wished for the pain to go away. He was very lonely. Yes, Jesus was a human being just like us. That is why he understands you.

Tell Jesus about everything that is in your heart, right now. He understands you because he was a human being just like you.

W.W.J.

Jesus became human in order to save us from our sin. He understands us completely.

The Disciples

WHO IS THE MOST IMPORTANT?

On the way they had argued about who was the greatest. (Mark 9:34)

One of our typically human problems is that we so much want to be important. We want to be the best. We want other people to sit up and take notice of us. We want to receive some recognition for who we are and what we do.

The disciples saw how humble Jesus was every day. They saw him serving other people. They saw how much he loved all people. And despite all of this, they still thought that they were very important because they were Jesus' followers. They even argued among themselves about which one of them was the most important.

One day, when they were walking along the road, they were once again busy arguing the matter. The one said that he was the most important of the disciples, and the other would reply by saying that he was definitely the greatest of the disciples.

Jesus called his disciples aside and sat down with them. He told them that if anyone wanted to be first, he had to be last, and he should furthermore be everyone's servant. He then took a little child and had him stand among the disciples. Then he said, *"Whoever welcomes one of these little children in my name welcomes me ..."* (Mark 9:37).

Jesus has no favorites. He doesn't regard some of us as more important than others. In Jesus' eyes, we are all equal. And every single one of us is important. You too!

W.W.J.

Jesus does not measure people's worth like the world does. All people are equal in his eyes.

September 18

Gabriel

A Very Important Angel

The angel answered, "I am Gabriel. I stand in the presence of God, and I have been sent to speak to you." (Luke 1:19)

Heaven is filled with angels, and they all belong to the Lord. They are God's messengers and servants, and they help him to rule over all creation. He sends them to give messages to people or to support and help them in times of need. Angels are mighty and powerful creatures.

One of the most important angels is named Gabriel. He was the one who explained Daniel's dream to him. He was also the angel who appeared to Zechariah in the temple and announced John's birth. Six months later, he appeared to Mary and told her that she would be the mother of Jesus.

We don't know who all the angels are. Very few people have actually been privileged enough to see an angel. But we know that they are there because the Bible says so. There are some spiritual leaders who believe that every person has a guardian angel that goes everywhere with him or her. The Word tells us that the angels watch over children. Thank God for sending his angels to protect and help you. One day, we will know everything there is to know about the angels. We might even find out about times when they helped us even when we didn't know about it!

W.W.J.

The angels helped Jesus after his temptation in the desert, and they comforted him in the garden of Gethsemane.

September 19

Christians

ARE YOU A FISH?

Then Jesus said to Simon, "Don't be afraid; from now on you will catch men." (Luke 5:10)

Have you ever tried to draw a fish? The easiest way to draw a fish is to draw two lines. One line should be drawn in an upwards curve, and the other should start at the same point, but be drawn in a downwards curve so that the two lines cross each other. The earliest Christians used the sign of the fish to identify themselves.

Perhaps you have seen a car with a bumper sticker of a fish on it. Sometimes there is also a verse from the Bible written on the sticker. Even today people still use the sign of the fish to show the world that they belong to Jesus. So why use the sign of the fish? Perhaps it is because Jesus said that we would be fishers of men. Many fishermen were also followers of Jesus. He told them that they should not spend all their time and energy on catching fish. Instead, they should give their everything to lead people to the Lord. They should be fishers of men.

The early Christians were often persecuted, and therefore they needed to communicate with one another in secret. If they wanted to make sure if someone was a Christian, they would draw a little fish in the dust. If the other person responded by doing the same thing, they knew that he or she was also a Christian. The Greek word for fish is "icthus." The letters in this word also stands for "Jesus Christ, Son of God, Savior."

If you are a Christian, you are Jesus' little fish. He has caught you in the net of his love.

W.W.J.

Jesus taught his disciples how to catch fish for the kingdom.

September 20

Mary Magdalene

RECEIVE THE PEACE OF JESUS

Mary (called Magdalene) from whom seven demons had come out ... (Luke 8:2)

The Bible tells of a number of women named Mary who knew and followed the Lord Jesus. One of them was a woman called Mary Magdalene. She was a woman who had many problems in her life.

At some point, Mary Magdalene must have allowed the devil to take a hold of her life. When Jesus met her for the first time, he immediately realized that she was a woman in terrible distress and need, and he released her from her suffering. She was possessed by not one, but seven demons, and Jesus cast out all seven. Can you imagine how terrible it must be when seven demons live inside one person? Mary Magdalene was completely in the power of the devil. But Jesus was her Redeemer and Savior. When Jesus helped her, she was freed of the devil's power. All the demons left her and she was emptied of all evil. Before Jesus helped her, her life was filled with chaos and confusion, but Jesus gave her peace.

Mary Magdalene was so happy about what Jesus had done for her that she became one of his most faithful followers. In Luke 8, we read that she, together with a number of other women, took care of Jesus and supported him. She was also one of the women who fulfilled a very important role after Jesus' burial and resurrection. She was the one to whom Jesus appeared after his resurrection. He instructed her to go and tell everyone that he had been resurrected; that he was no longer dead, but alive!

The Lord loves transforming people's chaos into peace. He is the Prince of Peace, who came to quiet the storms in our hearts, which are usually caused by the devil. Let us pray that every single person will receive the peace that only Jesus can give.

W.W.J.

Isaiah predicted long ago that Jesus would be the Prince of Peace. (Isaiah 9:6)

September 21

Mary

ALL EARS

Mary, who sat at the Lord's feet listening to what he said ... (Luke 10:39)

Jesus was visiting the home of the sisters Mary and Martha. Martha worked very hard to ensure that Jesus' stay in their home would be pleasant and comfortable. She cooked delicious food, served drinks, and made sure that Jesus felt at home. However, she was more than a little bit upset because Mary didn't really help with all of the work that needed to be done. So she spoke to Jesus about it.

Mary, Martha's sister, was so enthralled with Jesus' words that she could simply not tear herself away from him to help Martha with the preparations. She found it just too wonderful to sit at Jesus' feet and listen to everything he had to say. Mary's heart was probably filled with a hunger to hear the truth. She wanted to know everything about the Lord and his kingdom. She wanted to know what to do to have a better relationship with God. That is why she sat down at his feet, looked up at him, and listened to every word he spoke.

When Martha admonished her for not helping with the housework, Mary probably felt a little bit ashamed, but Jesus' answer took her by surprise. He told Martha that all the hustle and bustle was not the most important thing in the world and that Mary actually was doing the right thing in sitting down and listening to him. He also said, *"... it will not be taken away from her"* (Luke 10:42). By this, Jesus meant that all earthly things would eventually be taken from us. It will all pass away. But his words, the "bread of life," will never be taken away from us. They are eternal. That is why Mary's choice was the best choice.

Let's all make some time every day to listen to the Word of the Lord. Make his words a part of your heart and your spirit. Take in his words, think about them, and talk to others about them. His words belong to you eternally.

W.W.J.

Jesus said that people could not live on bread alone – they need the words of God to be truly alive. (Matthew 4:4)

September 22

Martha

STOP FIDGETING!

But Martha was distracted by all the preparations that had to be made. (Luke 10:40)

In the town of Bethany, Jesus was invited to be a guest in the home of Mary and Martha. Martha was very busy, trying to finish all the preparations that had to be made for Jesus' stay. She was hustling and bustling around the whole time because she wanted everything to be perfect for Jesus. Perhaps Martha became a little bit agitated about it all. It sounds as if she was quite stressed out about everything that had to be done.

Martha also had a sister, called Mary. While Martha was running about trying to get all the preparations done, Mary didn't help her at all. She was much too curious about everything Jesus had to say. Martha got very annoyed with her sister. She asked Jesus whether it didn't bother him that Mary left her all alone to do all the work by herself. She then said to Jesus that he should tell Mary to help her with the work.

I think Jesus was very grateful for all the work Martha did to make his stay pleasant. Jesus also knew that earthly things like food and clothes are important, but they are not the most important. That is what he wanted to teach Martha. He said that there are many earthly things that one can be worried and upset about, but these things were not nearly as important as listening to his words and following his instructions.

Does this mean that we should not be diligent and hardworking? Of course not! It simply means that we should not be so busy and overworked that we have no time for the Lord and his Word. Time spent with the Lord is the most important thing.

W.W.J.

Jesus taught us that the things of this earth pass, but that his words and his kingdom are eternal.

The Rich Man

Just a Drop of Water

"Send Lazarus to dip the tip of his finger in water and cool my tongue." (Luke 16:24)

Jesus told a story about a rich man who lived in the lap of luxury. He lived in a huge mansion, ate only the best food, and wore only the most beautiful clothes. At this rich man's gate sat a very poor man who begged for some food or money. His name was Lazarus. Every time the rich man went past him, Lazarus asked for a little something to eat. But the rich man was very haughty and simply pretended not to see Lazarus. The poor Lazarus also had sores all over his body, and the rich man's dogs came and licked his sores.

Then one day Lazarus died, and the angels came and carried him to heaven. Because he was a child of the Lord, God set aside a special place of honor for him, at Abraham's side. Shortly after this the rich man also died, but he went to hell, where he experienced terrible suffering. He saw Abraham, far away in heaven, and asked him to have pity on him and to send Lazarus to cool his tongue with a drop of water because he was in terrible agony in the fires of hell.

However, Abraham told the rich man that there was a big chasm between heaven and hell and that Lazarus could not cross it to help him. While he was on earth, the rich man received all the good things that life had to offer while Lazarus received nothing but suffering.

Then the rich man begged Abraham to send Lazarus to warn his family of what awaited them if they did not mend their ways. But Abraham could not do this either. He said that if all of the rich man's relatives had never listened to any of the prophets or teachers, then they weren't going to listen to him either.

We should love those in need with the love of the Lord. We should also tell people that if they do not accept Jesus as their Savior, they have no hope of eternal life in heaven.

W.W.J.

Jesus was always telling people about heaven, and he always loved those who were poor or in need.

September 24

The Blind Man

JESUS IS NEVER TOO BUSY

Jesus stopped and ordered the man to be brought to him. (Luke 18:40)

Jesus was walking along a road near Jericho. He was accompanied by a large group of people. In those days the teachers of the law often taught the people about the things of God as they were walking or traveling. Jesus probably did the same. On this particular day, he was surrounded by a large group of listeners and he was telling them all about his kingdom.

Next to the road sat a blind beggar. When he heard the crowd of people walking past him, he asked some of the people what was going on. They told him that it was Jesus of Nazareth passing by. The blind beggar had heard a great deal about Jesus, and called out, *"Jesus, Son of David, have mercy on me!"* (Luke 18:38). Some people in the crowd told him to be quiet, but he just kept on shouting louder and louder, asking the Lord to help him. The people thought that he was just making a nuisance of himself. How could he waste Jesus' time like that? Didn't he understand that the Lord was busy? Maybe Jesus was in a hurry to get to Jerusalem. So why would he stop to talk to the blind man? But the Bible tells us that Jesus suddenly stopped and asked the man to be brought to him. When the blind man came closer, Jesus asked him what he could do for him. The blind man answered that he wanted to see. Jesus healed him right then and there, and his sight was immediately restored. He became one of Jesus' followers.

Sometimes we think that Jesus is much too busy to think about us. How could our needs be important enough for him to pay attention to? But of course our needs are important to him! That is why he came to earth in the first place. He wants to help us. He is interested in every aspect of our lives. Jesus is never too busy to pay attention to us. And you can rest assured that he will pay attention to you and your needs today.

W. W. J.

Jesus sometimes went out of his way to help other people.

September 25

Zacchaeus

The Short, Curious Man

"Zacchaeus, come down immediately. I must stay at your house today."
(Luke 19:5)

Jesus arrived in the city of Jericho. In this city lived a man named Zacchaeus. He was the chief tax collector and a very wealthy man. The Jews didn't like the tax collectors, and it was regarded as shameful to be a tax collector or even be friends with one.

While Jesus was walking through the city, Zacchaeus tried very hard to catch a glimpse of him. A large crowd had gathered next to the road, however, and Zacchaeus could not see over their heads because he was a very short man. He then ran ahead of the procession and climbed a sycamore-fig tree so that he could see Jesus.

Was little Zacchaeus in for a surprise! When Jesus passed by under the tree, he suddenly stopped, looked up, and spoke to Zacchaeus. He told Zacchaeus to come down because he wanted to stay at Zacchaeus's house that day. What? A Jewish rabbi who wanted to visit the home of a Jewish tax collector? What a completely unheard-of thing!

Zacchaeus was very happy when he heard this because he was curious about Jesus. However, all the Jews who saw what had happened complained and said that it was wrong for Jesus to keep company with such a sinful man as Zacchaeus.

The Bible tells us that Zacchaeus's heart was completely changed. He decided to give half of all his possessions to the poor, and he also said that he would refund the money of everyone from whom he had taken more than he should have. Not only that, but he would give them four times the amount that he had taken from them!

Isn't it wonderful that Jesus loved even the sinners and the tax collectors so much that he reached out to them and helped them? As a result, their lives were completely changed. Today the Lord still wants to do exactly the same thing in people's lives.

W.W.J.

Jesus was never worried about what people would say or whether they would gossip about him. He always did what was right.

September 26

Rabbi

It Means Teacher

They said, "Rabbi" (which means Teacher) ... (John 1:38)

In Jesus' time, there were many Jews who were very knowledgeable about the Jewish law and the teachings of their forefathers. They were learned men, and they spent a lot of time studying and explaining the Holy Scriptures.

Because people wanted to know what the Lord said and what his will was, they listened to these teachers. The Jews had a special name for such teachers. This name was "Rabbi." It actually means "my teacher." Often a group of pupils went to a rabbi and asked him to teach them.

Today, there are still many people who study the Word of God so that they can teach other people everything about the will of the Lord. We should thank God for men and women who are willing to study the Lord's Word so that they can lead others to do the will of the Lord.

The fact that someone teaches God's Word does not mean that that person is more important than anyone else. It doesn't mean that person has more spiritual value than other people. Jesus once said a very interesting thing: *"But you are not to be called 'Rabbi,' for you have only one Master and you are all brothers. Nor are you to be called 'teacher,' for you have one Teacher, the Christ"* (Matthew 23: 8, 10). The title or the name is not important. The work that one does is the really important thing. And all people who work for the Lord are simply people who serve him.

W.W.J.

Jesus was the greatest and best Teacher ever.

September 27

Nicodemus

How Does One Find God?

He came to Jesus at night. (John 3:2)

The vast majority of the Pharisees and other teachers of the law refused to believe in Jesus. They were very hostile toward him and were constantly saying terrible things about him. However, there were a few of the Pharisees who were curious about Jesus and his teachings, and they sometimes went and listened to Jesus. There were even a few who asked him questions. One such man was Nicodemus.

Because Nicodemus was afraid of what the other Pharisees would say, he did not go to Jesus during the daytime. Instead, he waited until night fell and then went to see Jesus. Actually, Nicodemus went to Jesus and acknowledged his belief that Jesus was sent by God. Nicodemus said to Jesus, *"For no one could perform the miraculous signs you are doing if God were not with him"* (John 3:2).

Then Jesus told Nicodemus that he had to be born again, otherwise he would not be able to see the kingdom of God. Nicodemus wanted to know how it was possible for someone to be born again if he was already an old man. Jesus then explained to Nicodemus that it had nothing to do with a physical birth. Being born again had to do with a rebirth of the spirit. His heart had to be renewed. He had to be filled with the conviction that he had to follow Jesus, and in doing so his heart would be rejuvenated, and he would be a completely new person. And then Jesus spoke that beautiful verse which says that God loved the world so much that he gave his one and only Son so that all who believed in him could be saved (read John 3:16).

Even today we are surrounded by people who are skeptical, but we must never forget that there are also people who really want to know how to find God. And the answer to their question is very simple: Jesus. He is the One who helps us to be born again.

W.W.J.

Jesus also told Nicodemus that he would be crucified so that everyone who believed in him could have eternal life. (John 3:14-15)

The Samaritan Woman

Give Me Some Water

The woman said to him, "Sir, give me this water." (John 4:15)

One day Jesus came to a well in a little town called Sychar. Sychar was a Samaritan town. The Jews never really spoke to the Samaritans if they could help it, and they definitely did not keep company with them. They regarded it as shameful. But Jesus didn't think twice about talking to a Samaritan because he knew that she needed his help.

While Jesus was sitting beside the well in Sychar, a Samaritan woman came to draw some water from the well. Jesus asked her whether she could give him some water to drink. She was very surprised when she realized that it was a Jew who was speaking to her. Jesus then told her that he could give her living water, just as she gave him water to drink. But she didn't really understand what he meant.

Jesus continued to say that everyone who drank earthly water would inevitably grow thirsty again, but those who drank from the heavenly or living water would never again be thirsty. Jesus was talking about a life of peace and contentment with God. Jesus knew that only he could give it, and therefore he offered it to this woman. He then talked to her for a while about her life, and even though she had a bit of a reputation for being an immoral woman, she started to feel that there was a new life waiting for her.

Suddenly she realized that Jesus was sounding just like the Messiah was supposed to sound. She then said that when the Messiah came, he would explain everything to them. Jesus replied that he was the Christ, the Messiah. The woman was so excited about everything that Jesus had told her that she immediately went and told all her fellow townspeople about it. The Bible tells us that many of the Samaritans of that town came to believe in Jesus.

Thank Jesus for offering you his living water. Tell everyone you know that Jesus is the only source of living water.

W.W.J.

Jesus said that he came to earth so that we could worship him in spirit and truth. (John 4:24)

September 29

The Farmer

He Wants You to Bear Fruit

"This is to my Father's glory, that you bear much fruit." (John 15:8)

This book is written to help you bear more fruit for the Father. Jesus once said that his Father, who is also our Father, was like a farmer who planted a vineyard. A farmer does this with only one purpose: to harvest fruit.

We should bear fruit because we are Jesus' disciples. And Jesus himself teaches his followers how to bear fruit. He tells us about all the good things that should be in our lives. And what is more, he also sends us the Holy Spirit to help us bear fruit. Things like love, joy, and peace (and many more besides) are some of the fruits that people bear when Jesus is their Lord.

Jesus says three things about fruit: (1) We should bear fruit. (2) We should bear more fruit. (3) We should bear much fruit. Jesus is trying to tell us that we should not be satisfied with just a little bit of fruit. We should also be prepared to be pruned so that we can bear more fruit. When all is said and done, the Father wants to see much fruit in our lives. Do you bear his fruit? Let us pray for more fruit in our lives.

W.W.J.

Jesus said that we should remain in him as the branch remains in the vine. Only then will we be able to bear good fruit. (John 15:4)

The Disciples

Wait for Strength

"But you will receive power when the Holy Spirit comes on you." (Acts 1:8)

Jesus' short time on earth was over. It was time for him to return to his Father. However, he promised his disciples that he would not leave them behind all by themselves. He promised that he would send them Someone who would always be with them. He then told them to go to Jerusalem and to wait there for the gift that the Father promised them.

The disciples spent forty days waiting and praying in Jerusalem. They probably wondered what would happen. What could this gift possibly be? This gift was the Holy Spirit.

When Jesus was on earth, he walked around in a human body. Consequently, he could be in only one place at a time. But Jesus promised that he would send the Holy Spirit to live inside people, and in this way Jesus would be able to go everywhere with every single person.

This Holy Spirit would not merely live inside our hearts, but would also give us new strength and power: spiritual power to give us the courage that we need to live for Jesus. This power would also enable us to talk to other people about Jesus without being shy or afraid. When the Holy Spirit lives inside of us, we can be witnesses for the Lord. A witness is someone who tells other people about things that happened. We will be able to tell people about everything that Jesus did for us without being shy.

And this is how it came about that the Holy Spirit was poured out on the day of Pentecost. The disciples received the strength and power they needed. And you and I too – if we belong to Jesus, the Holy Spirit lives inside of us. The Holy Spirit leads us, strengthens us, and helps us to be witnesses for the Lord.

W.W.J.

Jesus promised that he would be with us always through the Holy Spirit.

October 1

The Disciples

CHOOSE ANOTHER ONE

So they proposed two men: Joseph and Matthias. (Acts 1:23)

Jesus chose twelve disciples to live with him while he was on earth. He taught them everything they needed to know about spreading the wonderful message of his kingdom. Judas was one of these disciples. He was the one who betrayed Jesus. Afterward, he regretted what he had done and was so filled with guilt and remorse that he killed himself. What a terrible end for someone who had spent so much time listening to Jesus' message of the truth.

After Jesus was resurrected and taken up to heaven to his Father, the disciples decided that they needed to choose a new disciple to take Judas's place. In this way they would once again be a full group of twelve disciples. Two men were proposed as possible candidates: Joseph and Matthias. How would they know which one to choose? The disciples came together and prayed. They told the Lord that he was the only one who knew everyone's heart, and therefore they asked him to show them the one that he had chosen to take over Judas's position in the apostolic ministry. (An apostle is someone who is an ambassador for the kingdom of Jesus, one who does the Lord's work, and someone who knew Jesus.)

After they had finished praying, they cast lots, and the lot fell to Matthias. Sometimes we also have the responsibility of choosing someone for a particular job. We should always pray to the Lord and ask him to show us the right person for the job, especially when it involves working for the kingdom of the Lord. God always knows who the right person for a particular job is. That is why we pray to him to give us the wisdom to know whom he wants us to choose.

W.W.J.

Jesus taught us that a person's heart and attitude is much more important than his or her external appearance. And he also prayed to his Father before choosing his disciples.

October 2

The Disciples

Wind and Fire

They saw what seemed to be tongues of fire that separated and came to rest on each of them. (Acts 2:3)

Jesus told the disciples to wait for the Lord's gift to be bestowed upon them from heaven. This gift was the Holy Spirit. God sent the Holy Spirit to strengthen the disciples and to help them to be powerful witnesses who could help to build Jesus' kingdom.

The disciples waited in Jerusalem for fifty days. On the fiftieth day a sound like the blowing of a violent wind suddenly came from heaven and filled the whole house in which the disciples and many of Jesus' other followers were sitting. They saw what appeared to be tongues of fire that separated and came to rest on each of them, just above their heads. This was a very strange, supernatural event.

At that exact moment, something also happened inside of them. They were filled with the Holy Spirit and suddenly started to speak in other languages. It must have sounded very strange because everyone was speaking a different language all at the same time. It must have been very mixed-up and confusing. The people outside in the streets heard this bewildering sound, and they were curious about what was going on. A crowd of people went into the house, and each person heard the disciples speaking in his or her own language. Everyone was very surprised and more than a little perplexed. Some people thought that the disciples were drunk and that this was why they were speaking so strangely. However, it was the work of the Holy Spirit, who enabled the disciples to tell as many people of as many nationalities as possible about the message of the gospel.

The Holy Spirit came down from heaven in tongues of fire. It is almost as if the Lord wants to use the Holy Spirit to set our hearts afire for him and his kingdom. He wants our hearts to be warm and excited about the gospel. I hope you're on fire for the Lord!

W.W.J.

Jesus doesn't like people who are lukewarm or filled with doubt. He prefers people to love him with a passionate, warm heart.

October 3

Peter

First Afraid, Then Brave

Then Peter stood up ... raised his voice and addressed the crowd. (Acts 2:14)

Do you remember how afraid Peter had been in the garden of Gethsemane? Yes, the same guy who said that he would never forsake Jesus ran away into the dark night when the soldiers came to arrest Jesus. He did, of course, first draw his sword and cut off the ear of a man named Malchus. But Jesus did not approve of Peter's violent behavior, and he healed Malchus's ear.

Later, Peter renounced Jesus and denied that he was his disciple. He was afraid that the people would have him arrested and do something terrible to him.

But on the day of Pentecost, a miracle happened. The Holy Spirit filled Peter's heart and suddenly this fearful man became brave. He no longer felt like running away, and he was no longer ashamed of being Jesus' follower. He suddenly became willing to tell everybody that he was Jesus' disciple. He was no longer afraid of being arrested or killed. Peter stood up, and under the guidance of the Holy Spirit, started to preach to the crowd. With great wisdom, he told them about Jesus' coming to the earth and about everything that happened to him during his life. He told them about Jesus' crucifixion and how he died so that people could be redeemed of their sins. The people were deeply moved by Peter's words and asked what they should do to be saved. Peter replied that they should repent and be baptized in the name of Jesus.

The Spirit of God gives fearful people courage. He gives us the courage and confidence to be his witnesses.

W.W.J.

Jesus knew that we needed the Holy Spirit in our hearts to help us to have the courage and ability to do his work in the world.

October 4

Peter and John

MIRACLE MEN

... and instantly the man's feet and ankles became strong. (Acts 3:7)

Jesus performed many miracles while he was here on earth. He taught people about God's power and about the kingdom of heaven, and then he showed them the reality of that power. That is why he healed many people and cast out many demons. It was very clear that Jesus possessed exceptional powers, and through his Holy Spirit, his followers are also able sometimes to do marvelous things.

One day, Peter and John went to the temple. A man who had been crippled from birth was lying by the temple gate. There he sat every single day, praying and begging. When he saw Peter and John, he asked them for some money. Peter replied that they did not have any money, but that he would gladly give the man what he had: *"In the name of Jesus Christ of Nazareth, walk"* (Acts 3:6).

The disciples were amazed at the powers that God had given to them through the Holy Spirit. You and I can also expect miracles when the Holy Spirit fills us and guides us to ask something in Jesus' name, the greatest of which is seeing people accept Jesus as Lord and Savior.

W.W.J.

Jesus performed many miracles to help people know how much God loves them.

Peter and John

Keep Quiet? Never!

Then they commanded them not to speak or teach at all in the name of Jesus. (Acts 4:18)

After Peter and John had healed the crippled man, everyone was very excited and praised and worshiped God. Crowds of people flocked to see Peter and John, and Peter spoke to them about Jesus. He also told them that they should repent and accept the Lord's forgiveness for their sins. This made the Sanhedrin, the council of Jewish elders, very angry. They had just had Jesus killed, and now all of a sudden a bunch of people appeared preaching and performing miracles in this same Jesus' name. So the Sanhedrin had Peter and John arrested, and the two men spent the night in jail. The next morning, Peter and John were brought before the Sanhedrin for questioning.

Peter was filled with the Holy Spirit and told them exactly how they miraculously healed the crippled man: in the name of Jesus. The Sanhedrin was not quite sure what to do with Peter and John, and in the end they commanded the two men not to speak or teach about Jesus anymore.

However, Peter and John replied *"... we cannot help speaking about what we have seen and heard"* (Acts 4:20).

Christians simply cannot keep quiet about God's miracles or about the redemption that only he can give. Sometimes people don't want to hear anything about the gospel, but Christians simply cannot help telling others about God's grace. We should always be willing to tell others about the wonderful new life that Jesus Christ can give us, but we should do so with love and not with arrogance or false pride.

W.W.J.

The Pharisees also told Jesus to stop teaching people, but it was impossible for him to keep quiet about God.

The High Priest

They arrested the apostles and put them in the public jail. (Acts 5:18)

The Pharisees probably thought that Jesus' crucifixion would finally put an end to all the trouble he had caused them. That is why they were very upset and dismayed when they found out that the disciples were preaching Jesus' message with renewed passion and fervor. The Pharisees couldn't quite understand what had brought about the remarkable change in the disciples, and neither could the ordinary people on the street. Jesus' disciples used to be shy, ordinary fishermen who did not really possess any special kind of wisdom. But all of a sudden, they became passionate as well as wise in everything they said. It was almost as if they were brand-new people. This dramatic change was the work of the Holy Spirit.

The Pharisees decided that it was time to start persecuting the disciples. Just as they had persecuted Jesus, they started to arrest and interrogate the disciples. This happened exactly as Jesus had predicted. Jesus said that those who preached the gospel and worked to build the kingdom of the Lord would be persecuted. But the disciples loved Jesus too much and were too convinced of the truth to stop telling people about him.

You and I will also encounter opposition when we tell others about Jesus' kingdom. Do you love Jesus enough to keep talking about him anyway?

W.W.J.

Jesus said that everyone who lived according to God's will would be persecuted. (John 15:20)

October 7

Gamaliel

Be Careful

"But if it is from God, you will not be able to stop these men." (Acts 5:39)

The kingdom of God is always victorious, even when the odds seem stacked against it. Regardless of how relentlessly people try to stop God's message from spreading, it will always continue to be taught and listened to. Yes, sometimes those who preach the gospel are subjected to much persecution and suffering. Some of God's messengers are even killed, but even this will not keep God from attaining his goal. The devil may try all kinds of tricks and make life very difficult for the Lord's children, but he will never be able to stop God's kingdom from growing.

When the high priest and his supporters started to persecute the apostles, many of the apostles were sent to jail. Once the religious leaders had accomplished this, they had another meeting to decide what to do with the disciples.

Gamaliel was a very clever man, a teacher of the law, and also a member of the Sanhedrin. God worked in his heart, and he spoke some very wise words during the meeting. He said that if the disciples' work was of human origin, it would definitely fail. But if the disciples' work was from God, no one would be able to stop them.

In this way, God ensured that the apostles could continue their work. The Lord often uses people to ensure that his work can be continued. And sometimes he may surprise us with who he decides to use!

W.W.J.

Jesus will enable you to play a part in building his kingdom.

October 8

Seven Deacons

FILLED WITH THE SPIRIT

"Brothers, choose seven men from among you." (Acts 6:3).

The first community of believers grew very fast. More and more people became curious about the disciples' teachings, and what is more, God used the Holy Spirit to change their hearts so that they decided to become part of the community of believers. Eventually, there were so many that the apostles found it difficult to pay attention to everybody's problems.

The twelve apostles then gathered all the believers together and said that it wouldn't be right for them to neglect the ministry of God's Word in order to take care of practical matters. The apostles suggested that seven men should be chosen from among the believers. These seven men should be known for their wisdom and should be filled with the Holy Spirit. These men would help the people with their problems, and the apostles would be able to devote all their time and attention to praying and ministering the word of God. This is how it came about that seven Christians were chosen to be deacons. The people prayed for the deacons and the deacons took care of the believers. The Bible tells us that the gospel spread rapidly during that time and the number of believers continued to grow. There were even some Jewish priests who became Christians.

Today we still need people to take care of the body of Christ. There are many people who are poor or destitute, and they need help and support. That is why many churches still choose deacons. However, it is important to remember that not just anybody can be a deacon. Everyone who works for the Lord must be filled with the Spirit. Deacons have to be people whose lives show that they love Jesus.

Every single one of us has our little place in the kingdom of God. Everyone can do something to help his kingdom here on earth to grow. Tell the Lord that you are available for his work today.

W.W.J.

Jesus knows that every person is unique and that everyone can serve in his kingdom in a special way.

October 9

Stephen

WHAT DID HE SEE?

But Stephen looked up to heaven and saw the glory of God, and Jesus standing at the right hand of God. (Acts 7:55)

The devil wasn't very happy that the first community of believers grew so rapidly. That is why he made sure that trouble came the Christians' way.

Stephen had been one of the seven deacons chosen to serve the early church. He received an extraordinary measure of grace, strength, and power from the Lord, and he performed many great miracles and signs. Some of the leaders and teachers of the synagogue argued with Stephen. However, the Holy Spirit gave Stephen so much wisdom that they were no match for him. In retaliation, they bribed some people to say that he was blaspheming against God and Moses. In this way, they stirred up the people, the elders, and the teachers of the law. They seized Stephen and brought him before the Sanhedrin. The Bible says that Stephen's face looked like that of an angel because the glory of God was upon him. Stephen then spoke to the teachers of the law about Jesus.

The Sanhedrin eventually became extremely angry with Stephen. But Stephen, filled with the Holy Spirit, looked up to heaven and saw the glory of God and Jesus standing at the right hand of God. He told them what he saw, and they became absolutely enraged. They refused to believe that an ordinary man could see the glory of God. They rushed at him, dragged him out of the city, and stoned him. While the stones were raining down on him, he called out, *"Lord Jesus, receive my spirit"* (Acts 7:59). Then he fell to his knees and cried out in a loud voice, asking the Lord to forgive them their sins. And then he died.

Stephen was the first martyr who died for Jesus' sake. But he was so filled with the Holy Spirit that he became a wonderful example of how a Christian should respond to suffering. When we are filled with the Spirit, we become braver than we ever thought possible.

W.W.J.

Jesus was filled with the Holy Spirit, and he radiated the glory of his Father.

October 10

Saul

The Man Before Christ

Meanwhile, the witnesses laid their clothes at the feet of a young man named Saul. (Acts 7:58)

The Bible often talks about people whose characters and lives were very different before they met Christ. However, after they had met the Lord and come to repentance, their thoughts and actions changed radically. In this way, they were different people before Christ than they were after Christ.

This is also true of Paul. He even underwent a change of name. Paul was initially called Saul. Saul was a very clever young man, and a student of the Law of Moses. He was a Pharisee who was very adept at arguing about religious matters. He had been a student of the respected rabbi Gamaliel.

Saul was very upset about the new teachings that the disciples were spreading about Jesus Christ. He was so angry that he decided to completely exterminate the disciples' teachings. That is why he started to persecute the Christians. When Stephen was stoned, the Bible tells us, the witnesses put Stephen's clothes at the feet of Saul. Saul was standing to one side, watching while the people stoned Stephen to death.

If we haven't given our lives to the Lord yet, we don't really love him and we don't really want to live for him. We might even go so far as being very mean and negative about the gospel and the Lord's work. Even today, there are still many Christians all around the world who are being persecuted by people who have not yet had a heartfelt encounter with Jesus Christ. We need to pray for these people. Are you still a Saul, or have you become a Paul? Have you given your life to the Lord? If you have, the Holy Spirit has taken up residence in your heart and has transformed you into a new person who belongs to Jesus Christ.

W.W.J.

Jesus changed the lives of many people here on earth by nothing more than a simple encounter.

An Ethiopian

SEEKING ANSWERS

"How can I," he said, "unless someone explains it to me?" (Acts 8:31)

There was once a man named Philip. He was an evangelist, meaning that he dedicated his life to sharing the gospel message so that people could accept Christ as their Savior.

One day, an angel of the Lord told Philip to go to a very quiet road, a desert road that went from Jerusalem to Gaza. Philip didn't quite understand why he had to do this, but he was obedient and did as the angel told him to do. On this road, he met an Ethiopian man who was on a journey. This Ethiopian was the minister of finance for the queen of Ethiopia. He was just on his way out of Jerusalem, where he had gone to worship. He was sitting in his chariot, busy reading the book of Isaiah.

Philip started to run alongside the chariot. He asked the Ethiopian if he understood what he was reading. The Ethiopian said that he couldn't possibly understand it because he knew no one who could explain it to him. He then invited Philip to get into the chariot with him and sit with him. Philip explained to the Ethiopian that the passage from Isaiah that he was reading was actually about Jesus. The Ethiopian listened to everything that Philip told him and accepted it as the truth. He also asked to be baptized then and there, in some water right next to the road. Then the official joyfully continued his journey back to his own country.

Because Philip was obedient when the Lord sent him, a very important man had the opportunity to hear the wonderful gospel of Jesus Christ and then to take that message to a far-off land. You and I are also the Lord's messengers. Sometimes the Lord sends us to a friend or a family member to tell them about his gospel. We should be willing to go to whomever we are sent and to talk to them. Perhaps we can answer some people's questions about Jesus so that they can give their hearts to him.

W.W.J.

Jesus said that we are a light for the world and salt for the earth. (Matthew 5:13-16)

October 12

Saul/Paul

THE MAN AFTER CHRIST

"Who are you, Lord?" Saul asked. "I am Jesus, whom you are persecuting," he replied. (Acts 9:5)

Saul was a devout Jew and Pharisee. The early Christians made him very angry because he thought the gospel message was wrong. His heart was completely closed and hardened to Christ's kingdom. He agreed with those who were persecuting the Christians; he approved of Stephen being killed. After that event, he was like a man with a mission – the wrong mission. The Bible says that Saul continued threatening the followers of the Lord with death (Acts 9:1).

He decided to take his persecution of believers to the city of Damascus. On his way there, however, a miracle happened. Suddenly a light from heaven flashed around him. The light was so powerful and bright that he fell to the ground. Then a voice from heaven said, *"Saul, Saul, why do you persecute me?"* (Acts 9:4). Saul was completely bewildered and wanted to know who was speaking to him. The voice replied that he was Jesus and that Saul was not only persecuting people, but also Jesus himself. For three days after that he was struck blind, and he could also not eat or drink. He had an amazing encounter with the Lord himself, and it changed his life.

Suddenly, Saul was transformed into Paul. From that day forward, he served the Lord and worked to build the kingdom of God. His heart had been changed, and he became a new man. The same thing happens to us. If we say yes to God and give ourselves and our lives to him, he fills us with his Spirit so that we can serve him.

Not everyone has a miraculous meeting with the Lord as Saul did. But you and I should nevertheless be certain that we have also said yes to the Lord.

W.W.J.

Even wicked and demon-possessed people had their lives completely transformed by their encounters with Jesus.

October 13

Cornelius

ALL KINDS OF ANIMALS

It contained all kinds of four-footed animals, as well as reptiles of the earth and birds of the air. (Acts 10:12)

After Jesus' resurrection and ascension, the disciples were still convinced that the gospel of redemption was only intended for the Jews. That is why they focused on telling only the Jews that Jesus Christ had died on the cross for them. However, God intended the gospel of Jesus' redemption to be heard and accepted by the whole world, not only the Jews. That is why he allowed the persecution of the Christians to take place – so that the disciples could also spread the gospel in other regions and among other people. However, the disciples still pretty much spoke only to the Jews.

The Lord wanted to change this. That is why he decided to appear to Peter in a vision. One afternoon, at about noon, Peter was on the roof of a house, resting and praying. Eventually, he became hungry and wanted something to eat. While the meal was being prepared, Peter fell into a trance. He saw heaven opened and something like a large sheet being let down to earth by its four corners. Inside the sheet were all kinds of four-footed animals, and also reptiles and wild birds. Then a voice told him to kill the animals and eat them.

Peter was very disturbed by this because many of these animals were the ones that the Law forbade the Jews to eat. These animals were considered unclean or impure. The voice replied that he should not call anything impure that God had made clean. This scene repeated itself three times. Then the sheet disappeared.

Right after that, a non-Jewish man knocked on the front door of the house and asked Peter to go to the Roman centurion Cornelius. Before the vision, Peter would never have done something like that. However, the vision made him understand that the Lord's gospel was also intended for non-Jewish people.

The gospel is for all people. For all nations. For all countries.

W.W.J.

Jesus knew that the earth, and everyone on it, belongs to the Lord.

October 14

The Believers

PERSECUTED AND SCATTERED

Those who had been scattered by the persecution in connection with Stephen ... (Acts 11:19)

Jesus' first followers lived in Jerusalem. You will remember that they waited in that city for fifty days before God's gift was given to them. This gift was the Holy Spirit, who filled them with the strength and power that they needed to be witnesses for Jesus.

The apostles worked mostly in and around Jerusalem. In this area, many people became followers of Jesus. However, shortly after this the persecution of the Christians started. The teachers of the law started devising plans to destroy the apostles and their teachings. Perhaps God allowed the persecution because he wanted the wonderful gospel of Jesus Christ to be spread even further afield.

After Stephen was stoned to death, the Christians were subjected to terrible persecution. They had to flee for their lives. They were scattered and many of them went to live in distant countries. But even in these new countries, they continued to spread the gospel of the Lord. They were filled with the Holy Spirit and simply could not keep quiet about the Lord. The Bible tells us that many people believed and turned to the Lord. A church was even established in a large city named Antioch.

Before Jesus had been taken up to heaven, he had told the disciples to spread the good news of the gospel among all people. In a way, the persecution of the Christians helped this to happen. You and I should pray today that the whole world will know that Jesus Christ is the Lord. Perhaps the Lord will send you to a distant country to preach the gospel to the people there. We should all work together to make sure that the whole world knows about Jesus Christ.

W.W.J.

God loved the world so much that he gave his only Son to pay for the sins of the world. Jesus' message is for everybody on earth.

October 15

Christians

The disciples were called Christians first at Antioch. (Acts 11:26)

There are many people who call themselves Christians. They think that they are Christians because they grew up in a Christian country. Or they decide that they are Christians simply because they are not Muslims or Buddhists. But what does the name "Christian" really mean?

The name "Christian" comes from the name "Christ," which means "Anointed One." In the Old Testament, people used to anoint prophets or priests or kings. If you were anointed, it meant that you were set aside for the service of the Lord. Christ was also anointed by the Holy Spirit, and he was set aside to do the Father's work of redemption so that you and I could be saved. He was therefore set aside for God. Christians are people who are anointed by the Holy Spirit to do the work of the kingdom.

The name "Christian" therefore means that Christ himself has come to live inside us. This is what makes our faith different from all the other faiths. The first time that followers of Jesus were called Christians was in Antioch, where one of the first churches was established. People knew who were followers of Jesus because they told others about Jesus and lived their lives to Jesus' glory.

Do people know that you are a Christian, not only in name, but also in word and deed? It is a wonderful name to bear: Christian. It tells others that Christ is the King of your life.

W.W.J.

People knew that the disciples were followers of Christ.

October 16

Peter

They came to the iron gate leading to the city. It opened for them by itself.
(Acts 12:10)

As the persecution of Christians continued in Jerusalem, King Herod
decided to have James, the brother of John, executed by the sword.
Some Jews were very pleased with this, and therefore King Herod
decided that it would be an even better idea to arrest Peter as well.
Herod intended to bring him out for public trial after the Passover.

So Peter was kept in prison, where he was guarded day and night.
The believers prayed for him continuously.

The night before Herod was to bring him to trial, Peter was sleeping, with two soldiers sitting beside him guarding him. He was bound
with two chains, and sentries stood guard at the entrance to the
prison.

Suddenly, an angel of the Lord appeared and a bright light shone in
the cell. The angel woke Peter and told him to get up. Suddenly, the
chains fell from Peter's wrists. The angel led Peter out of the prison.
They passed the first and the second guards, and when they came to
the iron gate leading to the city, it opened by itself. It was a miracle!

James had been taken to heaven, but God still had work for Peter
to do. This is why he sent an angel to lead Peter from the prison. It
was not yet his time to die. The Lord has the power to lead us safely
from even the most difficult situations. If it is God's will to save us, no
one can stop him from doing it.

W.W.J.

The Lord sends his angels to protect us every single day.

Rhoda

They Didn't Believe Her

"You're out of your mind," they told her. (Acts 12:15)

While Peter was in prison, all the believers were praying for him. They pleaded with the Lord to keep Peter safe. After all, Jesus taught them to pray so that they might receive. There is tremendous power in prayer.

While the Christians were still busy praying, an angel led Peter out of the prison. Before he knew what had happened, he was standing in the street outside the prison. He decided to go to Mary's house where he knew the believers would be busy praying for him. He knocked on the front door. A servant girl named Rhoda came to the door and immediately realized that it was Peter. She was so glad that she completely forgot to open the door for him! She ran back to the praying group saying that Peter was at the door. But they didn't believe her. They told her that she was out of her mind or simply imagining things.

Isn't this interesting? They were praying to the Lord to protect Peter and free him from prison, and when it happened, they didn't believe it! We do exactly the same sometimes. We pray for something, but we don't really believe that it will be given to us.

Peter continued knocking, and eventually they let him into the house. Everyone was completely astonished.

Let us have faith and trust that the Lord will answer our prayers if it is his will.

W.W.J.

Jesus invited us to pray and ask in his name so that we might receive what we ask for.

Manaen

ONE SAVED, ONE LOST

In the church at Antioch there were prophets and teachers: Barnabas, Simeon called Niger, Lucius of Cyrene, Manaen (who had been brought up with Herod the tetrarch) and Saul. (Acts 13:1)

One of the saddest things of all is that some people in a family know, love, and serve the Lord, while others have absolutely no interest in the Lord. Perhaps this is also true in your family. Some of your family members or friends may have given their hearts to the Lord, while others have not. This was the case with Manaen and Herod.

Manaen was a prophet and a teacher. He probably dedicated his life to Jesus as a consequence of Paul's ministry. Manaen lived in Antioch. We are told that he grew up in a very important and wealthy household. He had been childhood friends with Herod the tetrarch. This was the same Herod who was the governor when Jesus died on the cross. It is also the same Herod who had John the Baptist beheaded. He was a very evil man. He also took his brother's wife, Herodias, for himself.

Manaen accepted the Lord. Herod rejected him. This kind of thing often happens in families and between close friends. The most important thing is that you must be sure that you are a child of the Lord.

W.W.J.

Jesus said that two people could sleep on the same bed; the one would be saved and the other not. (Luke 17:34)

October 19

The Spirit

HE LEADS IN TRUTH

While they were worshiping the Lord the Holy Spirit said ... (Acts 13:2)

Jesus promised to send the Holy Spirit to his disciples so that they would know exactly what to do and how to act. The Holy Spirit would not only fill them with strength and power, but would also lead them in truth. In their hearts, the disciples would find the conviction they needed to guide their actions. The Holy Spirit would explain to them exactly what they needed to do.

One day, Jesus' followers gathered together to worship the Lord and to fast together. In their hearts, the Holy Spirit spoke to them. He told them to set apart Barnabas and Paul for the work to which the Lord had called them. This is how it came about that Barnabas and Paul were sent out by the Holy Spirit to do the Lord's work. They set out on their travels.

Their first destination was Cyprus. When they arrived at Salamis, they proclaimed the word of God in the Jewish synagogues. After that, they traveled throughout the whole island, and everywhere they told people about the gospel of Jesus Christ.

Each one of us has a special job to do in the kingdom of the Lord, and God knows exactly what it is. The Holy Spirit sets us apart to do this work. He leads us and gives us clarity about what is God's will for our lives. The Holy Spirit will lead you and show you how you can be of use in Jesus' kingdom.

W.W.J.

Jesus was also set apart to do the work of the Lord.

Bar-Jesus

Sorcerer and False Prophet

There they met a Jewish sorcerer and false prophet named Bar-Jesus. (Acts 13:6)

Paul and Barnabas were sent out by the Holy Spirit to minister the gospel of Jesus. In a town called Paphos, they met a sorcerer named Bar-Jesus.

The sorcerer tried to impress the governor, who was a very important and intelligent man named Sergius Paulus. Because he wanted to hear the word of God, the governor sent for Paul and Barnabas to tell him about Jesus. However, the sorcerer opposed them because he wanted to prevent the governor from believing in Jesus.

Paul was filled with the Holy Spirit and looked straight at Bar-Jesus. He then spoke to the sorcerer and said, *"You are a child of the devil and an enemy of everything that is right! You are full of all kinds of deceit and trickery. Will you never stop perverting the right ways of the Lord?"* (Acts. 13:10). The Holy Spirit led Paul to tell the sorcerer that the Lord would punish him. He would be struck with blindness and would be unable to see the light of the sun for a time. Immediately, mist and darkness came over Elymas, and he groped about until someone led him away by the hand.

Bar-Jesus (also called Elymas) had used evil powers and magical tricks. But God's power is much greater than the power of the devil. A wonderful thing happened. The important governor, who saw this take place before his eyes, gave his life to Jesus.

W.W.J.

The Bible tells us that he who is in us (the Holy Spirit) is stronger than he who is in the world (the devil). (1 John 4:4)

Paul and Barnabas

An Argument Caused Them to Part Company

They had such a sharp disagreement that they parted company. (Acts 15:39)

The Bible says that it is wonderful for people to live together in peace. It is truly marvelous when people are willing to give each other some leeway so that they can live together peacefully despite their different opinions and habits.

Unfortunately, we sometimes feel so strongly about something that we are not willing to compromise. The ensuing difference of opinion might cause us to be unable to continue a partnership with those with whom we differ. This is what happened with Paul and Barnabas.

Paul and Barnabas traveled together and ministered the gospel of Christ together. Their ministry helped many people to turn to Jesus. As the two of them prepared for another journey together, Barnabas suggested that they ask John, also called Mark, to join them on their journey. However, John Mark had previously traveled with them and had deserted them and returned home in the middle of the trip. Paul did not want John Mark to join them again. Barnabas said that John Mark should join them, and Paul said that he shouldn't. They had such a sharp disagreement that they decided to go their separate ways. Barnabas and Mark went to Cyprus. Paul took Silas on his next journey.

Sometimes you can only be friends with someone up to a point. Even Christians will have disagreements that cause them to part company. People are always growing and changing, and sometimes people grow apart. However, it is important not to part company in anger. Talk the matter through and decide to continue on your separate ways with peace in your hearts.

W. W. J.

Judas also parted company with Jesus, but for entirely the wrong reasons.

October 22

Lydia

A Chic Lady Says Yes!

One of those listening was a woman named Lydia, a dealer in purple cloth from the city of Thyatira. (Acts 16:14)

Everywhere they went, Paul and Silas talked to people about Jesus. One day, they arrived in an important city named Philippi. On the Sabbath they went to the river, just outside the city, because they thought that they would find a Jewish place of prayer there. They sat down by the river and began to speak to a number of women who had gathered there to pray. One of these women was Lydia.

Lydia was a businesswoman, and she dealt in purple cloth – an expensive cloth that only the rich could afford for making their clothing. She was probably a wealthy and chic lady, known far and wide as the lady who had beautiful purple cloth for sale.

While Paul was talking to the women, something happened in Lydia's heart. The Bible says that the Lord opened her heart to respond to Paul's message. This means that she could almost not help becoming a believer. She was hungry for the word of God. She desired to make it her own. She didn't just hear what Paul was saying, she decided to take possession of it and keep it in her heart. She gave her life to Jesus Christ and became his follower. She and her entire family were baptized that day.

From this passage, we learn that we should always be willing to talk to people about Jesus. We can never really know when the Lord will open other people's hearts to the gospel. We should pray to the Lord to open people's hearts and minds to the gospel of Jesus Christ.

W.W.J.

Jesus unlocks the door of the heart, and when he opens a door, no one can shut it again.

October 23

Paul and Silas

Music in Prison

About midnight Paul and Silas were praying and singing hymns to God. (Acts 16:25)

It is easy to sing when your heart is filled with joy and you are feeling happy. It is quite another thing to be able to sing when things go wrong. In the latter case, singing is in faith.

While Paul and Silas were talking to the people in Philippi, a slave-girl kept following them wherever they went. There was an evil spirit in her. This evil spirit helped her to predict the future. Paul and Silas cast out the evil spirit from her. However, after the evil spirit was cast out, her owners could no longer make any money from her by getting her to tell other people's fortunes. They were very angry about this.

They seized Paul and Silas and had them thrown in prison. They were severely beaten and then locked away in a heavily guarded part of the prison. Their hands were bound with chains and their feet were fastened in the stocks. Their bodies were probably bruised and battered, and it was cold, dark, and smelly in the prison. Just think of the discomfort and pain that they must have experienced. But the Bible tells us a very interesting thing about the two men's response to their unpleasant situation.

At about midnight, the other prisoners heard the sounds of beautiful singing, praising, and worshiping. It was none other than Paul and Silas, busy praising the Lord. The other prisoners listened in astonishment to the two singing men. They had probably never before heard anyone in such trouble singing so beautifully. Suddenly, God sent a violent earthquake and the prison doors flew open. All of the prisoners' chains came loose. The jailer saw this miracle. As a consequence, he and his entire household became followers of the Lord.

If you and I can sing even when we are in trouble, we are spiritual winners. Miracles may even happen, just because of our faith.

W.W.J.

Even when Jesus had to endure terrible pain and suffering, he still praised his Father.

October 24

The Jailer

First Afraid, Then Filled with Joy

He was filled with joy because he had come to believe in God – he and his whole family. (Acts 16:34)

Paul and Silas were in prison. At about midnight, they were singing songs of praise and worship to God. Their bodies were in pain, but their hearts were filled with the joy of the Lord. Then God performed a miracle. He sent a violent earthquake that caused the prison doors to open and the prisoners' chains to be loosened.

The jailer woke up because of the earthquake, and when he saw that the prison doors were standing wide open, he drew his sword to kill himself. He thought that the prisoners had all escaped and were long gone. He thought that he was certain to be in big trouble because of this.

But Paul shouted to the jailer not to harm himself, because they were all still there. The jailer called for lights to be brought and went into the cells. He then kneeled, trembling before Paul and Silas. He simply could not believe his eyes. The prison doors were open, yet all the prisoners were still inside their cells. Then he asked Paul and Silas what he had to do to be saved. Their answer was, *"Believe in the Lord Jesus, and you will be saved, you and your household"* (Acts 16:31).

This is how it happened that the jailer, who was initially trembling in fear, came to believe in Jesus Christ. Suddenly, his heart was filled with joy because he was now a child of God. The peace of the Holy Spirit filled his heart. Isn't it wonderful how God can change people? Praise him for this!

W. W. J.

Many people who went to Jesus with their questions, fears, and worries left with new peace and joy in their hearts.

October 25

Apollos

A FERVENT PREACHER

He spoke with great fervor and taught about Jesus accurately. (Acts 18:25)

Apollos was a Jew. Somewhere along the way, he had heard the gospel of Jesus and gave his life to God. The Holy Spirit filled his heart, and he longed to share the wonderful experience of his relationship with the Lord Jesus Christ with everyone who would listen.

He first learned everything he could about Jesus Christ's teachings by listening to the other disciples, and then he went out and told as many people as he could about Jesus and his kingdom. He spoke with great fervor and enthusiasm. The Bible tells us that he was a very good teacher, and he was also a very bold speaker.

When you are bold, you are not ashamed to speak to others or to act in a certain way. You are confident and you speak up without fear. The Holy Spirit likes to give people the confidence they need to be outspoken. Jesus promised that we would receive strength and power when the Holy Spirit lived inside us. That strength also gives us boldness and courage, just as it did Apollos.

Apollos was a very smart man and a good speaker. Yet he was humble enough to learn the rest of the story from Priscilla and Aquila. That made him an even more persuasive speaker! God gave him wisdom through the Holy Spirit. Later, he managed to convince many Jews, who still believed in the Law of Moses, that Jesus was the Son of God.

Today there are still people like Apollos who teach others about Jesus with great boldness and fervor. Pray for them and thank God for them.

W.W.J.

People were astonished by the fact that ordinary fishermen were able to teach with so much wisdom because of the power of the Spirit.

The Sons of Sceva

A Bad Idea

"Jesus I know, and I know about Paul, but who are you?" (Acts 19:15).

When some of the Jews saw the marvelous deeds that the Lord was doing through Paul, and how Paul even managed to cast out demons from people, they tried to imitate him. Some of them actually dared to use the name of Jesus to cast out demons, despite the fact that they did not believe in Jesus.

Among these Jews were the seven sons of a Jewish chief priest named Sceva. They imitated Paul, and when they met people who were demon-possessed, they said, *"In the name of Jesus, whom Paul preaches, I command you to come out"* (Acts 19:13). They thought these words were like a magic spell that anyone could say. When they tried it on a demon-possessed person, however, the person jumped on them and overpowered them all. The evil spirit gave them such a beating that they ran out of the house naked and bleeding.

The evil spirits did not know the sons of Sceva. However, they knew about Paul and they knew Jesus. If you and I try to do things in our own strength, the devil and his demons will always be too strong for us. But if we are filled with the Holy Spirit, as Paul was, and if we follow and serve Jesus Christ, the devil knows that we are too strong for him, and that is why he will be afraid of us. After all, Jesus has already conquered the devil by his death on the cross. Never try to overcome the devil's evil work in your own strength. Always do everything in the name of Jesus.

W.W.J.

Jesus gave his disciples power over demons, even before the Holy Spirit was poured out. (Luke 10:17)

October 27

Demetrius

"There is danger that our trade will lose its good name" (Acts 19:27)

In the big city of Ephesus lived and worked a silversmith named Demetrius. He made silver shrines and statues of a goddess named Artemis, and the sale of his silver statues made him a good living.

Then Paul arrived in Ephesus with the teaching that the Lord God was the only true and living God and that all other gods (and goddesses) were worthless, powerless idols. Paul was teaching that Artemis was no more than a false god who should not be worshiped.

When Demetrius heard this, he was very upset. His business was in danger because of Paul's teachings. He then called together all the other silversmiths. He told them all about Paul, who had gathered a large following in Ephesus. The problem was that so many people were turning to Paul's God that people would eventually stop buying the silver statues of Artemis. And then the silversmiths would no longer be able to make any money. This soon caused an uproar in the whole city. Some of the people were furious, and that put Paul's life in danger.

Many people make a profit from things that are not to the glory of our God. When the ministry of the gospel causes people to turn away from bad things, the people who make their money from these bad things and practices feel very threatened. Consequently, they may become infuriated at those who preach the gospel. Light and darkness clash, and as a consequence Christians usually become increasingly unpopular. But because we know the truth, we should be willing to do our work for the kingdom regardless of other people's negative responses.

W.W.J.

Jesus overturned the tables of the merchants in the temple. They were probably very angry with him. (John 2:14-16)

October 28

Eutychus

A Very Long Sermon

Seated in a window was a young man named Eutychus, who was sinking into a deep sleep as Paul talked on and on. (Acts 20:9)

Paul did a lot of traveling. When he came to a town named Troas, all the Christians came together to break bread with him. They had an enjoyable meal together and then Paul spoke to the Christians.

Because he intended to leave the next day, Paul had a lot that he wanted to tell the Christians. These believers also wanted to listen to what he had to say and learn as much as they could. So they sat and listened to everything he told them about Jesus and his kingdom. Paul talked on and on, until it was eventually near midnight. And still Paul continued to preach. A young man named Eutychus was sitting in a window, listening to Paul. However, he became increasingly drowsy, until he fell asleep. When he was sound asleep, he fell out the window to the ground from the third story. Everyone was frightened. When they ran down and picked him up, they found that he was dead. Right there, God gave Paul the power to restore the young man to life. Paul continued his sermon until daybreak, and all the believers were encouraged and strengthened by his words. Perhaps this incident took place so that the Christians' faith in God could grow even stronger.

W.W.J.

People who saw the miracles that Jesus performed praised God. It also helped their faith to grow stronger.

October 29

Paul

A Sad Farewell

They all wept as they embraced him and kissed him. (Acts 20:37)

The love of the Lord that infuses your heart when you give your life to Jesus is something truly extraordinary. There is a very special bond between people who share their faith in Jesus Christ. You really come to love the people who serve the Lord with you because they are your brothers and sisters in Christ.

While Paul was visiting the Christians in Ephesus, he spoke to them about Jesus Christ. After Paul had finished his sermon, it was time for him to leave.

Paul spoke a last few words of encouragement to the Christians of Ephesus. Then everyone kneeled together and prayed. Then they were filled with sadness. They all wept as they embraced and kissed Paul. They were especially sad because Paul had said that they would not see him again on this earth. After they had said their goodbyes, they accompanied him to his ship.

The ties that bind people together are very precious. Friendship with other children of the Lord is a wonderful thing. Thank God for giving you Christian friends whom you cherish close to your heart. And be sure to nurture these friendships.

W.W.J.

Jesus said that we should love one another just like he loves us.

Philip

FOUR EXCEPTIONAL DAUGHTERS

He had four unmarried daughters who prophesied. (Acts 21:9)

The Holy Spirit gives certain people certain gifts to do the work of the Lord. Some people are pastors who take care of God's people. Others are teachers, and their work is to teach the Lord's followers. There are also evangelists, who have received a special gift for preaching the gospel of the Lord in such a way that people want to give their lives to the Lord, and therefore make a choice to follow Jesus.

In Caesarea lived a man named Philip. He was one of the deacons in the early church. He also had the gift of evangelism. Previously, the Lord had sent him to speak with the Ethiopian about Jesus and his kingdom. When Philip followed the Lord's instructions, he was rewarded by the privilege of seeing the rich and important Ethiopian man give his heart and life to the Lord.

Philip also had four daughters. It is wonderful when a mother and father serve the Lord and their children also decide to give their lives to the Lord. It could just as easily not be the case. There are many children who do not believe as their parents do and who decide to go their own way. Philip's four daughters gave their lives to Jesus, and they received a special gift from the Spirit.

God gave them the special gift of being able to prophesy so that people were instructed and encouraged when they heard God's message. In this way they were able to tell people about God's message for the future. Philip's entire household, therefore, consisted of people who were in the service of the Lord. Philip's four daughters became well known as instruments of the Lord. I hope you are also well known as someone who is willing to be used by the Lord.

W.W.J.

Jesus regarded no one as too insignificant or unimportant to be used by him. Everyone who wants to be his servant and who is equipped with the Holy Spirit can be his instrument.

Felix

A Wily Old Fox

At the same time he was hoping that Paul would offer him a bribe, so he sent for him frequently and talked with him. (Acts 24:26)

Felix was the governor of Caesarea. He had to act as judge when Paul was charged and brought to trial. Felix was a wily old fox. His motives were not altogether pure. If you watch a fox running in the wild, you will see that it runs furtively, all the while trying to mislead its pursuers or its prey about its motives. Felix was exactly like this.

The Bible tells us that during the trial, Paul spoke to Felix about Jesus Christ and a righteous life characterized by obedience to God. Paul also talked to Felix about self-control and the judgment that was to come. But time and again, Felix would interrupt the trial and send Paul away, saying that he would call for Paul again later to continue the conversation. And so old Felix continued his little game.

Felix did this because he hoped that Paul would offer him a bribe to be set free. That is why he called for Paul to be brought to him as often as possible. Paul's trial, presided over by Felix, lasted for two years. Eventually, Felix was replaced by another governor. But because Felix wanted to grant a favor to the Jews, he left Paul in prison.

It is a pity that people sometimes have hidden agendas and motives. This means that they are never quite honest about their intentions. Felix's real motive was to extort money from Paul and to make a personal financial profit out of the situation. And of course, this created a lot of problems for Paul. The same kind of deceitful people are still around today. They are not honest and sincere toward others. Instead, they always try to get something from you or convince you to do them some kind of favor. You and I should not be like this. Be honest, sincere, and candid. And always make sure that your actions benefit others.

W.W.J.

Jesus always made sure that his actions benefited others. And he was always honest and frank with everyone.

November 1

The Sailors

SAFE IN THE STORM

"Do not be afraid, Paul ... God has graciously given you the lives of all who sail with you." (Acts 27:24)

God has a plan for every person's life. He also has a very important plan for his kingdom, and he wants to bring this plan to fulfillment. To achieve this end, God does a really wonderful thing: he uses people like us as instruments to bring his plan to fruition.

Paul was a very special instrument of the Lord. He was arrested for preaching about the kingdom of Jesus Christ. He was then sent to Rome to stand trial there. Together with a number of soldiers and other prisoners, he was taken to Rome by ship. However, on their way to Rome, they were caught in a terrible storm.

The wind in the storm became so strong that the ship could no longer keep on its course. The sailors had no choice but to simply allow themselves to be driven along. Everyone was afraid that the ship would run aground, and so they lowered the anchor. Eventually, the storm became so violent that the sailors were forced to throw some of the ship's cargo overboard. When this didn't help, they started throwing the ship's tackle overboard. Despite all their efforts, the situation seemed hopeless. The ship was sinking.

During the night, an angel appeared to Paul and told him that because God had a plan for his life, the ship would not sink. The lives of all the people on board would be saved for Paul's sake.

Isn't it wonderful that the Lord's hand rests in a very special way on his children? And when his children are among other people, God's favor is also upon these people. The lives of the unbelieving soldiers and prisoners were saved because they were on the same ship as Paul, who served the Lord. As a Christian, you are constantly among other people. If God's favor is upon you, you will bring blessing to your school, your community, and your family. In this way, you can bring God's light into this dark world.

W.W.J.

The disciples received God's favor because they walked with Jesus.

November 2

Priscilla and Aquila

A Reliable Couple

Greet Priscilla and Aquila, my fellow workers in Christ Jesus. (Romans 16:3)

It is truly wonderful when a husband and wife wholeheartedly serve the Lord together. Together they are a team, and they can support each other in doing the work of the Lord – not only because they love Christ, but also because they love each other as husband and wife.

Aquila and Priscilla were married. They initially lived in Rome, but then a Roman ruler expelled all the Jews from Rome. So they moved to Corinth. This is where they met Paul. Paul often stayed with them because he practiced the same trade as they did – tentmaking.

They became very good friends, and naturally Paul told them everything about Jesus. As a consequence, Aquila and Priscilla also became Christians.

From that day on, they worked for Jesus Christ. Wherever they went, they told people about the redemption that Jesus offers people. They later went to Ephesus, and there they taught Apollos what he needed to know about the Christian faith. They were true stalwarts of the faith.

Do you know married couples who have given their lives to Jesus? Isn't it wonderful when a family spends time praising, worshiping, and serving the Lord together? I hope this is the case in your family. If it isn't, pray for changes to take place. In any case, decide that one day, when you have a family of your own, yours will be a family that serves the Lord.

W.W.J.

Those who walk with Jesus discover the true meaning of life.

Apelles

Greet Apelles, tested and approved in Christ. (Romans 16:10)

There are many people in the Bible who are mentioned only once. The Bible has a lot to say about some people, like Paul or Peter or John, but other people are only given a brief mention, almost in passing.

Apelles is mentioned only once. But this single comment on Apelles is a very beautiful one. In this passage, Paul sends his greetings to Apelles, who is living in Rome. He also says that Apelles has been tested and approved in Christ. He did his work as a Christian well. This is a very nice thing to say of someone. It means that the person's life clearly shows other people that he is a Christian who serves only the Lord. It is also likely that Paul meant that Apelles stuck to his convictions even in hard times. His strength of character helped him to survive the difficult times. He acted with integrity, and people appreciated Apelles for his noble character. For all of this, Paul commends Apelles.

If people had to write down one line to describe your life, what do you think they would say? Would your testimonial be as wonderful as that of Apelles? May the Lord help us to show others that we truly serve the Lord, not only with our words, but also with our deeds. May others know that we are trustworthy and strong because our hearts and lives belong to Jesus.

W.W.J.

Jesus encouraged us to be the light of the world. A light isn't something that you hide away.

Tryphena and Tryphosa

Work Hard for Jesus

Greet Tryphena and Tryphosa, those women who work hard in the Lord. (Romans 16:12)

We don't know much about these two women, Tryphena and Tryphosa, except that they were acquaintances of Paul. They converted to Christianity and gave their lives to Christ.

There was a lot of work that needed to be done to help the apostles in their ministry. The number of people who became followers of Christ increased rapidly, but there were still many more who did not know him. Churches had to be established, leaders had to be taught and trained for their work, the believers had to be encouraged, the widows had to be taken care of, the false teachers who spread misleading teachings about Jesus had to be resisted, and much else besides. Building the kingdom required hard work. And it still does today.

Even though the church has existed for a long time, there is still a tremendous amount of work to be done. There are millions of people in the world who have never heard about Jesus. Christians in the churches still need encouragement and care. Even in your town and church, you will find that there is a lot of work that Jesus wants you to do.

Tryphena and Tryphosa were known as two women who worked hard for the Lord. They gave their all for Jesus. They expended all their energy and used all their strength to build the kingdom of the Lord. How about you? Are you willing to work hard in your church? What do you do for Jesus? Tell the Lord today that you are available to do his work.

W.W.J.

Jesus and his disciples worked long hours telling people about the kingdom, teaching them, and healing them.

November 5

Rufus's Mother

HOSPITALITY FOR THE SAKE OF THE KINGDOM

Greet Rufus ... and his mother, who has been a mother to me, too. (Romans 16:13)

Paul was a bachelor. When the Lord changed his life, he decided to dedicate his life to Christ's work completely, and therefore he never married. This doesn't mean that there was something wrong with Paul. He simply decided to devote all his attention to the kingdom of God. Elsewhere Paul wrote that it is good to get married, but it is even better to remain unmarried because then you can devote your entire life to the Lord!

Paul traveled a lot. He often stayed with fellow Christians and surely made some very close friendships. Apparently, he stayed at times with Rufus and his mother. Rufus worked very hard for the kingdom. When Paul sends his greetings to Rufus in Rome, he also sends his best wishes to Rufus's mother. He remembers her as a woman who loved him very much and had shown him kind hospitality on his visits. He is obviously filled with gratitude for everything she has done for him and wishes to acknowledge her good work. She was like a mother to him.

We should open our homes to those who dedicate their lives to serving the Lord. Pray for those who travel all over the world to minister the gospel.

W.W.J.

Peter's mother-in-law served Jesus when he came to her house. (Matthew 8:14-15)

November 6

The Corinthians

They Argued about Their Favorites

One of you says, "I follow Paul"; another, "I follow Apollos." (1 Corinthians 1:12)

We all have our favorites – people we like more than others. Just think about the singers or bands you like. You probably like the music of one singer or band, while your friend prefers the music of another. There is nothing wrong with having different preferences and tastes. The important thing is that we should not become angry with others for having a different opinion than ours. We should also not say mean things about other people's favorites. And our differences of opinion should definitely not cause dissension.

Paul was faced with a very difficult problem: the church members in Corinth had become divided into different groups. There were constant arguments and quarrels among the people. The reason for this division was that some of the people preferred Paul. Others liked Apollos better. Some said that Peter was their favorite, and yet others said that Jesus was definitely the person that they liked best. So the people could not agree whether they followed Paul, Apollos, Peter, or Jesus. Paul was indignant. How could there be such disagreement and division among people who served the Lord?

Paul told the Corinthians that they were acting very childishly. Mature Christians simply did not behave in such a childish way. After all, Paul and Apollos and Peter were all merely servants of the Lord. They were all just doing their little bit for the kingdom. The one was not more important than the other. The Lord never has favorites. In his eyes, everyone is equal. All people are co-workers in his kingdom.

Even though it might happen that we like one spiritual leader better than another, or one Christian singer better than another one, we must never allow our personal preferences to cause division within the Christian community. We are all working for the kingdom, and we are all equal in God's eyes.

W.W.J.

The disciples were also continually arguing about which one of them was the most important. Jesus was quick to admonish them. (Mark 9:34-35)

November 7

Paul

How Important is Baptism?

For Christ did not send me to baptize, but to preach the gospel. (1 Corinthians 1:17)

There are two ways in which Christians approach baptism. Some Christians feel that baptism should take place in infancy, because they believe that the entire family belongs to Christ when the mother and father are believers. Other Christians believe that it is better to baptize people once they are older and have decided for themselves to serve Jesus. Whatever you believe, don't argue with other Christians about this matter even though their beliefs might be different from your own. Being baptized is important, but it is not the most important aspect of the gospel of Jesus Christ.

Paul baptized a few people, but he never really felt that this was the work that he was sent out to do. He saw his work as preaching the gospel to people who had never had the opportunity to hear about Jesus. He did, however, baptize the household of Stephanas, as well as two other men, named Crispus and Gaius.

One of the causes of the discord in the Corinthian church was that some people were boasting that they had been baptized by this or that important man. This angered Paul. Being baptized is not nearly as important as following and serving God wholeheartedly. It must definitely never be the cause of discord.

W.W.J.

Jesus was baptized by John the Baptist, but as far as we know he never baptized anyone himself. (John 4:1-2)

November 8

Timothy

HE WAS SENT

For this reason I am sending to you Timothy. (1 Corinthians 4:17)

Paul's work in Corinth eventually led to a church being established in that city. Just think how interesting and difficult this must have been for him.

The church in Corinth continued to grow and expand, and Paul taught the new believers everything about Christ. However, Paul eventually had to continue his journey. He was probably concerned about the spiritual welfare of the believers in Corinth, and that is why he prayed for them and wrote letters to them.

At one point, he sent his co-worker Timothy to Corinth. Timothy's task was to remind the Corinthians of everything that Paul had taught them. Timothy would lead the Corinthians on the right path, encourage them, and help them to set right certain wrongs in their lives.

Today the Lord still wants people to help Christians all over the world by encouraging and strengthening them in their faith. Many believers also go to other countries to serve in their churches in order to encourage fellow Christians. Perhaps you will also get the opportunity to do so. This is one of the ways in which we can help others to stay on the Lord's path.

W.W.J.

Jesus often traveled long distances just to teach people.

Paul

COURT CASES

But instead, one brother goes to law against another – and this in front of unbelievers! (1 Corinthians 6:6)

Christians are people who have received the Holy Spirit. They are people who are led by the Holy Spirit, and when the Spirit has filled them, their lives produce the fruit of the Spirit. They have the Holy Spirit to guide them in their relationships with other people, and they also have their fellow Christians to give them advice and guidance.

Because Christians are not perfect people, they sometimes run into problems with other people, sometimes even with other Christians. The Bible says that when this happens, we should talk about the matter and try to resolve it as friends. If we cannot solve the problem by talking about it, we should involve a third Christian in the conversation and see if that will help us to find a solution.

The very last thing that we should do is to go to an unbelieving judge or court to resolve a problem between another Christian and ourselves. This is what happened in Corinth. The Christians who were arguing did not want to resolve the matter among themselves, and they dragged one another to court. This caused an even bigger fight. Paul says that this is not how Christians should go about solving the matter.

When we have a problem with someone, we should not be too quick to run to a lawyer or a court to bring charges against that person. Before we do anything else, we should talk about the matter in the forgiving spirit of Jesus Christ. If you have a problem with a friend, don't just run to your leaders and complain to them about your friend's behavior. First talk to him or her about the problem. It is likely that the Holy Spirit will help you solve the problem. We should always try to resolve our differences with others in a spirit of love and forgiveness.

W.W.J.

Jesus thought that we should obey the laws of our country as long as they do not go against the Bible.

November 10

Paul

I have become all things to all men so that by all possible means I might save some. (1 Corinthians 9:22)

Paul had a burning desire to tell people that they had the opportunity to become completely new because Jesus Christ had died for their sins. If they accepted him and had faith in him, they too would become Christians: new people in Christ.

Because Paul so much wanted to spread this message, he was willing to do just about anything to convince people that Jesus was their Savior. He spoke to many people, traveled long distances, and even endured terrible suffering for the sake of the gospel.

In order to win as many people as possible for Christ, Paul acted very wisely. The Bible tells us that to the Jews he became like a Jew, and to the Greeks he became like a Greek. This means that he tried to identify himself with whomever he was speaking. He tried to put himself in that person's shoes before he even attempted talking to him or her about Jesus. He tried to remove all possible obstacles so that nothing would stand in the way of the message of Jesus Christ being communicated clearly to that person.

If we want to speak about Jesus to gang members who live a tough life on the streets, we first need to understand them and their lifestyle. They must first feel comfortable in our company. If you talk to a child about Jesus, you cannot use the same language you would use for grownups. If you want to talk to a Chinese person about Jesus, you first have to be able to speak a language that the Chinese person would understand.

We as Christians should be adaptable so that we can reach and win more people for Jesus. Perhaps you need to get to know some of your classmates better and become their friends before you can really bring the message of the gospel across effectively. Ask the Lord to give you the wisdom you need to do this.

W.W.J.

Jesus understood people and talked to them on their level.

November 11

Paul

An Athlete for Jesus

Run in such a way as to get the prize. (1 Corinthians 9:24)

It is quite a sight to see athletes competing against one another. Each athlete tries his or her best, and every single one takes off from the starting block with the idea of winning. From the starting block to the finish line, they give everything in their efforts to win the prize.

Christians are also participating in a race every day. Our race is run on the track of life. We also do our very best to complete the race successfully. We too want to win the ultimate prize.

Running the race isn't always easy. We sweat and we grow tired, but we continue running. Before the race, we spent a lot of time exercising and practicing so that we could be fit and ready for the race. We ate food that would help our bodies grow strong, and we drank enough water so that we would not become thirsty. We also put on clothes that are suitable for running. After all, an athlete would never dream of running in boots and a heavy coat. He also doesn't try to run a race while carrying a large suitcase in his hand. An athlete has to rid himself of all unnecessary burdens before setting out to run the race.

All of this is applicable to the Christian running the Christian race. We cannot carry any unnecessary burdens with us because they will obstruct our progress. We cannot carry the heavy burden of sin upon our shoulders. We also exercise and practice for the race by reading the Bible and talking to God. The Holy Spirit is our trainer and he teaches us how to run well. We also do not run with uncertainty in our step. Instead, we reach out eagerly to what lies ahead. We follow Jesus, who has already finished his earthly race successfully.

Today you and I should do our very best, just like athletes running a race on a track. The Lord will give you the strength you need. Ask his Holy Spirit to help you. If we persevere, we will undoubtedly receive the prize from the hands of Jesus.

W.W.J.

Jesus completed his race on this earth and received the greatest prize of all.

November 12

Paul

FORGIVE AND COMFORT

Now instead, you ought to forgive and comfort him. (2 Corinthians 2:7)

We all make mistakes. Sometimes we feel like we could kick ourselves for doing something really foolish, but by then it is always too late to undo the damage. All we can do is to apologize for what we have done and to ask the people whom we have wronged to forgive us.

There was a man in Corinth who made some very bad mistakes. The other believers in Corinth admonished him for his wrongdoing and tried to get him to mend his ways. They told him that it was not right to act as he did. He then realized that he had made a mistake.

In this passage, Paul tells the Corinthians that they have admonished and punished this man enough. Because he has learned his lesson and repented, they ought to forgive him and comfort him, because otherwise he might become sad and dejected and lose all hope and courage. Sometimes we don't feel like really forgiving someone. We prefer to harp on that person's wrongdoing and continue to tell him that he made a mistake. Even when we don't do this with our words, we still do it with our actions and attitudes. We turn our backs on that person. It is as if we want to show him that we are not really willing to forgive him. However, this behavior is not worthy of a Christian.

Jesus Christ gladly forgives our sins, and therefore we should also be willing to forgive one another for our weaknesses and sins. If someone has made a mistake and is sorry for it, you should be willing to forgive. Show him that you love him. Show him that you have forgiven him. Show him that whatever happened is in the past, because it really is. Make friends with the person. Doing this is like giving clothes to someone who stands before you naked, vulnerable, and ashamed.

W. W. J.

Jesus told the adulterous woman that he did not condemn her. Instead he simply forgave her.

November 13

Paul

A Jar of Clay with a Precious Treasure Inside

But we have this treasure in jars of clay. (2 Corinthians 4:7)

Paul was all too aware of the fact that he was not perfect. He knew his shortcomings. He also sometimes felt very fragile. Just like us, Paul often suffered pain and humiliation at the hands of other people. He was rejected and misunderstood by others. He sometimes had to endure terrible beatings simply because he was a follower of Jesus. Like us, he was as fragile as a jar of clay.

Jars made of clay break quite easily. Have you ever had tea in a beautiful cup made of fine china? Fine china is very fragile, and if you drop one of your mother's expensive china cups, it will definitely break. A jar of clay is just as fragile.

Paul says that he is like a jar of clay that is cracked on the outside, but that has a great treasure inside. One can easily store jewelry and other precious things in a jar of clay. If you take a string of pearls or a diamond ring or a pair of golden earrings and put them in the jar, the contents of that humble jar make it something precious – despite the fact that the jar itself may be cracked. Even if the jar is not worth a great deal, its contents are still very precious.

Paul says that we are exactly like this jar of clay. We are fragile, breakable human beings. We have many shortcomings. We are easily hurt. We are imperfect. Nevertheless, what is inside of us is very valuable and precious. We carry the work of Jesus Christ inside us, and that is a very precious thing. Because the Holy Spirit lives inside us, we have a treasure in us. We make mistakes and we even sin, but he who lives inside us is a great and wonderful treasure.

We carry the kingdom and the message of Jesus inside us, and we need to make sure that the whole world can see these precious things inside us – even if it is through our cracks and chinks.

W.W.J.

Jesus was beaten and broken on the cross on Golgotha, but the message that he carried within him was so valuable that it could redeem all of mankind.

November 14

Paul and Peter

DOING DIFFERENT JOBS FOR THE LORD

For God, who was at work in the ministry of Peter as an apostle to the Jews, was also at work in my ministry as an apostle to the Gentiles. (Galatians 2:8)

We all look different. We all have different personalities. We all behave differently. Each and every person is unique. In the same way, each of us has a different calling. Every person does what his heart tells him to do, and every person has to be true to himself. If the Lord takes someone to be his child, he uses that person just as he or she is. He uses that person's personality and talents to serve him. He puts dreams and desires in our hearts so that we have aspirations regarding things that we would like to do, but he also makes sure that these things are aligned with what God wants us to do. For this reason, Christians do different kinds of work in the service of the Lord.

Peter was a Jew and he liked to work among the Jews. He devoted his entire life to sharing the message of Jesus with other Jews. He understood the Jews and could talk to them about Jesus. Preaching the gospel to the Jews was his work. Paul was also a Jew, but he had a different calling and desire. He wanted to preach the gospel to the Gentiles, or the non-Jews. He established Christian churches in many communities that were not Jewish. His heart's desire was to preach the gospel to these people.

The Lord still sends some people to Europe to preach the gospel there. Others go to Japan. Some go to America, and yet others travel to Russia. Every one of us has a particular circle or sphere within which we can do our work for the kingdom. The Lord has already started to work in your heart so that you can be equipped to share the gospel of Jesus with certain people. Ask him to show you where he wants you to work, and pray about the matter. Where does the Lord want to use you?

W.W.J.

Jesus initially kept company with the Jews only, but he knew that the entire world needed to hear his message. That is why he sent his disciples out into the world to spread the gospel.

November 15

Paul

Is God Your Abba?

Because you are sons, God sent the Spirit of his Son into our hearts, the Spirit who calls out, "Abba, Father." (Galatians 4:6)

One of the wonderful things that Paul discovered is that God is not only the God of law and order who lives somewhere far away in heaven. When the Lord spoke to Paul on the road to Damascus, Paul heard a voice filled with a wonderful love and profound strength. For the first time, he got to know God as a Person.

The more time Paul spent learning about Jesus and the Father, the more he realized that God was not somewhere far away, out of reach. Instead, he understood that God had come very near to us. Jesus came to live among people here on earth, and he sent his Holy Spirit to come and live in our hearts. Suddenly, God was no longer far away, but very close, and Paul got to know him as a God of deep and everlasting love.

Paul was so impressed by God's incredibly loving character that he called him "Abba." This was the word that young Jewish boys used to refer to their own beloved dads. If you have a father, what do you call him? Some say Dad, or Father, while others say Daddy, Pop, or Dadda. There are many different ways in which people address their fathers. But all these names are terms of endearment. They are names that show our awareness and gratitude that Dad is understanding, loving, and caring.

The Holy Spirit teaches us to call God our Dad. He understands us. He loves us. We can pour out our hearts to him. Because he loves us so much, we can feel free to love him. Call God your Abba today.

W.W.J.

Jesus had a very close relationship with his heavenly Dad.

November 16

Paul

A Soldier for the Lord

Put on the full armor of God. (Ephesians 6:11)

Throughout history, there have been soldiers. Soldiers fight for their country. Soldiers fight for their king. Soldiers ensure that the inhabitants of a country are safe and that enemies from beyond the borders of a country do not threaten its peace and order. History tells us about many wars that have taken place over the centuries.

Paul wants to teach us that we are like soldiers for the kingdom of God. We also fight against an enemy, and our enemy is the devil. He wants to destroy and conquer God's kingdom. He wants to hurt the people in God's kingdom and enslave them so that they will serve him. You and I cannot allow this to happen. That is why we are soldiers for Christ.

As Christians, we need weapons to fight the enemy. The best weapons we have are the Word of God and the name of Jesus. Because the Holy Spirit is with us, we needn't be afraid. He gives us all the courage we need. We also have other equipment, or armor, which the Lord has given us to help us be good soldiers. We have truth, we have been forgiven by God, and we are willing to preach the gospel. We have faith, and we know that we are redeemed. Therefore, we can take the Word of God in our hands and resist the devil and his evil spirits so that their attempts to destroy the kingdom will come to nothing. This is how we should go about being soldiers who emerge victorious from battle.

You are a soldier for God today. You are in Jesus' army. Put on his armor and be a winner for Jesus.

W.W.J.

Jesus was constantly fighting the enemy who wanted to destroy his kingdom.

Jesus

KNEEL BEFORE HIM

At the name of Jesus every knee should bow ... and every tongue confess that Jesus Christ is Lord, to the glory of God the Father. (Philippians 2: 10-11)

One of the most beautiful names of Jesus tells us that he is also Lord. This name comes from the Greek word *kyrios*, which means king or ruler.

Jesus' time here on earth as the Son of God culminated in his crucifixion on the cross so that he, as Lamb of God, could atone for our sins. However, after the Holy Spirit had resurrected him, he became the Conqueror who had defeated death. The Bible tells us that when he ascended to heaven to be with his Father, God gave him a name exalted above all other names. Upon hearing this name, all the people and all the creatures of heaven will kneel, and so will all the demonic creatures and the agents of the devil. Every tongue will confess and every knee will bow in recognition that Jesus is the Lord.

I have already bowed before Jesus in body and in spirit and have confessed that he is my Lord and King. Have you done so yet? If you are doubtful, you should bow down before him right now and acknowledge God as the Lord of your life. Ask him to live in your heart and to be the King of your life.

W. W. J.

Even those who spat on Jesus and those who kicked him and mocked him will one day have to acknowledge and confess that he is Lord.

November 18

Euodia

STOP ARGUING!

I plead with Euodia and I plead with Syntyche to agree with each other in the Lord. (Philippians 4:2)

It is to some extent understandable that non-Christians often fight and argue, because they do not have the Lord in their hearts. However, it is very unpleasant and disturbing when Christians argue and fight among themselves. After all, the God who gives peace to all people lives in all Christians' hearts, so how can they allow discord to disturb their peace with other people? Despite this fact, arguments and quarrels do occur among Christians.

In his letter to the Philippians, Paul writes that Euodia and Syntyche should stop arguing with each other. Paul says that they should decide to put an end to their fighting and agree with each other in the Lord.

These two women worked with Paul in the ministry of the gospel. They were serious about their commitment to the Lord. They wanted to help build his kingdom, but the devil made sure that they were distracted by quarrelling. Paul said that they should simply put an end to their fighting and no longer allow arguments to become obstacles to their work for the kingdom.

You and I should also decide not to be quarrelsome. Stop bickering and fighting. Make peace with the other person, especially if he or she is also a Christian. One person alone cannot sustain a fight. It takes two to fight. If you put an end to your side of the disagreement, the fight will immediately come to an end.

W. W. J.

Jesus taught that Christians' second name would be "peacemakers."

November 19

Epaphras

DEAR FELLOW SERVANT

Epaphras, our dear fellow servant. (Colossians 1:7)

Paul writes a letter to the Christians of Colosse. In this letter, he praises a man named Epaphras. He was the spiritual leader of the Christians of Colosse. What does Paul say about Epaphras?

The first thing that he says about Epaphras is that he was loved by his fellow Christians. Epaphras was filled with the love of Jesus and showed this love to everyone he met. That was why everyone loved him. It is easy to love someone who has the love of Christ in his heart.

The second thing that Paul says about Epaphras is that he led and taught the church of Colosse. Epaphras was a leader and a teacher. He wanted to teach people all about Jesus so that they would have the spiritual strength to live righteous lives. The Word of God strengthens us so that we can become good Christians.

The third thing that Paul says about Epaphras is that he was faithful in his work. Paul calls him a faithful servant of Christ. It is a joy to work with people who are faithful. You can depend on them because they will keep their promises and always stick to a task until it is finished.

The last comment that Paul makes is that Epaphras also told him that the Colossian Christians were doing very well in the faith. Epaphras was proud of the Colossians, and therefore he told Paul how well they were progressing. He said positive things about them. You and I should always try to say nice, positive, and encouraging things about other people.

W.W.J.

If Jesus is in our hearts, our good qualities will become increasingly visible.

November 20

Fathers

Don't be Faultfinders

Fathers, do not embitter your children, or they will become discouraged. (Colossians 3:21)

Dads are usually very proud of their kids. They want only the best for their children, and they also want their kids to be the best they can be. A father who really loves his children will do just about anything to make them happy. Sometimes he may even think that they can only be happy if they are always successful at everything they do or if they are always winners.

Because dads so much want their kids to be successful, they always correct their children when they see them doing something wrong. Kids need to be taught, and the Lord instructed fathers to teach their children the correct way of doing things. But sometimes a father is so anxious to correct his children that he becomes critical of them.

When you are critical, you keep a very close eye on what is right and what is wrong. You consciously seek out the errors and mistakes that people make. Paul writes that fathers should not be so critical of their children that their children become discouraged. If you are perpetually told about your many faults, you are bound to become discouraged. You will inevitably start thinking that you are completely worthless. You will feel as if you can't do anything right. You will begin to believe that you are an utter failure.

I don't think that fathers really want to discourage their children. Actually, fathers want to encourage their kids, but sometimes they go about doing it in an entirely wrong way. Forgive your dad if he is always finding fault with everything you do. Tell him that you really need his encouragement. Ask him if he is proud of you. Ask him if there is anything you do that he likes and approves of. But don't become angry with your dad; instead, try to understand him. Love him. And don't retaliate by finding fault with everything he does.

W. W. J.

Fortunately, Jesus accepts us just as we are without finding fault with us. He forgives us and encourages us.

November 21

Slaves

WORK HARD FOR HIM

Slaves, obey your earthly masters in everything; and do it, not only when their eye is on you ... but with ... reverence for the Lord. (Colossians 3:22)

In Bible times, many people were born into slavery. This is a very sad fact. Some people were bought to be in the service of others. People paid large sums of money to own a slave who would then have to work for his owner for the rest of his life.

Many of the slaves who lived in Paul's time also became followers of Jesus. They were still slaves who belonged to their masters, but they also belonged to the Lord.

There were good slaves and bad slaves. Some were hardworking, while others were lazy. Paul wrote to them and told them that, as Christians, they should have a completely new attitude toward their work because they had the Lord in their hearts. They should be doing their work so well that no one would be able to point a finger at them and accuse them of negligence. He also said that they should not simply work to win the favor of their masters. They shouldn't do their work in order to gain recognition and praise. They should do their work well even when no one is looking.

You are a truly good worker if you do your best even when no one is looking or keeping an eye on you. Paul says that we should not work for people, but for the Lord. He sees everything we do. His heart is filled with joy when he sees his children doing good work because they are good people who always want to do their very best.

You are not a slave, but you do have work to do. Give your utmost for the Lord. Do whatever you have to do with all your heart because you want to please the Lord, who is watching.

W.W.J.

Jesus taught people to live good lives even when no one is watching.

Friends

COMFORT AND ENCOURAGEMENT

They have proved a comfort to me. (Colossians 4:11)

Paul sometimes had to endure terrible suffering. He worked very hard for the Lord, and despite this, he was often misunderstood. He was also persecuted. Some days, he must have felt as if discouragement was about to overwhelm him. Some Christians, who were supposedly his friends, even spread nasty rumors about him behind his back.

Paul usually was accompanied by friends and co-workers on his journeys. We all need friends. Good company and conversation mean a great deal to all of us. And it means just as much to us when someone is there to offer us assistance when we need help. In his letter to the Colossians, Paul writes that he is very grateful for three men named Aristarchus, Mark, and Justus. They were three Jews who worked alongside him for the kingdom of God.

Because Paul was a Jew, he enjoyed being in the company of other Jews. They spoke his language and understood his culture. Birds of a feather flock together, as the saying goes. We enjoy being among people who understand us. This is also how Paul felt about his friends. In this letter, he writes that these three friends had been a great comfort to him, like a soothing balm that helped to heal the wounds of his suffering. When he was upset, his conversations with them comforted and calmed him.

Thank God for your friends. Be a good friend to others. Comfort your friends and encourage them; build them up with your words and your love. Do it today.

W.W.J.

Jesus' disciples were a great comfort to him during his time on earth.

November 23

Epaphras

HE PRAYED FOR THE CHRISTIANS

He is always wrestling in prayer for you. (Colossians 4:12)

One of the most wonderful things that the Lord does is to put it in people's hearts to pray for others. Prayer is important, and this includes prayer for certain issues and for other people. There is tremendous power in prayer. Jesus himself said that we should pray so that we may receive. If we pray to the Father in Jesus' name, and our request is in line with his will, we will receive whatever we pray for.

When you love someone, you care for that person. You want him or her to be happy. And because you are a Christian, you also know that if the Lord does not bless that person, he or she will never really be happy. That is why you pray to God the Father and ask him to bless that person.

Epaphras had the love of Jesus in his heart, and he was very concerned about his friends who lived in the city of Colosse. Paul saw how often Epaphras prayed faithfully and earnestly for the Christians. In his letter to the Colossians, Paul writes that they should be grateful for the fact that Epaphras prayed so earnestly for them. Epaphras asked God to help the Colossians stand firm in the will of God, especially when the devil attacked them. He also asked God to help the Colossians to be spiritually mature and completely obedient to the will of God.

Who needs your prayers today? Pray like Epaphras that people will continue to serve the Lord faithfully. Your prayer can make a big difference.

W.W.J.

Jesus prayed for his disciples, and he still prays for us. (John 17)

November 24

Luke

A Doctor for the Lord

Our dear friend Luke, the doctor ... (Colossians 4:14)

Doctors have a difficult but wonderful job. They spend many years studying so that they can understand the human body and help people who are ill. Doctors often work very long hours to help people who are ill, in pain, or dying.

One of Jesus' followers was a doctor. His name was Luke. Paul got to know and love Luke, and he and Luke traveled and worked together for the kingdom of the Lord.

When a doctor not only heals people's bodies, but also leads their spirits to Jesus, he or she becomes a very special instrument of God. People who are in physical pain also often carry a great deal of uncertainty in their hearts. They are often filled with anxiety or fear. Medicine alone can do nothing to alleviate these feelings. Only Jesus can help. We should be grateful for all the doctors who have a personal relationship with Jesus Christ. They not only heal people's bodies, but they can also tell people about the almighty Lord.

Pray for all the doctors you know. Pray that they will follow Jesus. Pray that God will use them to alleviate people's pain and suffering. It is God who gives doctors the wisdom to heal others. Doctors are also sometimes tired and discouraged. Let us ask the Lord to help them.

W.W.J.

Jesus said that he was like a great and powerful Physician who came to heal all the ill people of the world.

November 25

Nympha

THE GOOD HOSTESS

Give my greetings to ... Nympha and the church in her house. (Colossians 4:15).

Some people are known for their hospitality. People who are hospitable like to welcome other people into their homes. If you knock on a hospitable person's door, he or she usually opens the door and greets you with a smile and a friendly word of welcome. He or she immediately invites you in and makes you feel at home in no time.

Hospitable people put you at ease and make you feel that their house is a place in which you can just relax and be yourself. They are also very attuned to your needs: they ask whether you want something to drink or to eat; they show you where the bathroom and all the other amenities are. A visit with hospitable people is an absolute pleasure.

Paul often stayed with people. When he was in Laodicea, he often enjoyed the hospitality of a woman named Nympha. Nympha opened her house to all the Christians. I can imagine in my mind's eye how people used to drop in to visit at her house all the time. Her house was filled with warmth and love. The Christians often gathered there to share a meal and to worship the Lord together.

The Bible says that we should strive to be hospitable. You should always be hospitable toward your friends. Make them feel welcome in your home. Make sure that they enjoy visiting you.

W.W.J.

Jesus did not have a home of his own, but he often accepted other people's hospitality.

Archippus

Focus on Your Task!

Tell Archippus: "See to it that you complete the work you have received in the Lord." (Colossians 4:17)

Sometimes we are excited about something new and it may be easy to get started on a new task or project. At other times, we are excited when we see the end of a task in sight and we are working hard to finish. At other times, however, something that gets started doesn't get finished. People get tired, burn out, or run out of enthusiasm.

Someone once said that life is like a race. How you start isn't the important thing; how you finish the race is. Some athletes start out by running very fast, and before long they are dog-tired and out of breath. Consequently they finish last or never even finish the race at all. Life is exactly the same.

In his letter to the church of Colosse, Paul included a message to Archippus. He told Archippus that he should complete the task that he received from the Lord. Actually, he was simply telling Archippus to focus on the task at hand. When you are focused, you keep your eyes fixed on your goal. You know where you are going, and you are willing to persevere to reach your goal. "Yes," Paul was saying to Archippus, "you should focus on your task and complete it." Always finish the task at hand.

When we have decided to do something for the Lord, we should focus on it and complete it. Persevere until the job is done.

W.W.J.

Jesus persevered in the task that he received from God. He completed it even though it was a very difficult task.

November 27

Leaders

They Should Receive Recognition

Now we ask you ... to respect those who work hard among you. (1 Thessalonians 5:12)

Ungrateful people never show their appreciation for the sacrifices that others make for their sakes. They simply take everything for granted. They think they actually deserve the good things that other people do for them. They believe that they are entitled to others' good deeds and sacrifices. But if you give this matter some thought, you will realize that this isn't really the case.

We should learn to be grateful for all the good things that come our way. We should also learn to be appreciative and grateful toward those who are good to us. The fact that they care for us and love us is a wonderful gift. I hope that you show your gratitude toward your parents and friends and family who do so many small and big things to make you happy. Nothing brings so much joy as someone who shows his or her gratitude.

Paul writes to his friends and tells them to respect those who work hard among them. He also says that his friends should hold these people in the highest regard and love them for the hard work that they do and the sacrifices that they make. To whom can you say thank you today? To whom can you show your respect, gratitude, and appreciation? Your teachers? Your family? Your friends? Your minister?

Recognize and respect your leaders. Tell them that you are grateful for and appreciative of everything they do. Write it, say it, show it.

W.W.J.

Jesus taught us to say thank you for everything we receive. Receiving these good things is not our right, but a privilege.

November 28

The Thessalonians

LOAFERS SHOULD START WORKING

We were not idle when we were with you, nor did we eat anyone's food without paying for it. (2 Thessalonians 3:7-8)

Paul was really annoyed by Christians who were lazy and lived off other people. Some people believe that when you are a follower of the Lord, you can just sit back and the Lord will take care of all your needs. Such people think that Christians don't really have to do anything to make a living. However, this assumption is completely untrue. Even Paul, who worked for the Lord full time, did some manual labor so that he could make money to pay his living costs.

Some people use the Lord as an excuse to sit back and do nothing. They think that because they are followers of the Lord, other people have to take care of them. Exactly the same thing happened in Paul's time. Among the Christians in Thessalonica were a bunch of loafers who didn't want to work. They only wanted to sit around all day and pray. In this passage, Paul admonishes them and tells them to stop loafing about and start working. He says that he himself worked day and night just to make sure that he would not be a financial burden to anyone. And then he says, *"If a man will not work, he shall not eat"* (2 Thessalonians 3:10).

We should always be prepared to do our part in any chores that need to be done, and to work for the things we want, not just expecting other people to give them to us. As Christians, we should set an example. We should work hard, take care of ourselves, and help others.

W.W.J.

Jesus spent many years doing manual labor in his father's carpentry shop. Later he dedicated all his time to ministering the gospel of the kingdom, but he never begged for money.

November 29

Timothy

Make the Most of Your Gifts

Do not neglect your gift. (1 Timothy 4:14)

When the Lord changes our hearts, we make a decision to use all our gifts and talents in his service. He also gives us his Holy Spirit, who equips us to be even better servants for the Lord and his kingdom. Through the Holy Spirit, the Lord gives us the heartfelt conviction we need to fulfill the task for which we were created.

God's gift is a gift of grace. Despite the fact that it is a gift, we can use it to work for the Lord. Some people can preach. Others are talented at certain crafts. Others have the ability to help the poor. Others can sing beautifully. Every single one of us has received a gift from the Holy Spirit.

Paul says that we should not neglect whatever gift we have been given. We should make the most of it and use it as best we can. We should constantly learn how to use our gift more effectively. We should ask the Lord to make us even better at what we do. We should be the very best we can. You too should not neglect God's gift to you. Develop it and improve it. Pray about it and practice it. Sing or speak or pray or serve. Do it well. Do your very best.

W. W. J.

Jesus taught his disciples to develop and improve their gifts and talents.

November 30

Elders

In the Line of Fire

Do not entertain an accusation against an elder unless it is brought by two or three witnesses. (1 Timothy 5:19)

People will always be critical of other people. There will also always be those who will not understand the meaning and purpose of what you are doing. Consequently, they might speak ill of you or accuse you of things that aren't true.

People who are in leadership positions or who play important roles often receive much more criticism than others. There is a proverb that says this: Tall trees catch the most wind. When people in leadership positions do something wrong, everyone has something to say about it. In Paul's time, the leaders of the church, the elders, did very important work. As a result, they also came in for a lot of criticism.

Paul knew that the devil could use this kind of backhanded gossip to further his own ends. That is why he made a rule about it, and wrote it down in his letter to Timothy. This rule stipulates that if anyone has any accusation against an elder, he is not allowed to talk about it, except if it is corroborated by two or three witnesses. Only if two or three other people say that the accusation against the elder is true, can it be brought to the attention of the relevant people. Otherwise the accusation has to be kept quiet. This is a good rule, don't you think?

Never accuse anyone of anything unless two or three people can confirm that it is true. And first speak to the person about the problem.

W.W.J.

Jesus preferred not to accuse or condemn people. Instead he forgave and absolved them.

December 1

Timothy

MAN OF GOD

But you, man of God ... (1 Timothy 6:11)

Timothy was very young. He gave his heart and life to Jesus as a consequence of Paul's ministry, and he decided to dedicate his life to serving the Lord. He later became the leader of one of the new churches. In this letter, Paul calls him a "man of God."

There are a number of instances in the Bible where someone is described as a "man of God." This expression means that that person had a very special relationship with God. It means that the Lord gave that person a very special kind of authority and power. That person was backed by the authority of the Lord. He could act in the name of the Lord. The Bible calls Moses, Ezra, Elijah, Elisha, and a number of other people "men of God." And in this passage Paul addresses Timothy by the name "man of God."

All Christians are children of God. Some are called by the Lord to devote their lives to his ministry full-time. He gives them strength, power, and a very special calling. The Bible calls such people "men of God." However, this doesn't mean that women are excluded from this special calling. God also calls women to devote themselves to doing his work. We might call them "women of God."

The Lord has a task for each of us. He knows in what way he wants to use you. It might be that you will grow up to become a "man or woman of God." The Lord might have a special calling in mind for you. But always remember that in the kingdom of God no one is more important than anyone else. The fact that someone is a "man or woman of God" does not mean that he or she is better than anyone else. He or she isn't God's favorite. We are all equal in the eyes of the Lord. Thank God that you belong to him and can work for him.

W.W.J.

Jesus was also called "Rabbi." He is the Son of God but was also a teacher here on earth. He is our Savior.

December 2

The Rich

Rich in What Way?

Command them to do good, to be rich in good deeds. (1 Timothy 6:18)

It is wonderful when someone who is wealthy uses his or her money and possessions to serve the Lord. Such a person has the resources to further the work of the kingdom, and can also give away some of his or her possessions to help poor people. A Christian knows that whatever he or she has received is actually a gift from God's hand. It is therefore not intended to be used only for personal pleasure. Instead, it should be used to serve other people and to serve God. Christians ought to be generous people.

Paul writes to the wealthy members of the church that they should not be proud and arrogant. Unfortunately, wealth has a way of making people arrogant and haughty. You start believing that you are better than others because you have more than they do, and so you look down upon them. Paul also says that rich people should not put all their hope in their money or possessions. Many wealthy people have had to come to terms with losing all their possessions. There might be a natural disaster like a storm, or a fire might break out in your house. Burglars may steal all your possessions, or you may mismanage your funds and in the process lose everything. You should never place your trust in money as your only hope and security. God should be the source of our security.

Paul tells Timothy to encourage the wealthy members of the church to be rich not only in possessions, but also in good deeds. They should be generous and willing to share. In this way, they will not only accumulate treasure and wealth here on earth, but also in heaven. And this is, ultimately, the only way in which they will be able to inherit the true treasure – eternal life.

You and I should serve the Lord with our possessions. Learn to be generous and not stingy.

W.W.J.

Jesus taught his disciples not to be dependent on earthly possessions, but first to seek the kingdom of God. Then they would receive everything they needed.

December 3

Lois and Eunice

MOTHERS WHO KNEW JESUS

I have been reminded of your sincere faith, which first lived in your grandmother Lois and in your mother Eunice. (2 Timothy 1:5)

Timothy was a believer whose heart was truly on fire for the gospel. Paul was his teacher when he was still a spiritual infant, and he eventually grew to become a preacher who led one of the many Christian churches. Timothy was a very valuable asset to the kingdom of the Lord.

Timothy was a very lucky young man. His mother and grandmother not only raised him well, but also taught him about Jesus Christ, the Savior of the world. Paul writes to Timothy and says that he is very glad to see that Timothy's faith is sincere. Then he says that Timothy's faith is just as sincere as the faith that first lived in his grandmother Lois and his mother Eunice. Yes, Timothy learned true faith in Christ from his grandmother and his mother. When he was just a little boy, they taught him about the kingdom of God. He heard it from their mouths, and he probably also saw it in their deeds. They truly loved the Lord.

It is a privilege to grow up in a Christian home. It is wonderful if your father, or mother, or grandfather, or grandmother teaches you how to attain peace with God through Jesus Christ. Are your father and mother followers of the Lord? If they are, you should thank God. There are many children in the world who have never even heard of Jesus Christ. Their parents never got to know him, and therefore they were unable to introduce their children to Jesus. Thank God for your parents and appreciate it when they talk to you about Jesus Christ and take you to church.

Lois and Eunice were top-class mothers. They not only took care of Timothy and raised him, but also taught him all he needed to know about the Lord.

W. W. J.

Jesus was pleased when mothers brought their children to him.

December 4

Phygelus

HE DROPPED PAUL

You know that everyone in the province of Asia has deserted me, including Phygelus and Hermogenes. (2 Timothy 1:15)

There are many reliable, stalwart people upon whom you can always depend. When they say something, they are willing to substantiate their words with deeds. They never make promises that they can't keep. If they are for some reason unable to keep their promises, they are sure to inform you of the fact as soon as they can, and they are always very apologetic and sorry for not keeping their word. Reliable people keep the world going. They are people upon whom you can depend. Without them, the world would be a very unpleasant place.

It is also interesting to note that there are usually only a few stalwarts who are always willing to do the work. Most people prefer just to go with the flow and do nothing. They are like passengers in a vehicle. They are on their way somewhere, but they are not in control of their destination. They aren't in the driving seat. They don't do any actual work. They sit back and rely on others to get them to their destination. There are only a handful of people who are willing to roll up their sleeves and get to work: for the church, for the church fair, for the school, for the party, for the teachers, for the sports meeting ... Are you one of these reliable workers?

Paul writes to Timothy and says that a number of people deserted him while he was working in the province of Asia. He mentions two names in particular: Phygelus and Hermogenes. That's just about all that we are told about these two men. They dropped Paul. They bailed out when he needed them. They left him in the lurch. He could not depend on them.

I hope you are not in the habit of dropping people. If you made a promise, keep it. Do your part. Be reliable. Don't be one of those people who watch while things happen around them. Be someone who makes things happen.

W.W.J.

You can always rely on Jesus' words and deeds.

December 5

Onesiphorus

A Refreshing Friend

... because he often refreshed me. (1 Timothy 1:16)

Many things can have a destructive effect on us – such as negative comments and criticisms from others, unpleasant circumstances, or illness. We all sometimes feel as if our lives are falling apart, and this causes us a great deal of unhappiness.

Every single human being needs to be encouraged and refreshed. When you "refresh" someone, it means that you inspire that person with courage. You use your love and your words to restore and invigorate that person's spirit. You tell him or her that things will turn out fine and that he or she is a winner. You remind the person of all his or her good character traits. You show your appreciation for the person. You listen to him or her and give advice when appropriate.

The people who opposed Paul's work had a very destructive effect on him. There were even Christians who criticized him. Many of his friends and co-workers bailed out on their commitments and left him in the lurch. Despite this, he remained grateful to the Lord, especially for Onesiphorus and his household. Onesiphorus often came to see Paul in prison and encouraged and refreshed his spirit. He was also never ashamed to acknowledge Paul as his friend. When he was in Rome, he searched for Paul everywhere until he found him. He visited Paul regularly and encouraged him.

Wouldn't it be wonderful if you could also cheer up some people? Is there anyone who seems a bit dejected and dispirited to you? Is there someone who looks worried? Is there anyone who thinks that he or she is worthless? Bring some cheer and encouragement into that person's life!

W. W. J.

Jesus enjoyed nothing more than encouraging and refreshing people with his words and deeds.

December 6

Jannes and Jambres

TWO AGAINST TWO

Just as Jannes and Jambres opposed Moses. (2 Timothy 3:8)

When the Israelites were slaves in Egypt, God sent Moses to lead his people to freedom. Moses performed a number of miracles because the Lord wanted to convince Pharaoh of his power, strength, and greatness.

Time and again, Pharaoh called in his sorcerers to counter Moses' miracles and to perform miracles in the name of the Egyptian gods. The situation ultimately ended up being a battle of two against two. Pharaoh asked two of his magicians to use their sorcery and the devil's powers to perform miracles to counter God's miracles. The two magicians were called Jannes and Jambres. The two brothers responsible for performing God's miracles were Moses and Aaron. The Bible tells us that the two brothers whom the Lord chose to perform miracles in his name emerged as the victors in this battle. The two magicians lost the battle.

If you and I are on the side of the Lord, we will definitely emerge victorious from our battles with the devil. When the Lord wants to accomplish his goals through us, nothing can stop him. Choose to be on the Lord's side today, and be a conqueror.

W.W.J.

One of Jesus' names is "Conqueror." He is the ultimate winner.

Demas

Run with the Hares and Hunt with the Hounds

... for Demas, because he loved this world, has deserted me. (2 Timothy 4:10)

Demas told Paul that he wanted to accompany him on his travels and help him in his ministry of the gospel. However, one day, Demas decided that he actually wanted to do something else with his life. This is not necessarily wrong. You can decide to serve the Lord full-time, and then later change your mind and decide to work for the Lord in a different way. You need not necessarily devote your entire life to preaching his gospel in order to make a meaningful contribution to the Lord's kingdom. However, it seems as if Demas actually had a different problem altogether.

In this passage, Paul writes that Demas is no longer with him. Demas deserted Paul because he loved the world too much. What could this possibly mean? Paul probably knew Demas very well. He often had long conversations with him. He knew how Demas felt about certain matters. With time, Paul realized that Demas was struggling with many questions in his heart. He was no longer as enthusiastic about the Lord's work as he was in the beginning. He still just wanted to have some fun and enjoy life.

Young people want to enjoy their lives in particular ways. God also wants young people to enjoy their lives. However, if worldly things start to have such a powerful attraction that we drift away from the Lord in pursuit of worldly pleasure, we are actually choosing to reject the Lord as ruler of our lives.

There are many worldly things that can cause us to drift away from the Lord. We can enjoy life, but we should always enjoy it with Jesus in our hearts. Wherever you go, the Lord wants to go with you. Love Jesus more than anything else and never allow yourself to love the things around you more than you love him.

W.W.J.

When we follow Jesus we have life in abundance. Therefore, we can enjoy everything here on earth in the way the Lord meant for it to be enjoyed.

December 8

Alexander

He Opposed the Gospel

Alexander the metalworker did me a great deal of harm. (2 Timothy 4:14)

When someone decides to serve the Lord, he or she often encounters opposition from people who do not like the Lord's work. More often than not, it is actually the devil using his people to try and hinder God's work and prevent the building of his kingdom. Jesus promised his disciples that if they tried to live righteous and godly lives, they would inevitably be persecuted and have many troubles. After all, Jesus himself was persecuted. Therefore, all Christians will come face to face with opposition and will encounter all kinds of problems.

Paul encountered a great deal of opposition. One of the men who made his life very difficult was a metalworker named Alexander. While Paul was in prison, he wrote a letter to Timothy. In this letter, he mentions that Alexander did him a great deal of harm. He also warns Timothy to be on his guard against Alexander because Alexander would do anything to oppose the gospel.

However, note that Paul fosters no bitterness in his heart toward Alexander. He doesn't hate him. He doesn't curse him. No, instead he does what a mature Christian ought to do. He says, *"The Lord will repay him for what he has done"* (2 Timothy 4:14). He puts Alexander in the hands of the Lord and asks the Lord to do as he sees fit with Alexander. Ultimately, God is the One who has the power and authority to judge people. He is also the One who will repay every single person in accordance with what he or she has done.

Pray for those who oppose you, and leave them in the hands of the Lord. Don't become embittered toward them.

W.W.J.

Jesus taught us to love and bless our enemies.

December 9

Onesimus

A Slave Becomes a Christian

I am sending him – who is my very heart – back to you. (Philemon 1:12)

Christians are people whose hearts have been touched by God. Once they have given their hearts to Jesus, they change completely. They are completely different from the way they were before. This is how it ought to be. The Lord wants to remove all the bad and wicked parts of our lives. However, this does not mean that we are perfect once we have given our hearts to Jesus. Even though we are Christians, we still make many mistakes. But we have a new sense of focus and direction. Our goal is to do the right things so that we may glorify Jesus' name.

Onesimus was a slave. He belonged to a wealthy man named Philemon. Onesimus did not know God. He also didn't particularly like having to work long hours as a slave every day. That is why he one day decided to run away. In those days, slaves who deserted their masters were in deep trouble. Onesimus knew this and so he made sure that he ran as far away from his master's house as he could. But then something happened that changed his life completely. He met Paul, and Paul told him about Jesus Christ. The Holy Spirit opened his heart, and Onesimus accepted Jesus as his Lord. He became a Christian.

Paul taught Onesimus about Jesus. Paul also told Onesimus that he had to return to his master and apologize for running away. He had to set matters right. Paul gave Onesimus a letter to take with him so that apologizing would be easier for Onesimus.

When we give our lives to the Lord, we receive forgiveness for our sins. Then we often need to go to people whom we have wronged and apologize for what we did. Perhaps there is something that you need to confess to someone. You need to set the matter right. Speak to the person so that your heart may be at peace.

W.W.J.

After Zacchaeus met Jesus, he decided to do something to set the wrongs of his past right. (Luke 19:8)

December 10

Philemon

WILLING TO FORGIVE

Welcome him as you would welcome me. (Philemon 1:17)

Philemon was a wealthy citizen of the city of Colosse. In those times, rich men owned many slaves who worked for them. Philemon bought a slave named Onesimus. Philemon became a follower of Jesus as a result of Paul's ministry. Paul was the one who led him to the Lord.

However, one day the slave Onesimus ran away. A slave who deserted his master committed a very serious offense and he could be thrown in prison for a long time. That is why Onesimus decided to go to a faraway place. There he met Paul, and the same thing happened to him that happened to his master Philemon. Paul led Onesimus to the Lord. Paul also knew that Onesimus had to return to his master and apologize for running away. After all, a Christian has to do everything in his power to set right whatever he has done wrong.

Paul and Onesimus were probably not sure how Philemon would respond when Onesimus returned. He might still have been very angry with Onesimus, and he might have decided to have him thrown in prison. That is why Paul wrote a letter to Philemon and asked him to welcome Onesimus back, not only as a slave, but also as a brother in Jesus. Both Onesimus and Philemon were now Christians. They were brothers with the same Father.

Philemon had to forgive Onesimus. He also had to accept that Onesimus would be a better slave because he had Jesus in his heart. We too should be willing to forgive others.

W.W.J.

After people accepted him into their hearts, Jesus always told them that he forgave them their sins, but that they should repent and turn from their sins.

December 11

James

Live your Faith

What good is it if a man claims to have faith but has no deeds? (James 2:14)

This letter was written by Jesus' brother, James. He wrote this letter to all the Christians who lived in the province of Asia. Much of the letter is devoted to faith, but James also writes a lot about something else – deeds.

James says that it is impossible for someone to claim that he believes in Jesus Christ if his life and deeds do not prove his commitment to Christ. Sugared words are no use if your deeds don't correspond with your words. James says that faith without action or deeds is dead.

There are many people who like to say that they are Christians. They go to church. They sometimes read from the Bible. They may even pray. But this is the extent of their commitment to the Christian faith. When they are at work, or at a sports event, or at a party, you would never guess that they are supposedly Christians. They do things that are completely inappropriate for a Christian. The language that comes from their mouths doesn't sound like the language of Christians. They say nasty things, they gossip about others, and they even use blasphemous or rude language. James says that the faith of such people is worthless. Your faith should be evident in your life.

W.W.J.

Jesus said that a tree is known by its fruit. A peach tree does not bear prickly pears. Christians should not keep on sinning.

Jesus

HE ANNOUNCED HIS VICTORY

He was put to death in the body but made alive by the Spirit, through whom also he went and preached to the spirits in prison. (1 Peter 3:18-19)

Peter makes an interesting comment in this passage. He says that after Jesus Christ died on the cross for our sins, the Holy Spirit resurrected him. Then Jesus went to the spirits in prison and preached to them, announcing his victory to them.

When Jesus died on the cross, the devil probably thought that he had finally managed to destroy Jesus completely. But, says Peter, the Holy Spirit restored Jesus to life and then he went to the spirits in prison. He told them that he had won; that he had conquered death itself. Who were these spirits?

Peter tells us that these were the spirits of people from the time of Noah. While Noah was building the ark, these people laughed at him and mocked him. They all drowned when the rain and the flood came. These disobedient sinners were kept in prison in the realm of the dead. This is where Jesus went and told them that he was the Conqueror.

Jesus has power over death. He was resurrected from the dead and is the great Conqueror of death. He went to preach in the realm of the dead, among all the spirits of the dead. He went there to tell them that he is the only One that truly has eternal life. We share in this eternal life, and therefore we too will one day be resurrected. Death is no longer an enemy to be feared.

W.W.J.

Jesus said that he was the resurrection and the life. Anyone who believed in him would have eternal life. (John 11:25).

December 13

Peter

LIKE A ROARING LION

Be self-controlled and alert. Your enemy the devil prowls around like a roaring lion looking for someone to devour. (1 Peter 5:8)

Peter had had lots of experience with temptation from the devil. He had often said and done the wrong things, and he even denied that he knew Jesus. Jesus forgave him and Peter went on to become one of the most well-known leaders in the early church. Peter knew what it was like to let his emotions and feelings run away with him and lead him into trouble. And so here he warns people to be self-controlled, and to think carefully before they rush headlong into something wrong.

Peter tells us that it's easy to spot the devil and his temptations if you are aware that he wants to attack you. And he wants to attack all of God's children. Stay alert and on the lookout for the temptations of the devil. And remember that if a lion roars while it is looking for prey, the victims can hear him and will run away to safety. We have the Holy Spirit in our hearts and He acts like an amplifier, making sure we can hear the devil's roars.

So listen to the voice of the Holy Spirit, and block out the roars of the devil, and then you will not do the things that you know are wrong. In the strength of the Holy Spirit we can resist the devil and his roars. He will help us overcome the devil and his temptations.

W.W.J.

Even Jesus was tempted, but he recognized the voice of the devil and resisted him.

December 14

Peter

ARE PEOPLE LIKE PIGS?

"A sow that is washed goes back to her wallowing in the mud." (2 Peter 2:22)

Peter was very troubled about people who said that they knew and served Jesus, but whose attitude proved that this was not the case. In this passage, he calls such people false teachers or heretics.

These teachers despised and challenged authority and believed that they were more important than anyone else. They even went so far as to insult and slander celestial beings. Their teachings were nothing but nonsense, and yet they said that their teachings came directly from the mouth of God. They also exploited other people and swindled them out of a great deal of money. Peter says that they left the straight and narrow path and wandered from the Lord's way.

Peter also says that we should watch out for this kind of people. They like to pretend that they are free from the sin of this world because they know Jesus, but they are actually completely entangled in sin and overpowered by the devil. He describes them as pigs that were washed clean but returned to wallowing in the mud.

Pigs like mud. They enjoy rolling around in it. But cats or people don't really like mud. They immediately want to clean themselves when they are dirty and muddy. Christians are also like this. They don't like the mud and dirt of sin. When they have sinned, they immediately want to cleanse themselves from the sin. They confess their sin and are washed clean. Make sure that you always keep clean and don't develop a liking for the mud of sin.

W.W.J.

Jesus died so that our sins could be washed away.

Gaius

A Good Friend

To my dear friend Gaius, whom I love in the truth. (3 John 1:1)

Each one of us needs to have a good friend. John was no different than us in this respect. John was a disciple of Jesus. He was also a very special friend of Jesus. The Bible tells us that Jesus loved him very much.

John had a friend named Gaius, and in this letter he tells us that he truly loved Gaius. There are some friends who are closer to your heart than even your own family. Some friends are almost like brothers or sisters. John probably often visited Gaius. They probably talked a lot about Jesus, prayed together, and made plans for the future together.

John wrote a letter to Gaius, and in this letter he expresses his wish that many good things will come Gaius's way. We all want only the best for our friends. The first thing that John wishes for Gaius is good health. Of course, we want our friends to be happy and healthy. John also says that he hopes that in the future, all may go well with Gaius, just as at present everything is going well with his soul and his spiritual progress. John adds that he is very pleased to hear that Gaius is still following the way of the Lord faithfully and that he is still living in the truth. It is very sad to see our friends doing the wrong things and following the wrong path.

Then John thanks Gaius for all his hard work, especially in helping other Christians. He also warns him about a man named Diotrephes. And then John wishes Gaius peace and conveys the greetings of all the other friends to him.

I'm sure you also want only the best for your friends. Pray for them, encourage them, and bolster their courage. Thank God for your friends. And when you are spending time with your friends, be sure to enjoy it.

W. W. J.

Jesus called his disciples his friends. He loved them very much and wanted only the best for them.

December 16

Diotrephes

Spreading False Rumors

I will call attention to what he is doing, gossiping maliciously about us. Not satisfied with that, he refuses to welcome the brothers. (3 John 1:10)

In John's letter to his friend Gaius, he mentions a number of important matters. Among these matters is a warning that Gaius should be careful of a man named Diotrephes.

Diotrephes regarded himself as the leader of the Christians in the area where Gaius lived. But his heart was wicked. He had a very negative attitude and his behavior was definitely not in accordance with Christian principles. He spread nasty rumors about John and his friends. He also refused to welcome other Christians who wanted to visit his church. He told the members of his church to lock their houses to the traveling Christians who came to teach the people. Then John adds that Gaius should always remember, *"Anyone who does what is good is from God. Anyone who does what is evil has not seen God"* (3 John 1:11).

You are known by your deeds and your attitude. You can tell others that you are the leader of a church all you like, but if your deeds show people that the fruit of the Spirit is not in your life, it will do you no good whatsoever. The fruit of the Holy Spirit are all the pleasant and admirable qualities like love, patience, friendliness, faithfulness, peace, and self-control. If these characteristics are not visible in someone's life, he or she is most certainly not a child of God. This is exactly what happened with Diotrephes.

There is an easy way to test whether people really love the Lord. If their lives bear the fruit of the Spirit, we know that the Holy Spirit is in their hearts and that they belong to Jesus. We also know that we can work with them without fearing that they will betray us. If their lives do not bear the fruit of the Spirit, we should be wary and careful of them. Is the fruit of the Spirit visible in your life?

W.W.J.

Jesus said to be careful of people who appear pleasant on the outside, but who are evil and mean on the inside.

December 17

Demetrius

A Good Testimonial

Demetrius is well spoken of by everyone. (3 John 1:12)

Testimonials are written by one person who wishes to recommend another for a particular job or position. A person writing a testimonial writes down everything he knows about the other person. He testifies in writing about the other person's life. He describes the person's abilities, skills, and general behavior. You sometimes need a testimonial when you want to apply for a job. Your potential employers have no idea who you are and what abilities and skills you have. If you can give them a testimonial from someone else, they have a written description of you from someone who knows you. This puts them in a better position to judge whether you are the best person for the job.

God knows everything about us. He knows the contents of our hearts, and he knows all our thoughts and our deeds. That is why it is important that we should try to make our lives worthy and right in the sight of God. If you do this, he will underline only the good things in your life when he writes your testimonial.

In this letter, John writes about Demetrius and says that Demetrius is well spoken of by everyone. John also says that the testimony of people is corroborated by the truth. Demetrius's life clearly proved the goodness of his heart.

May this also be said of you. Let us ask the Lord to help us live good lives so that other people can see God's work in us and glorify the Father because of it.

W.W.J.

If people can see only bad things in our lives, we are actually dragging Jesus' name through the mud. If we follow Jesus, we should try to be just like him.

Ephesus

HOT OR COLD LOVE?

"Yet I hold this against you: You have forsaken your first love." (Revelation 2:4)

The Lord absolutely loves it when the people who belong to him show the world that they love him wholeheartedly.

Human beings have an inborn inclination not to want to love God. People are more inclined to love themselves than to love God. We want to live only for ourselves. We want to do only what is important to us. This love of ourselves is what really motivates us. However, when God changes our hearts, we learn to stop loving only ourselves. We learn to love Jesus instead.

The most important commandment in the Old Testament tells us that we should love the Lord with all our heart, soul, mind, and strength. It is really important to God that we should love him in this way. Loving God like this shows people that we honor and respect him, and also that we belong to him. How much do you love the Lord? Are you absolutely crazy about him? Do you enjoy being in his company? Do you like listening to his Word? Do you like talking to him? Do you enjoy singing songs of praise to him?

When Jesus writes a letter to the church in Ephesus, he says that there is one thing that he holds against them. They did not continue to love him as much as they loved him in the beginning. Their love for the Lord cooled. Perhaps they just got used to the Lord. They stopped spending so much time with him. They were no longer excited about him. They devoted more of their attention to things and people than they devoted to him.

You and I should always try to love the Lord even more than we did the day before. Think about everything that he has done for you. Think about how much he loves you. Thank him for his love and take some time to tell him how much you love him.

W.W.J.

Jesus asked Peter: "Do you love me?" (John 12:16)

Smyrna

RICH IN JESUS

"I know your afflictions and your poverty – yet you are rich!" (Revelation 2:9)

In this passage, Jesus sends a letter to the church in Smyrna. He says that he knows everything about them and that he is also aware that they suffer a great deal because of their faith in Christ. He knows that they are very poor, yet he also knows that they are actually rich. What does Jesus mean by this?

True riches have nothing to do with how much money you have in the bank or in your wallet. It has nothing to do with having beautiful clothes or living in a big, grand house. True riches are actually what you have in your heart: your relationship with the Lord. You can be extremely wealthy, and at the same time you can be unhappy and poor in your relationship with the Lord. Or you can be poor and yet rich in the eyes of the Lord, like the church members of Smyrna.

These Christians encountered a great deal of opposition from people who did not want to accept the fact that they followed Jesus. Many of the Christians were imprisoned. Jesus says that these people pretended to be Jews, but they actually belonged to Satan. He then tells the Christians of Smyrna that they need not be afraid of everything that would still happen to them. He says that they should be faithful even to the point of death. If they remain faithful, they will receive the crown of eternal life.

The Christians of Smyrna suffered here on earth, but they were as rich as can be in their relationship with Jesus. True treasures and riches are given only by Jesus, and we can experience these riches only in our relationship with him. I hope that you are rich in Jesus.

W.W.J.

Isaiah invited people to take possession of the riches of God, which have no price and cannot be bought with money (Isaiah 55:1). Jesus is the only one who can give these riches.

December 20

Mary

CHOSEN FOR A SPECIAL TASK

"You will be with child and give birth to a son, and you are to give him the name Jesus." (Luke 1:31)

Mary was a young woman who lived in Nazareth. She was engaged to Joseph. She must have been very excited at her impending wedding. One day, an angel appeared to her and greeted her. He called her "you who are highly favored." This means that she was very special. He then said to her that the Lord was with her. Mary was speechless with astonishment at these words and she wondered what they could mean. The angel told her not to be afraid because the Lord had a special task for her. She would become pregnant and bring a Child into the world. This Child would be Jesus Christ. He would be the Savior of all the people in this sinful world, if they chose to believe in him. He would also be the greatest King ever born.

Mary was obedient to the Lord and she accepted the task given to her. She was Jesus' mother. She had to raise the King of heaven and earth. You and I also have a task that we have to do for the Lord. We might think that our work isn't nearly as important as Mary's was. But the Lord regards our work as very important.

What does the Lord want you to do for him today? Even if your task is simply loving someone, it is important in his eyes.

W.W.J.

Jesus has an important job for you to do today. As you walk with him, he will show you what he expects of you.

December 21

Jesus

SENT TO SAVE US

"... and you are to give him the name Jesus, because he will save his people from their sins." (Matthew 1:21)

The Bible tells us that all people are trapped in the prison of sin. The devil managed to entice people to commit sin, thus making them guilty before God. This has been the case since the time of Adam and Eve. It is as if all people's hearts and souls are bound by the shackles of the devil so that they are unable to do God's will. They are trapped by their guilt. They are entangled in their sin.

However, God loves us so much that he decided to free us. He would come and unlock the doors of the prison of sin. How would he accomplish this? He decided to send Jesus to become a human being here on earth.

Just before Jesus was born, an angel appeared to Joseph and told him that the name of Mary's child should be Jesus. This name means "the Lord saves." Jesus would be the One to unlock the doors of the prison of sin. He would be the One to liberate people from their shackles. He would be the Savior. Jesus is the only One who can free people from the guilt of their sins. Only he can liberate them from the devil's powerful hold. Only he can unlock and open the doors of the prison of sin and hell and set them free. That is why his name is Savior.

Do you know Jesus as your personal Savior? If you ask him, he will save you from the guilt of sin and fear right now.

W . W . J .

Millions of people have experienced the joy of being saved by Jesus.

Joseph

A Family Scandal

He had in mind to divorce her quietly. (Matthew 1:19)

While Mary and Joseph were still engaged, Joseph found out that Mary was pregnant. She was expecting a baby, and it was very hard for Joseph to deal with this situation. He was obedient to the Law of Moses, and because he loved Mary he did not want to accuse her of anything in public. He probably thought that she had slept with another man and was expecting his baby. You can probably imagine how upset Joseph must have been. He decided to break off the engagement. It was a terrible family scandal, and poor Joseph was a broken man.

While he was still planning how to go about telling Mary that he could no longer be engaged to her, an angel appeared to him in a dream. The angel told him not to be afraid to marry Mary, because the baby that she was expecting was not the child of a man, but was from the Holy Spirit. The angel said that the child would be a boy, and that Joseph should name him Jesus because he would be the One to save people from their sins. Joseph had never heard of anything like this before. How could a woman be pregnant if she hadn't slept with a man? But it was God who made this miracle happen in Mary.

The Lord sometimes works in inexplicable ways. All we can do is listen to him carefully so that we can understand his will.

W. W. J.

Jesus told his disciples that they would not understand everything now, but one day they would.

December 23

Joseph

HE HAD TO HAVE FAITH

When Joseph woke up, he did what the angel of the Lord had commanded him. (Matthew 1:24)

After Mary had become pregnant through the work of the Holy Spirit, Joseph decided to break off his engagement to her because he didn't understand what had happened. However, the angel of the Lord visited him and told him that he should not be afraid and that he should still take Mary to be his wife.

Marrying a pregnant girl was unheard of in Joseph's time, especially if you were a religious man who abided by the Law of Moses. All Joseph could do in the end was to believe in God and to accept the Lord's message to him. Despite the fact that the people would gossip and say mean things about them, Joseph had to obey the Lord's command and marry Mary. So he went ahead and married her. He was obedient. He had faith.

As Christians, we often faithfully have to do what the Lord asks of us, even though other people might not understand it. Once there was another young man who had a very successful career. He was very wealthy. He was climbing the ladder of success. But then one day, while he was busy reading his Bible, the Lord called him to do the work of the kingdom. The Lord asked him to leave his successful career behind and to go to a faraway country and preach the gospel there full-time. His family did not understand this, and some of his family members even rejected him. They said mean things about him behind his back. He had no choice but to be obedient to the Lord's instructions. That is why he began his new life with faith and courage in his heart. He eventually became a very successful preacher, and the Lord used him in truly wonderful ways.

Sometimes we simply have to have faith in God and trust him. May you and I also have the same kind of faith that Joseph had.

W . W . J .

Jesus said that if we didn't have faith, we would be unable to enter into his kingdom.

December 24

The Magi

HOMAGE FROM A FARAWAY COUNTRY

After Jesus was born... Magi from the east came to Jerusalem. (Matthew 2:1)

The greatest miracle of all time has to be the fact that God the Father decided to send his Son Jesus to earth to save people from their sins. Even though the prophets of the Old Testament had already predicted this event a long time before, no one knew exactly when the Savior would come.

The Lord told a few wise men, or Magi, that something wonderful would happen. God touched their hearts, and they knew that something magnificent was about to happen. Someone special would be born, and he would change the world. They were so convinced of this fact that they set out on a very long journey from the East. Eventually, they arrived in Jerusalem.

In Jerusalem, they asked everyone they encountered, *"Where is the one who has been born king of the Jews?"* (Matthew 2:2). But no one could answer their question. They decided to continue their journey, and as they prepared to set out again, a star suddenly appeared in the sky. The star led them and eventually came to a standstill over Bethlehem, the place where Jesus was. They went into the building and there they saw Jesus with his mother Mary. They bowed down and worshiped him. They opened their bags and presented Jesus with gifts of gold, incense, and myrrh.

The King of kings had been born in Bethlehem, and most people didn't even know about this miracle that had happened. But God sent the Magi to worship and honor him. Today, you and I know that Jesus was born on that night so long ago. We pay homage to him, not only with gifts and money, but with our lives. And we don't only glorify him at Christmas, but every day of the year.

W.W.J.

Everyone who realized that Jesus was the Christ glorified and worshiped him.

December 25

Herod

WHERE IS HE?

"... for Herod is going to search for the child to kill him." (Matthew 2:13)

The Magi asked everyone they encountered in Jerusalem where they could find the Child who had been born king of the Jews. Herod heard about the Magi's enquiries. He was very upset and disturbed about it because he was afraid that the new king would usurp his throne. So he summoned the Magi and asked them about this Child that would be born. He also asked the priests and the teachers of the law to tell him everything they knew about the Child. They told him that the Child would be born in Bethlehem. Herod lied to the Magi. He told them to go to Bethlehem and search for the Child. If they found him they should immediately inform Herod because he too would like to worship him. Of course, this was not really what Herod wanted to do. He actually wanted to have the Child killed.

God warned the Magi in a dream that they should not return to Herod. Then Herod did a terrible thing. He issued a decree that all the boys age two years and younger living in Bethlehem and its vicinity had to be killed. Can you imagine how terribly sad the parents and families of those little boys must have been? It was an absolutely terrible thing to do. Because God knew about Herod's plan, he warned Joseph beforehand. He told Joseph to take Mary and Jesus and escape to Egypt. In this way, God made sure that Jesus was not killed along with all the other little boys.

The devil used Herod to try and kill Jesus. He did not want Jesus to save us. But the devil's plans were foiled. Jesus grew up and fulfilled his destiny. He died for us on the cross. Let us praise and worship him for this.

W.W.J.

The devil tried many times to prevent Jesus from doing what God had sent him to do. But Jesus fulfilled his destiny.

December 26

Sardis

The Living Dead

"You have a reputation of being alive, but you are dead." (Revelation 3:1)

Jesus writes to the church in Sardis that he is worried about them. He knows everything about them. He knows that they have a reputation of being alive, and yet they are actually dead. Why would the Lord say this to the church in Sardis?

Jesus says that they should wake up. This means that they had allowed themselves to fall asleep spiritually. They became lazy. Jesus continues to say that they should strengthen what remains and what is about to die. This means that they had become weak and sloppy in their faith. Another thing that Jesus says is that they had soiled their clothes. This means that they had dirtied themselves by sinning. They were no longer obedient to the Lord.

Jesus knows about every single thing we do. We can put on a spiritual or religious mask to impress other people, but before God, all masks come off. He can see into the deepest recesses of our hearts. He knows exactly what we feel. He sees everything we do. You can attend church, go to Sunday school, read your Bible, pray, and even talk to others about religious matters – and still be spiritually dead. However, if you follow the Lord with vigor and enthusiasm, remain strong in your faith, and ensure that your relationship with the Lord is healthy, you are spiritually alive. How alive is your spirit? I hope you are wide awake and on your toes for the Lord, unlike Sardis.

W.W.J.

The teachers of the law had a reputation of being alive, but they were spiritually dead.

Philadelphia

PERSEVERE DESPITE OPPOSITION

"I know that you have little strength, yet you have kept my word and have not denied my name." (Revelation 3:8)

The testimonial that Jesus sends to the church in Philadelphia is one of encouragement. Jesus tells them that he knows all their deeds. Then he says that he has placed before them an open door that no one can shut. He says that he knows that they have little strength, and yet they have held on to his message and have not denied his name.

The Christians of Philadelphia endured a great deal of opposition. There were many false prophets and teachers who said that the faith of the Philadelphian Christians was not the truth. Yet the Christians held on to the true gospel of Jesus Christ. They persevered even though they were persecuted. They were few in number, and they did not have much strength, but they persevered nonetheless.

Ultimately, it doesn't matter how much strength you have. What is really important is whether you can endure with what strength you have.

Strength also does not necessarily have anything to do with numbers. Even if you are part of a small group of Christians, you can still be strong in your faith. One of the most important qualities of the Christian life is the ability to persevere and endure. The Philadelphian Christians persevered, and Jesus was very pleased with them.

W.W.J.

Jesus said that where two or three are gathered in his name, he is present with them. (Matthew 18:20)

December 28

Laodicea

Neither Hot nor Cold

"So, because you are lukewarm – neither hot nor cold – I am about to spit you out of my mouth." (Revelation 3:16)

Jesus sent a letter to the Christians who lived in a city named Laodicea. Laodicea was a very prosperous city, and many of its residents were extremely wealthy. There was also a hot spring or thermal bath there, and people believed that the spring's water had the power to heal. The city was also known for producing exquisite fabrics from which beautiful clothing was made.

Jesus was worried about the Christians in Laodicea. Because he knew all their deeds and thoughts, he had a very clear and straightforward view of the state of their spiritual lives. His biggest problem with them was that they were rich in possessions, but were becoming increasingly poorer spiritually. They were lukewarm, just like the water from the spring that they drank to keep themselves healthy. This water had a very acrid taste, and people often spat it out because of the unappealing taste. In his letter to the Laodiceans, Jesus says that they had become lukewarm and no longer served him with warmth and passion in their hearts. Jesus tells them to put on clean, white clothes to cover their shame.

The Lord dislikes lukewarm Christians. He wants us to be on fire for him. He wants us to be passionate about his kingdom. We should be on fire for the King. Is there still passion and warmth for the Lord in your heart?

W.W.J.

Jesus sent the Holy Spirit like tongues of fire to ignite us for him and his work.

Jesus

The Bright Morning Star

"I am ... the bright Morning Star." (Revelation 22:16)

In the Old Testament, in Numbers 24:17, we read about the star of Jacob. Many scholars say that this reference was meant to tell people that Jesus would come like a star. The Jews also expected the Messiah who would save them to appear like a star.

Jesus is like the morning star, which announces the coming of a new day. When Jesus was born, he came to be the light of the world. The morning star shines brightly in heaven just before sunrise. And then the day breaks in all its glory and splendor. Jesus triumphed over the darkness of sin. He is like the rising morning sun that drives away the darkness. That is why he is also called the Morning Star. He brings a new day and new light for everyone who accepts him. In his light, we have life.

Peter says, *"And we have the word of the prophets made more certain, and you will do well to pay attention to it, as to a light shining in a dark place, until the day dawns and the morning star rises in your hearts"* (2 Peter 1:19). The Morning Star not only brought light to the world when he was born, but he will also rise in our hearts once more when Jesus returns from heaven. At that time, eternal light and eternal day will finally dawn. Never again will there be darkness. There will be no more sadness or pain or suffering. Everything will radiate light in the luminous presence of God. Now that's something to look forward to, isn't it?

Live with the light of Jesus in your heart. Sparkle brightly like a star because Jesus' light shines within you.

W.W.J.

Jesus said that if we looked carefully, we would be able to see signs that would tell us when all these wonderful things would happen.

December 30

The Bride

The Spirit and the bride say, "Come!" (Revelation 22:17)

Who is the bride of the Lord? The Bible says that we who belong to Jesus are the Lord's bride. A bride is someone who is ready to marry her bridegroom. A bride is usually radiant and filled with joy because the wedding day has arrived. She can't wait for her wedding day so that she can take her bridegroom to be her husband.

Jesus uses this image to illustrate how we will feel about him. We are like a bride who cannot wait to get married to our heavenly Bridegroom. When will this happen? When he returns for us from heaven. Just as a bridegroom takes a bride by the hand and leads her to the altar, Jesus will come back to earth to lead us to the Father and heaven. And then we will be with him eternally. The big wedding of the earthly bride and the heavenly Bridegroom will finally take place.

Here on earth we sometimes have to endure suffering. We often wish that all the painful and sad things of this life would just pass. We wish for all the hurt and suffering and pain to be over. We long for our heavenly Bridegroom. When will he come for us? We don't know for certain, but we do know that he promised that he will come.

Are you keeping your eyes peeled for the day when Jesus comes for us? Be ready for his coming. It could happen at any time.

W.W.J.

The angels promised that Jesus would return from heaven just as the disciples saw him ascending to heaven. (Acts 1:10-11)

Notes

Notes

Notes